D0720957

THE ROUGH GUIDE TO

Seoul

This second edition updated by

Martin Zatko

ROUGH
GUIDES

roughguides.com

Contents

OPPOSITE NEON LIGHTS, MYEONGDONG **PREVIOUS PAGE** BUKHANSAN NATIONAL PARK

Introduction to
Seoul

Want to wake up in a city that *really* never sleeps? An intoxicating mix of high-rise buildings and people-thronged streets, Seoul (서울) is one of the world's great 24-hour cities and a veritable assault on the senses. Even small streets are alive with frenzied activity by day and searing neon after sunset, while eardrums pound with clamouring shop assistants and the night-time thump of a thousand karaoke parlours. Within a single day, you can gaze out over Seoul from a mountaintop, set your tastebuds on fire with spicy Korean food, take in an absorbing cocktail of aromas at an open-air market, then recover in the hot pools and ice rooms of the ubiquitous *jjimjilbang* bathhouses, before bouncing the night away at a karaoke-style singing room. It's also a joy to see the city's other side – palaces, temples, royal tombs and ancestral shrines are evidence of Seoul's five centuries as a dynastic capital. This mix of ancient history combined with an open-all-hours culture gives the city an almost unmatched vitality, and the temptation to throw yourself in at the deep end is impossible to resist.

While Seoul itself is home to around 10 million people, the city has more or less swallowed up the neighbouring cities of Suwon and Incheon, giving it a combined urban mass of more than 25 million inhabitants – one of the largest on Earth. Ethnic Koreans dominate the population, with only 300,000 registered foreigners living here – two-thirds of these are Chinese, and many of the remainder are teachers from English-speaking nations.

That Seoul exists at all constitutes a minor miracle, since the Korean War saw it laid to waste in the early 1950s. The city sits just 30km from the border with North Korea, one day's march should the DMZ separating the countries ever be breached, and until the mid-1970s, Seoulites were poorer than their counterparts in the North Korean capital of Pyongyang. The city's transformation since then has been nothing short of

ABOVE VIEW OVER THE CITY **OPPOSITE** GEUNJONGJEON, GYEONGBOKGUNG

incredible – just a few generations down the line, it's one of the most modern and richest cities in the world, a major financial centre whose skyline is continually being enriched with gleaming skyscrapers.

But for all its nonstop consumption, Seoul is also a place of considerable tradition and history. Six wonderful **palaces** in the centre of the city proclaim its status as a seat of regal power from as far back as 1392 – the year that Seoul became capital of the **Joseon dynasty**, whose line of over two dozen kings ruled over all Korea until the country's annexation in 1910. Elsewhere, the tiled roofs of wooden *hanok* houses gently rise towards the ash-coloured granite crags north of Seoul, and the ancient songs and dances of farm hands and court performers are clashed out in a whirligig of sound and colour along Insadonggil, a traditional and tourist-friendly road in the palace district.

It's impossible to talk about Seoul without mentioning Korea's wonderful **cuisine**. Received Western knowledge tends to start with dog meat and end with *kimchi*; today, however, few Koreans eat dog (though some curious foreigners manage to hunt it down), and *kimchi* is a mere – if ubiquitous – side dish. Indeed, those in the know can **barbecue marinated beef** at tables inset with charcoal briquettes, stuff themselves with the dozens of side dishes available at a **royal banquet** and take their pick from a bewildering array of super-fresh **seafood**. In addition, Korea boasts Asia's best selection of indigenous alcoholic drinks, including the delicious milky rice-wine, **makgeolli**.

Seoulites themselves are a real highlight of any visit to the city: fiercely proud, and with a character almost as spicy as their food, they're keen to welcome foreigners. Within hours of arriving, you'll probably find yourself racing up a mountainside – new friends in

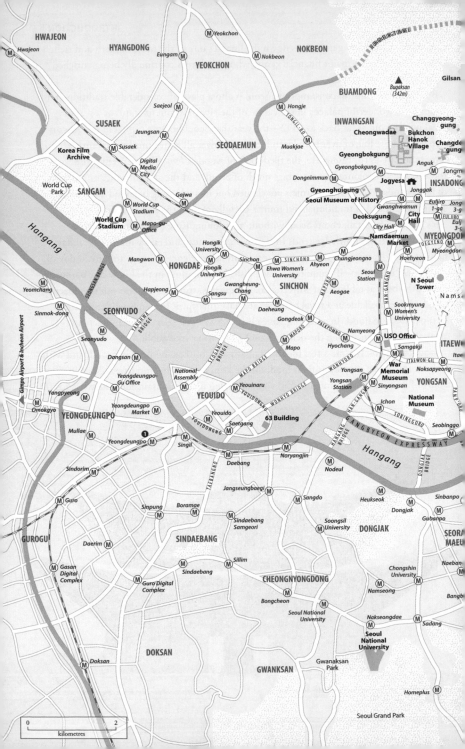

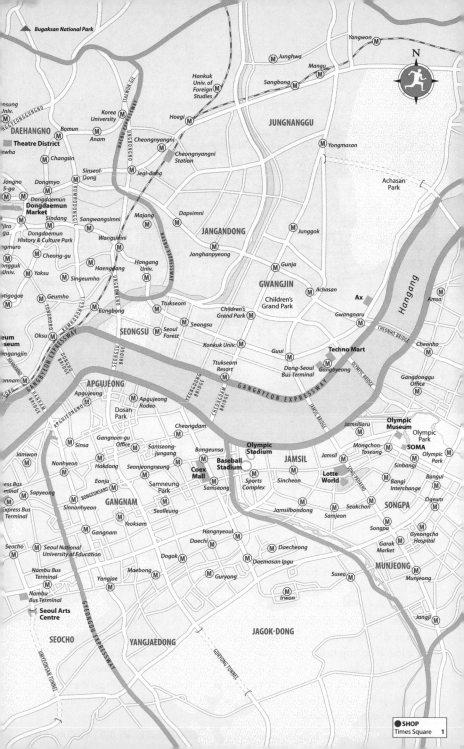

tow – lunching over a tasty barbecued *galbi*, throwing back *dongdongju* until dawn, or singing the night away at a *noraebang*. Few travellers leave without tales of the kindness of Korean strangers, and almost all wonder why the country isn't a more popular stop on the international travel circuit. Tourist numbers are, however, rising – the secret is well and truly out.

What to see

Although Seoul sprawls for kilometre after kilometre in every direction, most visitors venture no further than the compact city centre, where there are no fewer than six gorgeous palaces to stroll around, with **Gyeongbokgung** and **Changdeokgung** particularly popular with tourists. The others are all delightful in their own way, and those visiting **Changgyeonggung** can head by footbridge to **Jongmyo**, an ancient ancestral shrine venerated by the kings of the Joseon dynasty. In between Gyeongbokgung and Changdeokgung are two of Seoul's most notable districts, each possessing a distinctive appeal: **Samcheongdong** is a young, zesty area filled with trendy cafés, restaurants, clothing boutiques and art galleries, while neighbouring **Bukchondong** is one of the few places in Seoul where the city's traditional wooden buildings still stand.

ABOVE BANPO BRIDGE **OPPOSITE** BUKCHON HANOK VILLAGE

SEOUL'S WOODEN HEART

Though it may be hard to believe today, within living memory Seoul was a low-rise city. Its now-ubiquitous skyscrapers all went up over the past few decades, and as recently as the 1960s there was scarcely a multi-storey building in sight. On the fall of the Joseon kingdom in 1910, almost every Seoulite lived in the traditional form of housing – squat wooden houses now known as *hanokjip*, or **hanok** for short: the longer version means "Korean house" to distinguish these buildings from modern Western forms of accommodation. Although almost all *hanokjip* have now disappeared, a few clutches remain, particularly in the charming, hilly neighbourhood of **Bukchon Hanok Village** (see p.44).

Hanokjip are built almost exclusively from **local materials** – wood for the main framework, stone for the foundations and courtyard, and earth to fill the walls. Earth walls (*hwangteo*) have long been believed to have health benefits, as well as the practical advantage of insulation. Like Japanese houses, *hanokjip* make great use of handmade **paper** (*hanji*) – sliding doors and windows are covered with thin sheets and the walls with several layers, and even the flooring is made up of hundreds of sheets, each leaf varnished to produce a yellow-brown sheen mimicked by the yellow linoleum flooring found in most modern Korean apartments.

One feature which sets *hanokjip* apart is their use of underfloor heating, known as **ondol**. Rooms are raised above the courtyard, providing a space for wood fires; again, this feature has wormed its way into modern Korean housing, though today gas is used instead of flames.

Despite its central location, the charming area of **Insadong** exudes a markedly traditional atmosphere, with dozens of wonderful galleries, tearooms and restaurants – getting lost in its maze of winding side-streets is half the fun. A short walk to the west of Insadong is **Jogyesa**, a large temple that provides proof of Korea's Buddhist heritage, while just to the south is **Cheonggyecheon**, a recently developed creek whose pedestrian-only banks are arguably Seoul's best walking territory.

UNRAVELLING KOREAN PLACE NAMES

Many foreign visitors to Seoul struggle with the lengthy transliterated Korean place names, but armed with a few facts – and some practice – you'll be able to distinguish your Insadonggils from your Samcheongdongs, and perhaps even Changgyeonggung from Changdeokgung. The key lies in the **suffixes** to these long words: **gung**, for example, means "palace", and once removed you're left with the slightly less bewildering two-syllable name of the complex in question – Gyeongbok Palace, and so on. The **dong** suffix means "district", while **gil** means "road" – all of a sudden, it's possible to break Samcheongdonggil down, and identify it as a thoroughfare in the Samcheong district. Others that may be of use are **gang** and **cheon**, respectively used for waterways large (the Hangang, for example) and small (Cheonggyecheon); **mun**, which means "gate" (Dongdaemun); and **dae**, which usually signifies a university (Hongdae).

South of Cheonggyecheon is the capital's prime **business district**, and home to innumerable skyscrapers and other trappings of commerce. Hidden among the tower blocks are scores of buildings dating from the Japanese occupation period, these elegant **colonial structures** now incongruous in their modern surroundings. This is also the main shopping area, and includes Korea's two largest markets, **Dongdaemun** and **Namdaemun**. Both of these are colossal, with a mixture of mall-style buildings and open-air sections. The **market food**, utterly alien to the average traveller, is by far the best reason to visit, though there are also dozens of quality **museums** in this area, and the mini-mountain of **Namsan** provides wonderful views of the capital.

As you travel further out from the business and palace districts, the buildings become smaller in both size and number, thanks to the rugged – even mountainous – topography of the area. In fact, northern Seoul is home to a tremendously popular national park: **Bukhansan**, whose tree-lined trails are steep but surprisingly easy to navigate. Nestled among the western foothills, laidback **Buamdong** is Seoul's most relaxing district, with a plethora of galleries and restaurants. In contrast, heading east will bring you to **Daehangno**, a student-filled zone whose hectic street life and cheap restaurants have made it the long-established base of choice for backpackers.

Seoul is bisected by the **Hangang**, whose car-free banks are great for **cycling**, while you can also take a ferry tour, or even a trip by **river taxi**. The river slides gently past two of Seoul's most popular nightlife areas, studenty **Hongdae** and cosmopolitan **Itaewon**. Hongdae has more vitality and Itaewon more variety – it's best to visit both, though your liver may disagree.

Relatively few visitors venture south of the Hangang, but there are certainly reasons to do so. The fascinating district of **Apgujeong** is where the city's rich and beautiful come to party, dine and shop, and you can get a glimpse of certain facets of Seoul's high society, most notably fashion from the city's new wave of designers. In addition, this is the best place in which to sample **neo-Korean cuisine**, a new take on traditional styles.

Seoul also has a pleasing range of sights within easy day-trip range. Foreign travellers leap at the chance to visit the **DMZ**, the chilling 4km-wide buffer zone separating North and South Korea. In fact, on some tours it's technically possible to walk across the border, under the watchful eyes of rifle-toting soldiers. Two major cities are easily accessible from

OPPOSITE FROM TOP KOREAN BARBECUE; KARAOKE IN A *NORAEBANG*; JOGYESA TEMPLE

Seoul, and actually on the city's subway system. **Incheon** to the west has a thriving Chinatown and serves as a travel base for trips to dozens of **islands** in the **West Sea**, while **Suwon** to the south is home to a stunning fortress. There's an even better fortress in **Gongju**, a small city further south again; this was once the capital of the **Baekje kingdom**, whose astonishingly beautiful jewellery can be admired in a fantastic museum.

When to go

In Seoul, **spring** generally lasts from April to June, and is one of the best times of the year to visit: flowers are in bloom, and a fluffy cloak of cherry blossom washes a brief wave of pinkish white over the city. Locals head for the hills by day, and riverside barbecues by night, and the change in weather is also celebrated in a number of interesting festivals.

The **summer** can be unbearably muggy, and you may find yourself leaping from one air-conditioned sanctuary to the next. You'll wonder how Koreans can persist with their uniformly fiery food at this time, but be grateful for the ubiquitous water fountains. It's best to avoid the **monsoon** season: more than half of the country's annual rain falls from early July to late August. Although Japan and China protect Korea from most of the area's typhoons, one or two manage to squeeze through the gap each year.

The best time of the year to visit is **autumn** (Sept to Nov), when temperatures are mild, rainfall is generally low and the mountains that encircle the city erupt in a magnificent array of reds, yellows and oranges. Locals flock to national parks to picnic surrounded by these fiery leaf tones, and there are plenty of festivals livening things up. T-shirt weather can continue long into October, though you're likely to need some extra layers by the end.

Seoul's **winter** is long and cold, though visiting at this time is far from impossible, even on the many occasions on which the capital finds itself under a thick blanket of snow. There's almost no change to public transport, underfloor heating systems are cranked up, and the lack of rain creates photogenic contrasts between powdery snow, crisp blue skies, off-black pine trees and the earthy yellow of dead grass.

SEOUL'S AVERAGE TEMPERATURES AND RAINFALL

	Jan	Feb	Mar	Apr	May	Jun	Jul	Aug	Sep	Oct	Nov	Dec
Max/min (°C)	0/-9	3/-7	8/-2	17/5	22/11	27/16	29/21	31/22	26/15	19/7	11/0	3/-7
Rainfall (mm)	31	20	38	76	81	130	376	267	119	41	46	25

Author picks

Our intrepid author has explored almost every street, alley, nook and cranny in central Seoul, in a quest to better understand this fascinating city. Here are some of his favourite discoveries…

Meokgeorichon Seoul has a wealth of trendy places in which to enjoy *makgeolli* rice-beer and *pajeon* pancakes, but this semi-legal Insadong institution (p.112) is the most fun – like a small aircraft hangar hung with fishing lights, its many stalls are alive with merriment each evening.

A jog down the Cheonggyecheon The banks of this pretty stream (p.53) are a great place to run – though busy with people at the beginning, you'll be alone with cyclists and other joggers by the time the Cheonggyecheon's waters pour into the Hangang.

Craft beer Beer lovers rejoice! In a nation once known for its poor-quality beers, a small team of microbreweries in and around Itaewon (box, p.92) is now producing some great ales, shaking up the once stagnant local beer scene.

Galbi in Jongno 3-ga The small knot of tiny, earthy restaurants north of Jongno 3-ga subway station (p.112) is the city's most atmospheric spot to try barbecued meat Korean-style.

Sunset from Namsan The peak of Seoul's mini-mountain (p.66) is a prime spot to head at dusk, when you can marvel at the city's rapid transformation from grey to pulsating neon.

Joseon-era palaces Of Seoul's half-a-dozen immensely appealing palaces from the days of dynasty, Changgyeonggung (p.71) is chock-full of historical note, yet not as full of tourists as the other palaces.

Ssamziegil Tucked away in tourist-friendly Insadong, this spiral-market (p.133) is a pleasing, highly photogenic piece of modern architecture – you're also guaranteed to find some fantastic souvenirs here.

> Our author recommendations don't end here. We've flagged up our favourite places – a perfectly sited hotel, an atmospheric café, a special restaurant – throughout the guide, highlighted with the ★ symbol.

FROM TOP *PAJEON* PANCAKES; SSAMZIEGIL

18

things not to miss

It's not possible to see everything that Seoul has to offer on a short trip – and we don't suggest you try. What follows is a selective taste of the city's highlights: fascinating markets, spectacular palaces and a few ways just to indulge yourself. All entries have a page reference to take you straight into the Guide, where you can find out more. Coloured numbers refer to chapters in the Guide section.

1 NORYANGJIN FISH MARKET

Page 88

There's a mind-boggling variety of ultra-fresh seafood available at this highly atmospheric fish market, which brings together the best produce from Korea's East, West and South seas.

2 POTTERY

Pages 133 & 134

Some pottery styles that the world thinks of as Japanese actually originated in Korea – browse through the many shops around Insadong, and take home a tea set whose design mirrors these dynastic-era styles.

3 HUWON

Page 46

Relax by the pond just as kings once did at this secluded "Secret Garden", which nestles at the back of Changdeokgung, a UNESCO World Heritage-listed palace.

4 NAMSANGOL

Page 66

This re-created Joseon-era village is a delightful place for a wander, especially in the evening, when it's gently illuminated by paper lanterns.

5 SAMNEUNG PARK

Page 97

The burial place of three Joseon-dynasty royals, and one of Seoul's most pleasant parks to boot.

6 YANGSU-RI
Page 157

A complete antithesis to bustling Seoul, this riverside village is a prime spot for those seeking a little serenity.

7 BUKCHON HANOK VILLAGE
Page 44

Sleep in a traditional wooden *hanok* house heated by underfloor flames.

8 THE DMZ
Page 143

Step inside the world's most heavily armed border area – the 4km-wide Demilitarized Zone separating North and South Korea.

9 GWANGJANG MARKET
Page 113

Gwangjang is a Seoul institution, with sights and smells redolent of decades gone by.

10 MAKGEOLLI
Page 125

This dynastic rice-beer is as popular with young Koreans as it is with the older generation, and comes in a mind-boggling array of brands and flavours.

11 COLONIAL ARCHITECTURE
Page 57

The buildings constructed during the brutal Japanese annexation of Korea are some of the most beautiful and elegant in the city.

12 NAMSAN
Page 66

Take a short ride up on Namsan's cable car for great views of the city.

13

14

15

16

17

A ROYAL FEAST
Page 113

Seoul gives visitors the rare opportunity to eat like a king: feast like the Joseon monarchs, with your table creaking under the weight of up to forty dishes.

ART GALLERIES
Page 43

Seoul is crammed with a truly astonishing number of galleries, such as the National Museum of Art, which show why Korean art is gaining an ever-growing global reputation.

GYEONGBOKGUNG
Page 37

Enjoy the colourful spectacle of the Changing of the Guard at the most popular of Seoul's six palaces.

JJIMJILBANG
Page 107

Take a scrub the Korean way at these sauna-like facilities.

INSADONG TEAROOMS
Page 121

The traditional Insadong district remains home to well over a dozen classy tearooms – a rare opportunity to try Korea's fantastic range of domestic infusions.

GANGHWADO
Page 152

Thousands of years old, the Neolithic dolmens on this island are the area's earliest signs of human habitation.

18

GANGNAM SUBWAY STATION

Basics

Getting there

It may come as something of a surprise to learn that Seoul is not Korea's main international transport hub: that honour goes to Incheon, a city just to the west, yet essentially part of the same gigantic urban conurbation. Incheon is home to the country's main international airport (often referred to as "Seoul Incheon" on departure boards), as well as a couple of international port terminals handling ferries to various cities on China's eastern seaboard. There is no way to arrive in Seoul by land, since such opportunities are choked off by the spiky frontier with North Korea, though there are ferry links to Korea from both China and Japan.

The vast majority of visitors, however, fly in with the two big Korean **airlines**, Korean Air and Asiana, both of which operate direct flights from a number of destinations around the world. Seoul increasingly features as a stopover on round-the-world trips, and the country is also well served by dozens of international carriers. **Fares** increase for travel in the summer months and at Christmas time, when it's common for all flights to be fully booked weeks in advance. A **departure tax** applies when leaving Korea, but will almost certainly be factored in to your ticket price.

Flights from the UK and Ireland

Korean Air and Asiana have **direct connections** from London Heathrow to Incheon – Korean Air has a daily service, while Asiana flies five times a week. The journey takes eleven hours, with return fares costing around £600, though this can rise to over £800 in summer and at Christmas. You can save money by taking an indirect flight, with prices often dipping to around £400 return during low season; good options include Finnair via Helsinki, Qatar Airways via Doha, Aeroflot via Moscow and Emirates via Dubai. It's also worth checking deals

with KLM and Air France, whose routes are as close to direct as possible.

There are no direct flights to Korea from **Ireland** so you'll have to transfer in the UK or in mainland Europe.

Flights from the US and Canada

If you are coming from the **US** you have a number of options: there are direct flights to Incheon from New York, Dallas, Las Vegas, Los Angeles, San Francisco, Detroit, Seattle, Chicago, Atlanta, Houston, Washington and Honolulu; carriers include Delta and United, as well as Asiana and Korean Air. Sample low-season return fares are $1400 from New York (a journey of around 14hr), $1200 from Chicago (14hr) and $1150 from Los Angeles (13hr). In all cases you may save hundreds of dollars by transferring – Beijing and Tokyo are popular hubs.

Korean Air has direct flights to Incheon from both Vancouver and Toronto in **Canada**, though these can be very expensive in peak season (over Can$2500); low-season prices can drop under Can$1000. Again, you're likely to save money by taking an indirect flight.

Flights from Australia, New Zealand and South Africa

From **Australia**, the only direct connections to Korea are Korean Air and Asiana flights from Sydney (10hr) and Korean Air flights from Brisbane (9hr). There have, in the past, also been direct flights from Melbourne and Cairns, so it's worth checking to see whether these have restarted. The number of Koreans going to Australia means that direct flights tend to be pricey, so check around for indirect flights via a Southeast Asian hub; return prices via Kuala Lumpur, Singapore or Hong Kong can often drop below Aus$1000.

From **New Zealand**, Korean Air flies direct from Auckland (12hr), and there have been direct flights from Christchurch in the past, too – fares may drop as low as NZ$1400, but you'll probably pay nearer NZ$1900.

At the time of writing, there were no direct flights from **South Africa**.

Flights from other Asian countries

There are flights to Incheon from many cities across **Japan** (from $150 return) and **China** (around $250 from the major East-Coast cities). It's also worth considering connections to other Korean international airports, such as Busan's Gimhae airport, Jeju, Daegu and Gwangju. There's also a handy, and extremely regular, connection between Seoul's Gimpo airport and Tokyo Haneda, both of which are closer to the centre of their respective capitals than the larger hubs, Incheon and Narita.

China and Japan aside, Incheon is also served by flights from an ever-increasing number of other **Asian cities**, with many routes run by budget airlines – local carriers Eastar Jet, Jin Air and Jeju Air have services from Thailand, the Philippines, Hong Kong, Vietnam, Laos, Cambodia and more besides.

AIRLINES

Aeroflot Ⓦ aeroflot.ru
Air France Ⓦ airfrance.com
Asiana Airlines Ⓦ flyasiana.com
British Airways Ⓦ ba.com
Delta Ⓦ delta.com
Eastar Jet Ⓦ eastarjet.com
Emirates Ⓦ emirates.com
Finnair Ⓦ finnair.com
JAL (Japan Air Lines) Ⓦ jal.com
Jeju Air Ⓦ en.jejuair.net
Jin Air Ⓦ jinair.com
KLM Ⓦ klm.com
Korean Air Ⓦ koreanair.com
Qatar Airways Ⓦ qatarairways.com
United Airlines Ⓦ united.com

INTERNATIONAL TRAVEL AGENTS

ebookers Ⓦ ebookers.com. Low fares on an extensive selection of scheduled flights and package deals.
North South Travel Ⓦ northsouthtravel.co.uk. Friendly, competitive travel agency, offering discounted fares worldwide. Profits are used to support projects in the developing world, especially the promotion of sustainable tourism.
STA Travel Ⓦ statravel.com. Worldwide specialists in independent travel; also student IDs, travel insurance, car rental, rail passes, and more. Good discounts for students and under-26s.
Trailfinders Ⓦ trailfinders.com. One of the best-informed and most efficient agents for independent travellers.

LOCAL TOUR OPERATORS

Aju Tours Ⓦ ajutours.co.kr. A few interesting additions to the regular Seoul tours and DMZ trips, including birdwatching, oriental health or a tour of shamanistic sites.
Grace Travel Ⓦ english.triptokorea.com. Outfit offering a wide range of good-value tours, including ski trips, Jeju excursions, hiking adventures and a "Royal Relics" journey.
O'ngo Ⓦ ongofood.com. Interesting food tours, mostly focused on Seoul but sometimes heading to the hinterlands; you'll be able to wrap up the experience with a cooking class or two.
Rye Tour Ⓦ ryetour.com. In addition to a few Korea-only itineraries, this group also offers week-long tours which combine Seoul and Busan with Beijing, Shanghai or Tokyo.

By ferry from China and Japan

Despite the fact that South Korea is part of the Eurasian landmass, and technically connected to the rest of it by rail, the DMZ and North Korean red tape means that the country is currently **inaccessible by land**. Two old railway lines across the DMZ have been renovated, and 2007 saw trains rumble across the border as part of a peace ceremony, but overnight trains from Beijing to Seoul remain a distant prospect. Therefore access from the continent takes the form of **ferries from Japan or China**. Access from China can possibly be combined with a ride on the Trans-Siberian Railway (see Ⓦ seat61.com for more information), while, if you're arriving from China or Japan, a **combined rail and ferry ticket** gives substantial discounts on what you'd pay separately (see Ⓦ letsko rail.com for details).

Ferries from China

There are several **ferry routes** from **China**'s East Coast to Incheon's international terminals (see below). All the ferries have numerous classes of comfort, with one-way tickets starting at around 850 RMB. The most popular connections are from Dalian, Qingdao, and Tianjin's port in Tanggu, which is the most convenient if you're coming from Beijing.

FERRIES TO INCHEON FROM CHINESE PORTS

From Dalian Mon, Wed & Fri at 6pm; 17hr
From Dandong Tues & Thurs at 6pm; Sun 3pm; 16hr
From Qingdao Mon, Wed & Fri at 4pm; 17hr
From Qinhuangdao Wed & Sun at 1pm; 24hr
From Shidao Tues, Thurs & Sun at 6pm; 14hr
From Tanggu (Tianjin) Thurs & Sun at 11am; 24hr
From Weihai Tues, Thurs & Sun at 6pm; 14hr
From Yantai Mon, Wed & Fri at 6.30pm; 14hr
From Yingkou Mon & Thurs at 11am; 24hr

Ferries from Japan

Services from **Japan** depart from Fukuoka and Shimonoseki to the southern city of Busan: they arrive reasonably close to Busan train station, from where a high-speed service leaves every 10–20 minutes for Seoul (2hr 45min). Fukuoka is by far the better choice, since there are two different services to Korea – a regular ferry, departing Fukuoka every day except Sunday (6hr; ¥9000; Ⓦ koreaferry.co.kr), and a faster jetfoil with at least five services a day (3hr; ¥13,000; Ⓦ jrbeetle.co.jp). There's also a longer ferry from Osaka (19hr; from ¥14,000; Ⓦ panstar.co.kr), three days a week – a beautiful ride through Japan's island-studded inland sea.

Arrival

Getting into Seoul from the airport or ferry terminals is simple. The airports are a little removed from the city centre, but the presence of tourist booths and English-language signage facilitates matters. For those arriving from elsewhere in Korea, Seoul's train stations are all very central, and each is connected to at least one subway line; the main bus stations also have direct connections to the subway, but unfortunately they're all rather awkwardly located to the south and east of the centre.

By plane

Most people take **the bus** from Incheon Airport to Seoul, which takes about an hour, depending on your destination. There are no fewer than fifteen bus routes from the airport to the capital (W10,000), each stopping off at numerous locations, while more expensive **limousine buses** head straight to many of the top hotels (around W15,000); ask at an airport tourist booth for details of which bus to take.

Alternatively, the rather slow **AREX** (airport express) **train** runs from Incheon Airport to Seoul train station (45min–1hr), where you can connect to the Seoul underground network (lines 1 and 4). The AREX train also connects to the underground at Gimpo airport (the terminus for most domestic flights and a few short-haul international services) and Gongdeok for line 5, Digital Media City or Gongdeok for line 6 and Hongik University for line 2, though most people head straight to the terminal at Seoul Station. A high-speed KTX train is also planned from the airport to Seoul Station.

A **taxi from the airport** will take around thirty minutes to get to central Seoul and cost W70,000– 120,000 depending upon your destination and the time of day; the black "deluxe" taxis are more costly.

By ferry

Ferries from China all land in the city of Incheon (see p.149), just west of Seoul. To get to Seoul from Incheon, take a taxi to Dongincheon station, which is on line 1 of the capital's subway network – the journey to central Seoul will take around an hour.

Getting around

With Seoul's hectic streets making car rental almost tantamount to suicide, and bicycle riding even more so in most places, it's lucky that the city is covered by a cheap, clean and highly comprehensive public transport system – the subway network is one of the best developed in the world, not least because of the sheer number of workers it has to speed from A to B. Buses dash around the city every which way, and even taxis are cheap enough to be viable for many routes.

Busy roads and noxious emissions mean that **walking** through Seoul is rarely pleasurable, though Insadonggil is closed to traffic on Sundays; the shopping district of Myeongdong and club-heavy Hongdae are so swamped with people that vehicles tend to avoid these areas; and there are innumerable malls and underground shopping arcades around the city. Riding a **bike** is only really advisable on a specially designed route along the Han River (see box, p.87 for further details).

By subway

Seoul's **subway system** consists of eighteen lines and over 300 stations, and is still growing – it's one of the most comprehensive on earth, and in terms of annual passenger numbers, second only to Beijing. In the area bounded by the circular 2 line, you'll never be more than a short walk or taxi ride from the nearest station, while line 1 runs for a whole third of the country's length, stretching well over 100km from Soyosan in the north to Sinchang in the south. It's also possible to get to Suwon (see p.154) or Incheon (see p.149) by subway. Running from around 5.30am to midnight (slightly earlier on

TRANSPORT CARDS

Those staying in the city for anything more than a few days should buy a **T-money transport card**, available for W3000 (refundable) at all subway stations and some street-level kiosks. After loading it with credit (easiest at machines in the subway station), you'll save W100 on each subway or bus journey, and any remaining balance can be refunded at the end of your stay. These cards make it possible to switch at no extra cost from bus to subway – or vice versa – should a combination be needed to complete your journey. In addition, you can use these handy cards to pay **taxi fares**, make **phone calls** from most street-side booths, and even pay your bill at **convenience stores**.

weekends), trains are extremely frequent but are packed to bursting at rush hour, and often livened up by hawkers selling anything from hand cream to folk music.

Fares are extremely reasonable, starting at W1150 for rides of less than 10km, and very rarely costing more than W2000. **Ticket purchase** can be tricky; unless you have one of the highly recommended transport cards (see box above), you'll have to buy a single-use card from a machine – though the operating system is a little curious, you should get there in the end. Each card requires a deposit of W500, retrievable from machines outside the turnstiles when you've completed your journey. The subway system itself is very user-friendly: **network maps** are conveniently located around the stations, which are made easily navigable by multi-language signage. You'll be able to find maps of the surrounding area on walls near the station exits, though be warned that north only faces upwards a quarter of the time, since each map is oriented to the direction that it happens to be facing.

By bus

In comparison with the subway system, Seoul's **bus network** often proves too complicated for foreign guests – English-language signage is rare, and some of the route numbers would look more at home in a telephone directory (for instance, the #9009-1 to City Hall). The buses are split into four coloured categories – **blue** buses travel long distances along major arterial roads, **green** buses

are for shorter hops, **red** ones travel out to the suburbs and **yellow** ones run tight loop routes. **Fares** start at W1150 for blue and green buses, W1950 for red buses and W950 for yellow buses, increasing on longer journeys; cash is not accepted on most buses, so you'll need a travel card (see box above). Handily, a bus-plus-subway-plus-bus journey often counts as just one trip; scan your card when you exit the bus to take advantage of this. For more information on routes go to Ⓦ bus.seoul.go.kr, or call ☎ 1330.

By taxi

Seoul's taxis are **cheap** and ubiquitous. A W3000 fare covers the first 2km, and goes up in W100 increments every 142m – given that bus and subway fares start at W1150, it often works out almost as cheap for groups of three or four to travel short distances by cab rather than public transport. Note that a twenty percent surcharge is added between midnight and 4am. There are also deluxe *mobeom* cabs, which are black with a yellow stripe; these usually congregate around expensive hotels, charging W5000 for the first 3km and W200 for each additional 164m. You should never have to wait long for a cab. Drivers do not expect tips, but it's unlikely that they'll speak any **English** – having your destination written in *hangeul* is the easiest way to get the information across, though many drivers will be both willing and able to call an interpreter on their phone.

ONLINE TRAVEL RESOURCES

Incheon International Airport Ⓦ www.airport.or.kr. Information on flights into and out of Korea's main airport.

Korail Ⓦ letskorail.com. Information on train times and passes, including discounted combined train and ferry tickets to Japan.

Korean Airports Corporation Ⓦ airport.co.kr. Almost identical to the Incheon site, this also has details of domestic and international flights for the smaller Korean airports.

Seoul Metropolitan Rapid Transport (SMRT) Ⓦ smrt.co.kr. Timetables, and a useful best-route subway map.

Visit Korea Ⓦ english.visitkorea.or.kr. Good for bus connections between major cities, and has cursory information on trains and ferries.

The media

Korean media has come a long way since bursting out of the dictatorial strait-jacket of the 1970s and 1980s, but most of it is only accessible to those fluent in Korean.

English-language media

The two big English-language **newspapers** are the *Korea Times* (W koreatimes.co.kr) and *Korea Herald* (W koreaherald.com), near-identical dailies publishing near-identical news agency output and dull business statistics. This said, both have decent listings sections in their weekend editions, which detail events around the country, as well as the goings-on in Seoul's restaurant, film and club scenes. The *International Herald Tribune* is pretty easy to find in top hotels, with copies containing the eight-page *Joongang Daily* (W korea joongangdaily.joins.com), an interesting local news supplement. You should also be able to hunt down the previous week's *Time* or *Economist* in most Korean cities – try the larger bookstores, or the book section of a large department store.

For Korean news translated into English, try the **websites** of *Yonhap News* (W english.yonhapnews.co.kr), or *Dong-a Ilbo* (W english.donga.com); the *Chosun Ilbo* (W english.chosun.com) has a translated version too, but it's rather conservative in nature. Lastly, Seoul has its own clutch of useful websites and **magazines** (see below), some of which also cover destinations elsewhere in Korea.

Television

Korean **television** is a gaudy feast of madcap game shows and soppy period dramas, and there are few more accessible windows into the true nature of local society. **Arirang** (W arirang.co.kr) is a 24hr English-language television network based in Seoul, which promotes the country with occasionally interesting (but often propaganda-like) documentaries, and has regular news bulletins. Arirang TV is free-to-air throughout much of the world, and though not free in Korea itself, it comes as part of most cable packages.

SEOUL ON THE WEB

10 Magazine W 10mag.com. A fun publication with good listings sections for Seoul and other Korean cities.
Eloquence W eloquence.co.kr. Stylish magazine that focuses on upper-class Seoul society.
Marmot's Hole W rjkoehler.com. This personal blog of long-time expat Robert Koehler is full of interesting, extremely informative snippets about Seoul's culture and history.
Roboseyo W roboseyo.blogspot.com. Expat blog that takes an often offbeat view of Seoul society.
Seoul W magazine.seoulselection.com. City-sponsored magazine that's usually much more interesting than its name may suggest.
Seoul Eats W seouleats.com. Food blog with an admirable selection of restaurant reviews, though not updated as often as it once was.

The Seoul Times W theseoultimes.com. Though the news itself is stale to say the least, the site has good job listings and is a useful place to hunt for flatmates.
Visit Seoul W visitseoul.net. Much improved in recent years, this is the official tourist site of Seoul's city government.
Zen Kimchi W zenkimchi.com. Another food blog, with a pleasingly user-friendly interface.

Festivals

Most of Seoul's festivals are concentrated around spring and autumn, but a whole host are spread throughout the year. If you're heading to one, don't be shy – the locals love to see foreigners joining in with traditional Korean events, and those who dare to get stuck in may finish the day with a whole gang of new friends.

It must be said that a large proportion of **Korean festivals** are quite unappealing: many are brazenly commercial in nature, making no bones about being held to "promote the salted seafood industry", for example. Other festivals include those dedicated to agricultural utensils, clean peppers and the "Joy of Rolled Laver" – you'll easily be able to spot the duds. The most interesting events are highlighted below, though bear in mind that celebrations for two of the big national festivals – Seollal, the Lunar New Year, and a Korean version of Thanksgiving named Chuseok – are family affairs that generally take place behind closed doors. As long as you're not in Seoul during the long, cold winter, you'll almost certainly be able to catch a festival of some kind. In addition to the traditional parades and street performances on Insadonggil (usually every Thurs, Fri and Sat), there are a whole host of events, of which a selection is detailed below.

APRIL

Cherry Blossom Though the exact dates are determined by the weather, Seoulites get their picnicking equipment together as soon as the soft pink flowers are fluted through the cherry trees. Yeouido is the most popular place to go – bring a bottle of *soju* and make a bunch of friends.
International Women's Film Festival W wffis.or.kr. A week-long succession of films that "see the world through women's eyes" (even if they were created by men).

MAY

Jongmyo Daeje First Sunday of the month. Korean kings performed their ancestral rites at the Jongmyo shrine for hundreds of years prior to the end of the monarchy, and it's been carried forward to this day; the event is necessarily sober but very interesting, and is followed by traditional court dances.

Hi Seoul Festival Ⓦ hiseoulfest.org. Myriad events take place in this ten-day-long celebration of the coming of summer. From choreographed firework displays and tea ceremonies to men walking across the Han River by tightrope, there's simply no better time to be in Seoul, and the event also incorporates the Seoul World DJ festival.

Buddha's Birthday Late May. With their courtyards strewn with colourful paper lanterns, temples are the place to be at this age-old event, which is also a national holiday. In the evening a huge lantern parade heads to Jogyesa temple along Jongno; get window-space early in one of the cafés overlooking the street.

Seoul International Cartoon & Animation Festival Late May Ⓦ en.sicaf.org. Koreans young and old are major cartoon addicts, but while most of the national fix is sated by Japanese fare, there's still a lot of local talent – *The Simpsons*, *Family Guy* and *Spongebob Squarepants* are among the shows inked and lined here. Screenings take place in several locations.

JUNE

Dano An age-old event centred around the shamanist rituals still practised by many Koreans, this takes place at locations across the city, but is best experienced in the Namsangol Hanok Village (see p.66). It's also your best chance to see *ssireum*, a Korean form of wrestling.

Korean Queer Culture Festival Ⓦ kqcf.org. Not exactly an event trumpeted by the local tourist authorities – in fact, not so long ago the police were still trying to ban it – this is a great way to see Korea crawling out of its Confucian shell. A fortnight-long programme includes a film festival, art exhibitions and the obligatory street parade.

JULY

Jisan Valley and Pentaport Rock Festivals Ⓦ valleyrockfestival .com and Ⓦ pentaportrock.com. Two competing European-style music festivals (think tents, mud and portable toilets) which manage to rope in major international acts, though admittedly ones usually on the wane in their homelands. Both events stretch across three alcohol-fuelled nights, the revelry running non-stop.

AUGUST

Seoul Fringe Festival Ⓦ seoulfringefestival.net. This fortnight-long platform for all things alternative is very popular with local students, and its semi-international nature means that certain events will appeal to visitors from overseas, with Hongdae usually the best place to be.

SEPTEMBER

Seoul Performing Arts Festival Late September and early October Ⓦ spaf.or.kr. This increasingly acclaimed event has seen performances from as far afield as Latvia and Israel, though its main aim is to showcase Korean talent. It takes place in various locations around Seoul over a three-week period.

OCTOBER

Global Gathering Early October Ⓦ globalgatheringkorea.co.kr. The Korean edition of the international electronic music event takes place on the banks of the Hangang, near World Cup Stadium, and should be staying in Korea for some time to come.

Seoul Drum Festival Early October Ⓦ seouldrum.go.kr. The crashes and bangs of all things percussive ring out at this annual event, which takes place in the Gwanghwamun area.

Seoul Fashion Week Ⓦ seoulfashionweek.org. Since it first opened in 2000, this has become Asia's largest fashion event, functioning as a great showcase for Seoul's up-and-coming designers.

NOVEMBER

Pepero Day November 11. A crass marketing ploy, but an amusing one nonetheless – like Pocky, their Japanese cousins, Pepero are thin sticks of chocolate-coated biscuit, and on this date in the year when it looks as if four of them are standing together, millions of Koreans say "I love you" by giving a box to their sweethearts, friends, parents or pets.

Culture and etiquette

You may have mastered the art of the polite bow, worked out how to use the tricky steel chopsticks, and learnt a few words of the Korean language, but beware, you may upset new friends by accepting gifts with your hand in the wrong place. While even seasoned expats receive heartfelt congratulations for getting the easy bits right (some are even surprised when foreigners are able to use Korean money), there are still innumerable ways to offend the locals, and unfortunately it's the things that are hardest to guess that are most likely to see you come a cropper.

Korea is often said to be the world's most **Confucian** nation, such values having been instilled for over a thousand years across several dynasties (see p.174). Elements of Confucianism still linger on today – it's still basically true that anyone older, richer or more important than you (or just male as opposed to female) is simply "better" and deserving of more respect, a fact that becomes sorely clear to many working in Korea. Perhaps most evident to foreigners will be what amounts to a national obsession with **age** – you're likely to be asked how old you are soon after your first meeting with any Korean, and any similarity of birth years is likely to be greeted with a genuine whoop of delight (note that Koreans count years differently from Westerners – children are already 1 when they're born, and gain another digit at Lunar New Year, meaning that those born on December 31 become two years old the very next day). Women have traditionally been treated as inferior to men, and were expected to ditch their job as soon as they gave birth to their first child; however, recent years have shown a marked shift towards gender equality, with males more forgiving in the home and females more assertive in the workplace. **Foreigners** are largely exempt from the code of conduct that would be required of both parties following their knowledge of age, employment and background, and little is expected of them in such terms, but this does have its drawbacks – in such an ethnically homogeneous society, those who aren't Korean will always remain "outsiders", even if they speak the language fluently or have actually spent their whole lives in the country. Meanwhile, foreigners with Korean blood will be expected to behave as a local would, even if they can't speak a word of the language.

Conduct

The East Asian concept of "face" is very important in Korea, and known here as **gibun** (기분); the main goal is to avoid the **embarrassment** of self or others. Great lengths are taken to smooth out awkward situations, and foreigners getting unnecessarily angry are unlikely to invoke much sympathy. This occasionally happens as the result of an embarrassed smile, the traditional Korean retort to an uncomfortable question or incident; remember that they're not laughing at you (even if they've just dropped something on your head), merely trying to show empathy or move the topic onto safer ground. Foreigners may also see Koreans as disrespectful: nobody's going to thank you for holding open a door, and you're unlikely to get an apology if bumped into (which is almost inevitable on the subway). **Dressing well** has long been important, but while pretty much anything goes for local girls these days, foreign women may be assumed to be brazen hussies (or Russian prostitutes) if they wear revealing clothing.

Meeting and greeting

Foreigners will see Koreans **bowing** all the time, even during telephone conversations. Though doing likewise will do much to endear you to locals, don't go overboard – a full, right-angled bow would only be appropriate for meeting royalty (and the monarchy ended in 1910). Generally, a short bow with eyes closed and the head directed downwards will do just fine, but it's best to observe the Koreans themselves, and the action will become quite natural after a short time; many visitors find themselves inadvertently maintaining the habit long after they've left. **Attracting attention** is also done differently here – you beckon with fingers fluttering beneath a downward-facing palm, rather than with your index fingers protruding hook-like from an upturned one.

Koreans are great lovers of **business cards**, which are exchanged in all meetings that have even a whiff of commerce about them. The humble rectangles garner far greater respect than they do in the West, and folding or stuffing one into a pocket or wallet is a huge *faux pas* – accept your card with profuse thanks, leave it on the table for the duration of the meeting, and file it away with respect (a card-holder is an essential purchase for anyone here on business). Also note that it's seen as incredibly rude to write someone's name in red ink – this colour is reserved for names of those who have died, a practice that most Koreans seem to think goes on all around the world.

If you're lucky enough to be invited to a Korean home, try to bring a **gift** – fruit, chocolates and flowers go down well. The offering is likely to be refused at first, and probably on the second attempt too – persevere and it will eventually be accepted with thanks. The manner of receiving is also important – the receiving hand should be held from underneath by the non-receiving one, the distance up or down the arm dependent on exactly how polite you want to be. This will only come with experience and will not be expected of most foreigners, but you will be expected to take your **shoes off** once inside the house or apartment, so try to ensure that your socks are clean and hole-free.

Dining

Korea's Confucian legacy can often be a great boon to foreigners, as it has long been customary for hosts (usually "betters") to **pay** – as with the rest of the local workforce, many English teachers get taken out for regular slap-up meals by their bosses, and don't have to pay a dime. Koreans also tend to make a big show of trying to pay, with the bill passing rapidly from hand to hand until the right person coughs up. Nowadays things are changing slowly – "going Dutch" is increasingly common where it would once have been unthinkable – but there are still innumerable codes of conduct; Koreans will usually guide foreigners through the various dos and don'ts.

Table manners

Many Korean meals are group affairs, and this has given rise to a number of rules surrounding who **serves the food** from the communal trays to the individual ones – it's usually the youngest woman at the table. Foreign women finding themselves in this position will be able to mop up a great deal of respect by performing the duty, though as there are particular ways to serve each kind of food, it's probably best to watch first. The **serving of drinks** is a little less formal, though again the minutiae of recommended conduct could fill a small book – basically, you should never refill your own cup or glass, and should endeavour to keep topped up those belonging to others. The position of the hands is important – watch to see how the Koreans are doing it (both the pourer and the recipient), and you'll be increasing your "face" value in no time.

One big no-no is to **blow your nose** during the meal – preposterously unfair, given the spice level of pretty much every Korean dish. Should you need to do so, make your excuses and head to the toilets. It's also proper form to wait for the **head of the table** – the one who is paying, in other words – to sit down first, as well as to allow them to be the first to stand at the end of the meal. The latter can be quite tricky, as many Korean restaurants are sit-on-the-floor affairs that play havoc on the knees and backs of foreigners unaccustomed to the practice. It's almost impossible, too, to avoid the Korean Catch-22: locals love to ask foreigners questions during a meal, but anyone stopping to answer will likely fail to keep pace with the fast-eating Koreans, who will then assume that your dish is not disappearing quickly because you don't like it.

Using chopsticks

Many rules surround the use of **chopsticks** – don't use these to point or to pick your teeth, and try not to spear food with them unless your skills are really poor. It's also bad form, as natural as it may seem, to leave your chopsticks in the bowl: this is said to resemble incense sticks used after a death, but to most Koreans it just looks wrong (just as many Westerners obey unwritten and seemingly meaningless rules governing cutlery positions). Just leave the sticks balanced on the rim of the bowl.

All in all, Koreans will tolerate anything viewed as a "mistake" on the part of the foreigner, and offer great encouragement to those who are at least attempting to get things right – you're likely to be praised for your chopstick-handling abilities however long you've been in the country.

Living and working in Seoul

There are two main subspecies of Westerner in Seoul: English teachers and American soldiers. Other jobs are hard to come by, though today's Korea is becoming ever more prominent in global business, with the resulting foreign contingent gradually permeating Seoul's army of suits. It's still fairly easy to land a teaching job, though to do this legally a degree certificate is nigh-on essential; wages are good, and Korea is a popular port of call for those wishing to pay off their student loan quickly while seeing a bit of the world. The cost of living, though rising, is still way below that in most English-speaking countries, and many teachers are able to put financial considerations out of their mind for the duration of their stay – many slowly realize that they've inadvertently been saving more than half of their salary.

Seoul is the most obvious target for those wishing to teach English in Korea, and with the number of **teaching jobs** on offer, it's quite possible to handpick the area of the city you'd like to live in. Doing so may save unnecessary disappointment: those who fail to do their research often end up living in the suburbs (Bundang, for example, has a veritable army of English teachers), which are an hour or so from the city centre. As well as teaching, some come to **study**. Korea has given a number of martial arts to the world, and continues to draw in students keen to learn directly from the horse's mouth; others choose to learn the local language.

Teaching English

Uncomplicated entry requirements, low tax and decent pay cheques make Korea one of the most popular stops on the **English-teaching** circuit. Demand for native speakers is high and still growing; English-teaching qualifications are far from essential (though they certainly help), and all that is usually required is a degree certificate, and a copy of your passport – many people have been taken on by a Korean school without so much as a telephone interview. Most new entrants start off by teaching kids at a **language school** (학원; *hagwon*). There are several pan-national chains, with YBM and Pagoda among the biggest; like the smaller operations, they pay around W2,500,000 per month. After a year or two, many teachers tire of kids and puny holiday allowances (typically less than two weeks a year), and make their way to a university teaching post; pay is usually lower and responsibilities higher than at a *hagwon*, though the holiday allowances (as much as five months a year) are hard to resist. Most teachers give their bank balance a nudge in the right direction by offering **private lessons** on the side – an illegal practice, but largely tolerated unless you start organizing them for others. To land a full-time job from outside Korea you'll have to go online, and it's still the best option if you're already in Korea – popular sites include Dave's ESL Café (Ⓦeslcafe.com) and HiTeacher (Ⓦhiteacher.com), though a thorough web search will yield more.

One of the most regular *hagwon*-related **complaints** is the long hours many teachers have to work – up to 30 per week. This may include Saturdays, or be spread quite liberally across the day from 9am to 9pm – try to find jobs with "no split shift" if possible. Questionable school policies also come in for stick; for example, teachers are often expected to be present at the school for show even if they have no lessons on. Real scare stories are ten-a-penny, too – every teacher knows an unfortunate fellow-foreigner whose school suddenly closed, the manager having ridden off into the sunset with a pay cheque or two. That said, most schools are reputable; you can typically expect them to organize **free accommodation**, and to do the legwork with your **visa** application. Some countries operate Working Holiday visa schemes with Korea, but others will need a full working visa to be legally employed; those unable to collect this in their home country are usually given a plane ticket and directions for a quick visa-run to Japan (the closest embassy is in Fukuoka).

Studying in Seoul

Korea has long been a popular place for the study of **martial arts**, while the country's ever-stronger ties with global business are also prompting many to gain a competitive advantage by studying the Korean language.

Language

Those looking to study **Korean** in Seoul have a full range of options to choose from, depending on what linguistic depth they require and how long they have to attain it. Students wanting fluency may consider attending one of the institutes run by the larger **universities**, though even these vary in terms of price, study time, skill level and accommodation.

Most of the year-long courses start in March – apply in good time. There's a good list at Ⓦenglish.visit korea.or.kr, while information on study visas and how to apply for them can be found on the Ministry of Education's website (Ⓦstudyinkorea.go.kr). There are **private institutes** dotted around Seoul and other major cities – Ⓦenglish.seoul.go.kr has a list of safe recommendations in the capital. Those who are working in Korea may find they have no time for intensive study, so opt to take language lessons from friends or colleagues.

Cooking

Seoul has a range of excellent Korean **cooking classes** aimed at novice foreigners. The best classes are run by **O'ngo** (Ⓦongofood.com), a cooking school just east of Insadonggil; beginner classes include *bulgogi*, *pajeon* and *kimchi* techniques, and cost from W45,000 per person. More refined are the classes at the **Institute of Traditional Korean Food** (Ⓦkfr.or.kr) north of Anguk station, which include lessons on royal cuisine. At the other end of the scale is **Yoo's Family** (Ⓦyoosfamily.com) near Jongmyo, who run simple *kimchi*-making classes from W20,000.

Martial arts

Finding classes for the most popular styles (including **taekwondo**, *hapkido* and *geomdo*) isn't hard, but very few cater for foreigners – it's best to go hunting on the expat circuit. Those looking for something more advanced should seek advice from their home country's own federations, rather than just turning up in Seoul.

Buddhist teachings

Many **temples** around the country offer teaching and templestay programmes for around W50,000 per night, a wonderful opportunity to see Seoul at its most serene (as long as you can stand the early mornings). Some temples are able to provide English-language instruction, and some not – see Ⓦeng.templestay.com for more details. Alternatively, the **Ahnkook Zen Academy**, north of Anguk station (Ⓦahnkookzen.org), runs English-language programmes every Saturday afternoon, though it gets mixed reports: the teachings themselves are good, but the ugly building tends to dash any thoughts of true Zen. Simpler, but perhaps more enjoyable for some, are the classes run by **Jogyesa** temple (see p.50), which charges W10,000 for a programme including Buddhist painting and lotus lantern-making; reserve as far in advance as possible through a tourist office. Lastly, and perhaps most suitable for spiritualism given its out-of-Seoul location, is the **Lotus Lantern Meditation Centre** (Ⓦlotuslantern.net) on the island of Ganghwado (see p.152), which runs weekend-long meditation programmes (W50,000) most weeks.

Travel essentials

Costs

Some people come to Korea expecting it to be a budget destination on a par with the Southeast Asian countries, while others arrive with expectations of Japanese-style levels. The truth is somewhere on the latter side of the scale – those staying at five-star hotels and eating at top restaurants will spend almost as much as they would in other developed countries, though there are numerous ways for budget travellers to make their trip a cheap one. Your biggest outlay is likely to be **accommodation** – Seoul has some grand places to stay costing upwards of W400,000 as well as cheaper tourist hotels for around W100,000. Though they're not to everyone's taste, motels (see p.103) usually make acceptable places to stay, costing W30,000–50,000, while the capital also has a fair few backpacker flophouses where prices start at W15,000 for a dorm bed. Real scrimpers can stay at a *jjimjilbang* (see box, p.107), where overnight entry fees start at around W7000.

Transport is unlikely to make too much of a dent in your wallet – even a taxi ride right across the city shouldn't cost more than W20,000, and short rides are under W5000. Public transport is even cheaper, usually W1000 per journey. **Sightseeing** is also affordable, with many sights free, and many more costing a nominal W1000–3000. The easiest thing to splurge on is **food**: Seoul has an ever-growing number of top-class restaurants, whose prices are generally far lower than they would be in other developed countries. For those fond of Korean cuisine, cheaper restaurants are plentiful, and a good meal can be had for W5000.

By staying in motels or guesthouses and eating at reasonably cheap restaurants, you should be able to survive easily on a **daily budget** of W40,000, or even half this if seriously pushed. After you've added in transport costs and a few entry tickets, a more realistic daily figure may be W60,000.

Tipping plays almost no part in Korean transactions – try not to leave unwanted change in the hands of a cashier, lest they feel forced to abandon their duties and chase you down the street with it. Exceptions are tourist hotels, most of which tack a ten percent service charge onto the room bill; these are also among the few places in the country to omit **tax** – also levied at ten percent – from their quoted prices.

Crime and personal safety

Korea is one of those countries in which you're far more likely to see someone running towards you with a dropped wallet than away with a stolen one – tales abound of travellers who have left a valuable possession on a restaurant table or park bench and returned hours later to find it in the same place. Though you'd be very unlucky to fall victim to a crime, it's prudent to take a few simple precautions regarding personal safety. One involves the country's awful **road accident** record, the gruesome statistics heightened by the number of vehicles that use pavements as short cuts or parking spaces. Caution should also be exercised around any **street fights** that you may have the misfortune to come across: since Korean men practise taekwondo to a fairly high level during their compulsory national service, Seoul is not a great place to get caught in a scuffle. In general, female travellers have little to worry about, and though some locals caution against taking night-time taxi rides alone, you'd be extremely unfortunate to come to harm in this (or indeed, any other) situation.

Electricity

The electrical **current** runs at 220v, 60Hz throughout the country, and requires European-style plugs with two round pins, though some older buildings, including many cheap guesthouses, may still take flat-pinned plugs at 110v.

Entry requirements

Citizens of almost any Western nation can enter Korea visa-free with an onward ticket, though the duration of the permit varies. Most EU nationals, including UK citizens, qualify for a visa exemption of three months or 90 days, as do citizens of the US, New Zealand and Australia; the Portuguese are allowed sixty days, South Africans just thirty, and Canadians a full six months. If you need longer than this, apply before entering Korea. **Overstaying** your visa will result in a large fine (up to W500,000 per day), with exceptions only being made in emergencies such as illness or loss of passport. Getting a new passport is time-consuming and troublesome, though the process will be simplified if your passport has been registered with your embassy in Seoul, or if you can prove your identity with a birth certificate or copy of your old passport.

Work visas

Work visas, valid for one year and extendable for at least one more, can be applied for before or after entering Korea. Applications can take up to a month to be processed by Korean embassies, but once inside the country it can take as little as a week. Your **employer** will do all the hard work with the authorities, then provide you with a visa confirmation slip; the visa must be picked up outside Korea (the nearest consulate is in Fukuoka, Japan; visas here can be issued on the day of application). Visas with the same employer can be extended without leaving Korea. An **alien card** must be applied for at the local immigration office within ninety days of arrival – again, this is usually taken care of by the employer. Work visas are forfeited on leaving Korea, though re-entry visas can be applied for at your provincial immigration office. Citizens of seventeen countries – including Americans, Australians, Brits, Canadians and New Zealanders – can apply for a **working holiday** visa at their local South Korean embassy, as long as they're aged between 18 and 30.

SOUTH KOREAN EMBASSIES AND CONSULATES ABROAD

Australia 113 Empire Circuit, Yarralumla, ACT 2600 ☎ 02 6270 4100, ⓦ aus-act.mofa.go.kr.
Canada 150 Boteler St, Ottawa, Ontario K1N 5A6 ☎ 613 244 5010, ⓦ can-ottawa.mofa.go.kr.
China No 3, 4th Avenue East, Sanlitun, Chaoyang District, Beijing 100600 ☎ 10 6532 0290.
Ireland 20 Clyde Rd, Ballsbridge, Dublin 4 ☎ 01 660 8800, ⓦ irl.mofa.go.kr.
Japan 1-2-5 Minami-Azabu, 1-chome, Minato-ku, Tokyo 106 ☎ 03 3452 7611, ⓦ jpn-tokyo.mofa.go.kr.
New Zealand 11th Floor, ASB Bank Tower, 2 Hunter St, Wellington ☎ 04 473 9073, ⓦ nzl-wellington.mofa.go.kr.
Singapore 47 Scotts Rd #08-00 Goldbell Towers, Singapore 228233 ☎ 6256 1188, ⓦ koreaembassy.org.sg.
South Africa Green Park Estates, Building 3, 27 George Storrar Drive, Groenkloof, Pretoria ☎ 012 460 2508, ⓦ zaf.mofa.go.kr.
UK 60 Buckingham Gate, London SW1E 6AJ ☎ 020 7227 5500, ⓦ gbr.mofa.go.kr.
US 2450 Massachusetts Ave NW, Washington, DC 20008 ☎ 202 939 5600, ⓦ usa.mofa.go.kr.

Gay and lesbian travellers

Despite Goryeo-era evidence suggesting that undisguised homosexuality was common in Royal and Buddhist circles, the **gay community** in today's Korea forms a small, alienated section of society. Indeed, many locals genuinely seem to believe that Korean homosexuality simply does not exist, regarding it instead as a "foreign disease" that instantly gives people AIDS. The prevalent traditional attitudes, together with the lack of a decent gay scene, have been the bane of many a queer expat's life in the country.

For Korean homosexuals, the problems are more serious – although the law makes no explicit reference to the legality of sexual intercourse between adults of the same sex, this is less a tacit nod of consent than a refusal of officialdom to discuss such matters, and gay activities may be punishable as sexual harassment, or even, shockingly, "mutual rape" if it takes place in the military. In the early 1990s, the first few **gay and lesbian websites** were cracked down on by a government that, during the course of the subsequent appeal, made it clear that human rights did not fully apply to homosexuals – all the more reason for the "different people" (*iban-in*), already fearful of losing their jobs, friends and family, to lock themselves firmly in the closet.

Korean society is, however, slowly but surely becoming more liberal, particularly in Seoul. With more and more high-profile homosexuals coming out, a critical mass has been reached, and younger generations are markedly less prejudiced against – and more willing to discuss – the pink issue. Gay clubs and bars, while still generally low-key outside "Homo Hill" in Itaewon, can now be found in other parts of the city too (see p.126). Finally, the **Korean Queer Culture Festival** takes place over a fortnight in early June at locations across Seoul (see p.26).

GAY INFORMATION SOURCES

Chingusai ⓦ chingusai.net. Loosely meaning "Among Friends", *Chingusai*'s trailblazing magazine is available at many gay bars in the capital. Mainly in Korean, but with some English-language information.
Travel Gay Asia ⓦ travelgayasia.com. Pan-Asian site featuring listings of bars, clubs and saunas, mainly focused on Seoul and Busan.
Utopia Asia ⓦ utopia-asia.com. Useful information about bars, clubs and saunas, including a good selection in Seoul.

Health

South Korea is pretty high up in the world rankings as far as **healthcare** goes, and there are no compulsory vaccinations or diseases worth getting too worried about. Hospitals are clean and well staffed, and most doctors can speak English, so the main health concerns for foreign travellers are likely to be financial – without adequate insurance cover, a large bill may rub salt into your healing wounds if you end up in hospital (see box, p.21). It would be wise to bring along any medicines that you might need, especially for drugs that need to be prescribed – bring a copy of your prescription, as well as the generic name of the drug in question, as brand names may vary from country to country.

Drinking Korean **tap water** is not the best idea, and with free drinking fountains in every restaurant, hotel, supermarket, police station, department store and internet café in the country, there really should be no need; in addition, the ubiquitous convenience stores sell bottles of water for W700. Restaurant food will almost always be prepared and cooked adequately (and all necessary precautions taken with raw fish), however bad it looks, though it's worth bearing in mind that the incredible amount of red pepper paste consumed by the average Korean has made stomach cancer the country's number one killer.

In an **emergency**, you should first try to ask a local to call for an ambulance. Should you need to do so yourself, the number is ☎119, though it's possible that no English-speaker will be available to take your call. Alternatively, try the tourist information line on ☎1330, or if all else fails dial English directory assistance on ☎080 211 0114. If the problem isn't life-threatening, the local tourist office should be able to point you in the direction of the most suitable doctor or hospital. Once there, you may find it surprisingly hard to get information about what's wrong with you – as in much of East Asia, patients are expected to trust doctors to do their jobs properly, and any sign that this trust is not in place results in a loss of face for the practitioner.

For minor complaints or medical advice, there are **pharmacies** all over the place, usually distinguished by the Korean character "yak" (약) at the entrance, though English-speakers are few and far between. Travellers can also visit a practitioner of **oriental medicine**, who will use acupuncture and pressure-point massage, among other techniques. If you have Korean friends, ask around for a personal recommendation in order to find a reputable practitioner.

Insurance

The price of hospital treatment in Korea can be quite high and, therefore, it's advisable to take out a decent **travel insurance** policy before you go. Keep the emergency number of your insurance company handy in the event of an accident and, as in any country, if you have anything stolen make sure you obtain a copy of the police report, as you will need this to make a claim.

Internet

You should have no problem getting online in South Korea, possibly the most connected nation on the planet. **Wi-fi** access is becoming ever more common, with many cafés allowing customers to use their connection for free. Tom N' Toms and Hollys are generally the best chains for this (though the coffee at the former is pretty poor). You may also be able to get online at your accommodation, though ironically the cheaper places are better: most modern motels have free-to-use terminals in the rooms, while hotels generally charge extortionate rates of over W20,000 per day.

If wi-fi fails, **PC rooms** (PC 방; pronounced "pishi-bang") are everywhere; though declining in number with each passing year, there should always be one within walking distance – just look for the letters "PC" in Roman characters. These cafés charge around W1500 per hour, with a one-hour minimum charge.

Laundry

Almost all tourist hotels provide a **laundry** service, and some of the backpacker hostels will wash your smalls for free. Public laundries are very thin on the ground, so those staying elsewhere may have to resort to a spot of DIY cleaning. All motels have

24-hour hot water, as well as soap, body lotion and/or shampoo in the bathrooms, and in the winter clothes dry in no time on the heated *ondol* floors. Summer is a different story, with the humidity making it very hard to dry clothes in a hurry. Dry-cleaning is straightforward, since there'll always be a *setakso* (세탁소) within walking distance.

Mail

The Korean postal system is cheap and trustworthy, and there are **post offices** in every district of Seoul. Most are open Monday to Friday 9am–6pm; all should be able to handle international mail, and the larger ones offer free internet access. The main problem facing many travellers is the relative dearth of **postcards** for sale, though if you do track some down, postal rates are cheap, at around W400 per card. Letters cost a little more, though as with **parcels** the tariff varies depending on their destination – the largest box you can send (20kg) will cost about W150,000 to mail to the UK or US, though this price drops to about W50,000 if you post via **surface mail**, a process that can take up to three months. All post offices have the necessary boxes for sale, and will even do your packing for a small fee.

Maps

Free maps, many of which are available in English, can be picked up at any tourist office or higher-end hotel, as well as most travel terminals. The main drawback with them is that distances and exact street patterns are hard to gauge, though it's a complaint the powers that be are slowly taking on board. Mercifully, maps for Bukhansan National Park are excellent and drawn to scale, and can be bought for W1000 at the park entrances. Those looking for professional maps will find plenty (although mostly in Korean) in the city's major bookshops (see p.134).

Money

The **Korean currency** is the won (W), which comes in notes of W1000, W5000, W10,000 and W50,000, and coins of W10, W50, W100 and W500. At the time of writing the **exchange rate** was approximately W1700 to £1, W1250 to €1, and W1100 to US$1.

Travellers occasionally encounter difficulties when attempting to withdraw money from **ATMs** (there are several different systems in operation, even within the same banking chains), but most should be able to withdraw cash using an international debit or credit card. The official advice is to head to an ATM marked

"Global", which are easiest to find in branches of KB Bank. Global ATMs and similar machines are also commonplace in the ubiquitous 24-hour convenience stores such as Family Mart, 7-Eleven or LG25. Most machines capable of dealing with foreign cards are able to switch to English-language mode.

Though you shouldn't rely on them, foreign **credit cards** are being accepted in more and more hotels, restaurants and shops. It shouldn't be too hard to **exchange** foreign notes or travellers' cheques for Korean cash once in the country; banks are all over the place, and the only likely problem when dealing in dollars, pounds or euros is how long it takes – some places simply won't have exchanged money before. **Leaving Korea** with local currency is not advisable, as it's hard to exchange outside the country – get it changed before you head to the airport if you want a good rate.

Opening hours and public holidays

Seoul is one of the world's truest 24-hour cities – **opening hours** are such that almost everything you need is likely to be available when you require it. Most shops and almost all restaurants are open daily, often until late, as are tourist information offices. A quite incredible number of establishments are open 24/7, including convenience stores, saunas, internet cafés and some of the busier shops and restaurants. Post offices (Mon–Fri 9am–6pm) and banks (Mon–Fri 9.30am–4pm) keep more sensible hours.

Until recently, the country was one of the few in the world to have a **six-day working week**; though this has been officially reduced to five, the changes haven't filtered through to all workers, and Korea's place at the top of the world's "average hours worked per year" table has not been affected. The number of **national holidays** has fallen, however, in an attempt to make up the slack, and as most of the country's population are forced to take their holiday at the same times, there can be chaos on the roads and rails. Three of the biggest holidays – Lunar New Year, Buddha's birthday and *Chuseok* – are based on the lunar calendar, and have no fixed dates (see box, p.34).

Phones

Getting hold of a **mobile phone** while you're in the country is easy – there are 24-hour rental booths at Incheon Airport. Using your own phone is more problematic, but you'll be able to rent a data-only SIM at the same places, or switch on roaming.

SOUTH KOREAN PUBLIC HOLIDAYS

Sinjeong (New Year's Day) January 1. Seoul celebrates New Year in much the same fashion as Western countries, with huge crowds gathering around City Hall.

Seollal (Lunar New Year) Usually early February. One of the most important holidays on the calendar, Lunar New Year sees Koreans flock to their home towns for a three-day holiday of relaxed celebration, and many businesses close up.

Independence Movement Day March 1.

Children's Day May 5. Koreans make an even bigger fuss over their kids than usual on this national holiday – expect parks, zoos and amusement parks to be jam-packed.

Memorial Day June 6. Little more than a day off for most Koreans, this day honours those who fell in battle, and is best observed in the National Cemetery.

Constitution Day July 17.

Independence Day August 15. The country becomes a sea of Korean flags on this holiday celebrating the end of Japanese rule in 1945.

Chuseok Late September or early October. One of the biggest events on the Korean calendar is this three-day national holiday, similar to Thanksgiving; families head to their home towns to venerate their ancestors in low-key ceremonies, and eat a special crescent-shaped rice-cake.

National Foundation Day October 3. Celebrates the 2333 BC birth of Dangun, the legendary founder of the Korean nation. Shamanist celebrations take place at shrines around Seoul, with the most important on Inwangsan mountain (see p.83).

Christmas Day December 25. Every evening looks like Christmas in neon-drenched Seoul, but on this occasion Santa Haraboji (Grandpa Santa) finally arrives.

If you're going to be in Korea for a while, you may want to buy a secondhand mobile phone; the best places to look are shopping districts, electrical stores or underground malls. After purchase you'll need to register with a major service provider – KT and SK Telecom are two of the biggest chains, and so ubiquitous that the nearest store is likely to be within walking distance. Registration is free, though

you'll need a Korean ID of some sort (bring a Korean friend along if you're not legally employed in the country); you can top up pay-as-you-go accounts in increments of W10,000.

Despite the prevalence of mobile phones, you'll still see **payphones** on every major street; many of these ageing units only take coins, meaning that you'll have to pump in change at a furious pace to avoid the deafening squawks that signal the end of your call-time. Pre-paid travel cards (see box, p.24) will work with some of these machines.

PHONE CODES

To call Seoul from abroad, use the **Korean international dialling code** (❶82), followed by 2, then the seven- or eight-digit number. When dialling the UK, Ireland, Australia and New Zealand from Seoul, dial 001 to get **an international connection**, then dial the relevant country code (see below), and omit the initial zero from the area code.

Australia International access code + 61 + city code.

Ireland International access code + 353 + city code.

New Zealand International access code + 64 + city code.

South Africa International access code + 27 + city code.

UK International access code + 44 + city code.

US and Canada International access code + 1 + area code.

Photography

Photography is a national obsession in Korea – at tourist sights around the country, and even at every café in the land, locals feed their cameras as they would hungry pets. Few Koreans will mind being photographed, though of course it's polite to ask first. One serious no-no is to go snap-happy on a tour of the DMZ (see p.143) – this can land tourists in trouble, and has indeed done so. You may also see temple-keepers and monks poised ready to admonish would-be photographers of sacrosanct areas.

Smoking

Many Korean men smoke, as well as a growing number of younger women – no real surprise, with packets of twenty starting at around W3000 in any convenience store. In line with international norms, it's illegal – at least in theory – to light up in a restaurant or bar, though some larger cafés have dedicated smoking sections. Many Koreans retreat to public toilets for a cigarette; curiously, many have signs on the doors forbidding such activities, yet also ashtrays or paper cups on hand for those who break the rules.

Time

The Korean peninsula shares a **time zone** with Japan – one hour ahead of China, nine hours ahead of Greenwich Mean Time, seven hours ahead of South Africa, fourteen hours ahead of Eastern Standard Time in the US or Canada, and one hour behind Sydney. Bear in mind that daylight saving hours are not observed, so though noon in London will be 9pm in Seoul for much of the year, the difference drops to eight hours during British Summer Time.

Tourist information

The Korean tourist authorities churn out a commendable number of English-language maps, pamphlets and books, most of which are handed out at **information booths** which you can find all over Seoul including at the city's train and bus stations. Not all of these have English-speakers, but you'll be able to get 24-hour assistance and advice on the dedicated **tourist information line** – dial ☎02 1330 and you'll be put through to helpful call-centre staff who speak a number of languages and can advise on transport, sights, accommodation, theatre ticket prices and much more. The official **Korean tourist website** (Ⓦenglish.visitkorea.or.kr) is also quite useful.

KTO Tourist Information Center Cheonggyecheonno ☎02 1330; map p.56. On the basement level of the Korea Tourist Organization's HQ, this is the largest and most info-packed tourist office in town. They're able to help with anything from accommodation to tours, and have handy pamphlets detailing sights around the city. English spoken. Daily 9am–8pm.

Insadong Tourist Information Center Yulgongno; map p.49. Right at the north end of Insadonggil, and conveniently located for an array of surrounding sights, this small office can help with basic sightseeing queries. Daily 9am–6pm.

Itaewon Tourist Information Center Itaewon station ☎02 3785 0942; map p.91. Within Itaewon subway station itself, this small office is handy if you're looking for something local. Daily 9am–6pm.

Myeongdong Tourist Information Center Euljiro 2-ga 171 ☎02 778 0333; map p.64. The largest of Seoul's tourist offices, and also very helpful when trying to glean advice for destinations around the country. English-speakers always on hand. Daily 9am–8pm.

Travelling with children

Seoul has high standards of **health and hygiene**, low levels of crime and plenty to see and do – bringing children of any age should pose no special problems. Koreans dote upon their children, no real surprise given that the birth rate is among the lowest on earth. Locals make enough fuss over their own kids, but foreign children (particularly those with fair hair) are likely to find themselves the star of plenty of photographs.

Changing facilities are common in public toilets (department stores are particularly good for this), and classier restaurants have highchairs. Unfortunately, baby food labelled in English is almost non-existent. A few hotels provide a babysitting service, though those in need can also ask their concierge for a newspaper with babysitter adverts (see p.25). There are also cinemas (see p.129), theme parks (see p.98 & p.101) and a zoo or two (see p.101) to keep children amused.

Finally, a few words of warning. It's essential to note that some of the restaurants listed in this guide – especially those serving *galbi*, a self-barbecued meat – have hotplates or charcoal in the centre of the table, which poses an obvious danger to little hands. Additionally, in a country where it's perfectly normal for cars to drive on the pavements, you may want to exercise a little more caution than normal when walking around town with your children. Note that breastfeeding in public may still cause grave offence.

Travellers with disabilities

Despite its First World status, Korea can be filed under "developing countries" as far as **disabled accessibility** is concerned, and with rushing traffic and crowded streets, it's not the easiest destination to get around. Until recently, very little attention was paid to those with disabilities, but things are changing. Streets are being made more wheelchair-friendly, and many subway and train stations have been fitted with lifts. Almost all motels and tourist hotels have lifts, too, though occasionally you'll come across an entrance that hasn't been built with wheelchairs in mind. Some museums and tourist attractions will be able to provide a helper if necessary, but wherever you are, Koreans are likely to jump at the chance to help travellers in obvious need of assistance.

GEUNJEONGJEON THRONE HALL, GYEONGBOKGUNG

Gyeongbokgung and around

Seoul is one of the world's largest urban agglomerations, racing out for kilometre after kilometre in every direction, and swallowing up whole cities well beyond its own official limits. As such, it's hard to imagine that the Korean capital was once a much smaller place, bounded by fortress walls erected shortly after the nascent Joseon dynasty chose it as their seat of power in 1392. The palace of Gyeongbokgung was built during these fledgling years, and centuries down the line its environs are still the seat of national power. The oldest and most historically important of Seoul's five palaces, Gyeongbokgung attracts the greatest number of visitors and boasts a splendid mountain backdrop, as well as two great museums.

BEST OF GYEONGBOKGUNG AND AROUND

Gyeongbokgung The daddy of Seoul's palaces, and a must-see on any itinerary. See below
National Museum of Modern and Contemporary Art With its creative exhibitions, this
new museum is the best of Gyeongbokgung's many galleries. See p.43
Bukchon Hanok Village Meander through this neighbourhood of traditional Korean houses,
many of which have been converted into tourist accommodation. See p.44
Traditional workshops and classes Learn a Korean art or craft – create your own embroidery,
woodwork, dolls, *kimchi* and more. See box, p.45
Secret Garden The most attractive place in Seoul, this secluded patch of greenery lies at the
back of Changdeokgung palace. See p.46
Tongin Market A hit with local youngsters, this atmospheric market operates a quirky meal
scheme in which you pay for your food with tokens, fashioned like old-style coins. See p.110

Abutting **Gyeongbokgung** to the northeast is the neighbourhood of **Samcheongdong**,
a trendy, laidback area filled with cafés, galleries, wine bars and clothing boutiques.
Across a small ridge, hilly **Bukchon Hanok Village** is one of the few pockets of
traditional architecture remaining in the city – its wooden buildings with their tiled
rooftops shelter plenty of tearooms and traditional culture. Beyond Bukchon Hanok
Village, the palace of **Changdeokgung** is the only one of Seoul's palaces to have been
awarded UNESCO World Heritage status: a little more refined than Gyeongbokgung,
it has superb architecture and a charming garden. Heading west from Gyeongbokgung
will bring you to **Seochon**, currently Seoul's most trendy area.

Gyeongbokgung

경복궁 • Sajingno 161 • March–Oct daily 9am–6pm; Nov–Feb Wed–Sat 9am–5pm; Free English-language tours at 11am, 1.30pm &
3.30pm • W3000; also on combination ticket (see box, p.39) • Changing of the guard Wed–Mon at 10am, 1pm & 3pm • ⓦ royalpalace.go.kr •
Gyeongbokgung subway (line 3)

The glorious palace of **Gyeongbokgung** is, with good reason, the most popular tourist
sight in the city, and a focal point of the country as a whole. The place is quite
absorbing, and the chance to stroll the dusty paths between its delicate tile-roofed
buildings is one of the most enjoyable experiences Seoul has to offer. Gyeongbokgung
was ground zero for Seoul's emergence as a place of power, having been built to house
the royal family of the embryonic **Joseon dynasty**, shortly after they transferred their
capital here in 1392. The complex has witnessed fires, repeated destruction and even
a royal assassination (see p.166), but careful reconstruction means that the regal
atmosphere of old is still palpable, aided no end by the suitably majestic crags of
Bugaksan to the north. A large historical complex with excellent on-site **museums** (see
p.42), it will easily eat up the best part of a day to see it all.

Substantial **reconstruction** of Gyeongbokgung began in earnest in 1989, when the city
government embarked on a mammoth forty-year campaign to re-create the hundreds of
buildings that once filled the palace walls. The Seoul Capitol, which was used after the
war as the Korean National Assembly, then the National Museum, was finally torn
down on Independence Day (see p.34) in 1995. More than half of Gyeongbokgung's
former buildings have now been rebuilt, and the results are extremely pleasing.
Particularly noteworthy was the **reopening of Gwanghwamun** in 2010, since this was the
first time Korea's most famous palace gate had been present in its original position, and
built with traditional materials, since the fall of Joseon.

Brief history

Construction of the "Palace of Shining Happiness" was ordered by **King Taejo** in 1394
and completed in 1399: it then held the regal throne for over two hundred years. At
the peak of its importance, the palace housed over four hundred buildings within its

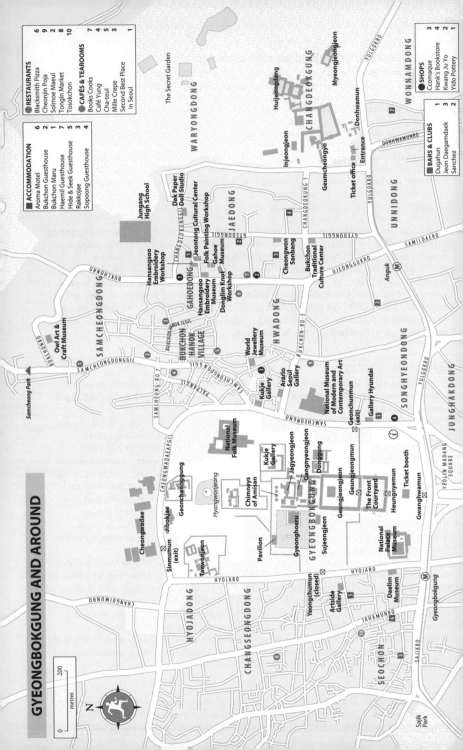

GYEONGBOKGUNG AND AROUND

N

0   200
metres

■ ACCOMMODATION	
Aroma Motel	6
Bukchon Guesthouse	2
Bukchon Maru	1
Haemil Guesthouse	7
Hide & Seek Guesthouse	5
Rakkojae	3
Sopoong Guesthouse	4

● RESTAURANTS	
Blacksmith Pizza	6
Cheonjin Poja	9
Solmoe Maeul	2
Tongin Market	8
Tosokchon	10
● CAFÉS & TEAROOMS	
Books Cooks	7
Café Yung	4
Cha-teul	5
Mille Crepe	3
Second Best Place	
in Seoul	1

● SHOPS	
Ccomaque	3
Hank's Bookstore	4
Kwang Ju Yo	2
Yido Pottery	1

■ BARS & CLUBS	
Dugahun	1
Jeon Daegamdaek	3
Sanchez	2

1

VISITING SEOUL'S PALACES

Entrance to four of Seoul's palaces – Gyeongbokgung (see p.37), Changdeokgung including the Secret Garden (see p.46), Changgyeonggung (see p.71) and Deoksugung (see p.60) – plus the Jongmyo shrine (see p.50), is included on a W10,000 **combination ticket**. The ticket can be bought at all the venues, and is valid for a month from first usage – you only have to visit Gyeongbokgung, Changdeokgung and the Secret Garden to get your money's worth. Note that some of the palaces are closed on Mondays or Tuesdays.

vaguely rectangular perimeter walls, but most were burnt down during the Japanese invasions in the 1590s. Though few Koreans will admit it, the invaders were not always to blame – the arsonists in one major fire were actually a group of local slaves, angered by their living and working conditions, and aware that their records were kept locked up in the palace. The palace was only rebuilt following the coronation of child-king **Gojong** in 1863, but these renovations were destined to be short-lived thanks to the expansionist ideas of contemporary Japan, who in 1895 removed one major obstacle to power by assassinating Gojong's wife, Empress Myeongsong (see box, p.40), in the Gyeongbokgung grounds. Following this murder, the Japanese slowly increased their standing in Korea, before making a formal annexation of the peninsula in 1910. Gyeongbokgung, beating heart of an occupied nation, was first in the line of fire and, all in all, only a dozen of the palace's buildings survived the occupation period.

Under Japanese rule, the palace was used for police interrogation and torture, and numerous structural changes were made in an apparent effort to destroy Korean pride. The front gate, Gwanghwamun, was moved to the east of the complex, destroying the north–south geometric principles followed during the palace's creation, while 1926 saw the construction of the **Seoul Capitol**, a huge Neoclassical Japanese construction that became the city's largest building at the time, dwarfing the former royal structures around it, and making a rather obvious stamp of authority. Other insinuations were more subtle – viewed from above, the building's shape was identical to the Japanese written character for "sun" (日). One interesting suggestion, and one certainly not beyond the scope of Japanese thinking at that time, is that Bukhansan mountain to the north resembled the character for "big" (大) and City Hall to the south – also built by the Japanese – that of "root" (本), thereby emblazoning Seoul's most prominent points with the three characters that made up the written name of the **Empire of the Rising Sun** (大日本).

Gyeongbokgung remained a locus of power after the Japanese occupation ended with **World War II** in 1945; the American military received the official Japanese surrender at the Seoul Capitol, and in 1948 **Syngman Rhee**, the first president of Korea, took his oath on the building's front steps. Then, of course, came the Korean War (1950–53, though technically still going on), during which Seoul changed hands four times – it will suffice to say that the palace complex, one of Asia's most wonderful royal abodes just a few decades previously, resembled a bomb site by the time full-scale warfare ceased.

Geunjeongjeon

Most visitors start their tour at the palace's southern gate, **Gwanghwamun** (광화문), though there's another small entrance on the eastern side of Gyeongbokgung. Entering through the first courtyard – now minus the Japanese command post – you'll see **Geunjeongjeon** (금정전), the palace's former throne room, looming ahead. Despite being the largest wooden structure in the country, this two-level construction remains surprisingly graceful, the corners of its gently sloping roof home to lines of small guardian figurines, beneath which dangle tiny bells. The central path leading up to the building was once used only by the king, but is now open to all. However, the best views of Geunjeongjeon's interior are actually from the sides – from here you'll see the

1

TROUBLE AT THE PALACE

Rarely have troubles with the in-laws achieved as much significance as those endured by the Joseon royalty during the latter part of the nineteenth century. Korea was, at the time, ruled by **King Gojong** (r.1863–1907), a weak leader destined to be his country's penultimate monarch. Gojong took the throne when he was just eleven years of age, with his father **Heungseon** acting as regent and de facto ruler of the country. Heungseon was deeply Confucian and suspicious of foreigners: in 1866, he incurred a military invasion from France after ordering the execution of nine French missionaries. King Gojong reached marriageable age at 14, and took **Myeongseong** as a wife. With no powerful relatives, Heungseon assumed that the empress would be as malleable as his son, but the two quickly became enemies – favouring modernization, Myeongseong's beliefs ran contrary to those of her father-in-law, and by 1872 she had forced him to retire from the court. Her attempts at reform were stymied by the Japanese, who had their own plans for power in Seoul and ratcheted up their standing on the peninsula during the 1880s and 1890s. Attempting one final hurrah, Heungseon cosied up to the Japanese, but he underestimated the scale of their ambition, which became clear in October 1895. A team of **Japanese agents** entered the palace by force early one morning, murdering Myeongseong and two other women. Over fifty men were charged, but none was convicted. An obstacle to the Japanese until the end, it's no surprise that Myeongseong – posthumously made **empress** in 1902, and referred to by the Japanese as "Queen Min" – is now venerated as a national heroine.

Her shady tale has been told in countless movies and soap operas, as well as in *The Last Empress*, Korea's first original musical, the success of which spawned versions in New York and London's West End.

golden dragons on the hall ceiling, as well as the throne itself, backed by its traditional folding screen.

The living quarters

After Geunjeongjeon you can take one of a number of routes around the complex. To the east of the throne room are the buildings that once housed **crown princes**, deliberately placed here to give these regal pups the day's first light, while behind is **Gangnyeongjeon** (강녕전), the former living quarters of the king and queen, furnished with replica furniture. Also worth seeking out is **Jagyeongjeon** (자경전), a building backed by a beautiful stone wall, and chimneys decorated with animal figures – used to direct smoke outwards from the living quarters' *ondol* (an ingenious underfloor heating system still employed in Korean apartments today), these flues were made from pink-red brick, and look slightly incongruous in their surroundings.

Gyeonghoeru

West of the throne room is **Gyeonghoeru** (경회루), a colossal pavilion looking out over a tranquil **lotus pond** that was a favourite with artists in imperial times; it remains so today, though only from the periphery, since the pavilion itself is almost always closed to visitors. Its surrounding pond was also used as a ready source of water for the fires that regularly broke out around the palace (an unfortunate by-product of heating buildings using burning wood or charcoal under the floor), while the pavilion itself was used for events as varied as royal banquets and civil service examinations, the latter an integral part of life in the Confucian kingdom of Joseon (see p.174 for more on Confucianism in Korea).

The rear of the complex

To the north again, and past another pond, is **Geoncheonggung** (건청궁), a freshly renovated miniature palace famed as the venue of Empress Myeongseong's assassination (see box above). At the beginning of the twentieth century, there was actually a Western-style building on these grounds, providing evidence of how the reclusive

1

"Hermit Kingdom" of Joseon opened up to foreign ideas in its final years. This building, now destroyed, was designed by Russian architect A.S. Seredin-Sabatin, who was visiting at the time of the assassination, and witnessed the murder himself.

One foreign-themed building still in existence is **Jibokjae** (지복재), just to the west, a miniature palace constructed in 1888 during the rule of King Gojong to house books and works of art. Designed in the Chinese style that was the height of fashion at the time, this building is markedly different from any other structures around the palace, particularly the two-storey octagonal pavilion on its western end. Geoncheonggung sits right next to the palace's northern exit, but if you still have a little energy to spare, press on further west to **Taewonjeon** (태원전), a relatively new clutch of buildings. Though there's little of historical interest here, the area's mountain views and relative dearth of visitors make it the perfect end to a tour around the palace.

The National Folk Museum

국립민속박물관 • March–April, Sept & Oct Wed–Sun 9am–6pm; May–Aug Mon, Tues, Thurs & Fri 9am–6pm, Sat & Sun 9am–7pm; Nov–Feb Wed–Sun 9am–5pm • Entrance included in palace ticket • Ⓦ nfm.go.kr

On the east of the palace complex is the diverting **National Folk Museum**, a traditionally styled, multi-tier structure that fits in nicely with the palatial buildings. Despite its size, there's only one level, but this is stuffed with dioramas and explanations of Korean ways of life long since gone, from fishing and farming practices to examples of clothing worn during the Three Kingdoms era (c.57 BC – 668 AD). Children may well find the exhibits more interesting than slogging around the palace buildings, plus there's a gift shop and small café near the entrance, which makes it an excellent pit stop for those who need to take a break.

The National Palace Museum

국립고궁박물관 • Tues–Fri 9am–6pm, Sat & Sun 9am–7pm • Free • Free English-language tours at 11am & 2.30pm • Ⓦ gogung.go.kr

At the far southwest of the palace grounds is the **National Palace Museum**. This was the site of the National Museum (see p.92) until 2005, when it moved to a new location, leaving behind exhibits related to the Seoul palaces. The star of the show here is a **Ilwolobongdo**, a folding screen which would have once been placed behind the imperial throne, and features the sun (the *il* from the name), moon (that's the *wol*) and five peaks (*obong*) painted onto a dark blue background, symbolically positioning the seated kings at the nexus of heaven and earth. It's a glorious, significant piece of art that deserves to be better known. Other items in the fascinating display include a jade book belonging to King Taejo, some paraphernalia relating to ancestral rites, and some of the wooden dragons taken from the temple eaves, whose size and detail can be better appreciated when seen up close. Equally meticulous is a map of the heavens, engraved onto a stone slab in 1395.

Seochon

서촌

Immediately to the west of Gyeongbokgung is a mix of eclectic neighbourhoods – these are often banded together under the name **Seochon**, which means "west village". As recently as 2013, few non-locals ventured here, yet today it is one of Seoul's trendiest locales. Most come to eat, drink and be merry in **Sejong Maeul**, a small but popular street lined with charming restaurants; it was named after King Sejong, the creator of the Korean alphabet (see p.181), and you'll see that businesses lining the main road to the east all sport signs in *hangeul*, rather than Roman letters. Elsewhere, **Artside** and the **Daelim Museum** are the best of the area's many gallery spaces, while the Tongin Market (see p.110) lures locals with its earthy vibe, and an admirably zany meal scheme.

Daelim Museum

다림미술관 • Jahamunno 4-gil 21 • Tues–Sun 10am–6pm • W5000 • ⓦ daelimmuseum.org • Gyeongbokgung subway (line 3)

One of Seoul's most highly regarded galleries, the **Daelim Museum** hosts a string of
fascinating temporary exhibitions, with the focus on photography. Past contributors
have included Karl Lagerfeld and Stella McCartney, though the curators also branch off
into other fields: clothes from Paul Smith and furniture from Jean Prouve have been on
display during past exhibitions.

Artside Gallery

아트사이드갤러리 • Tonguidong 33 • Tues–Sun 10am–6pm • Free, though fee occasionally levied for special exhibitions •
ⓦ artside.org • Gyeongbokgung subway (line 3)

With a sister gallery in Beijing, the **Artside Gallery** is one of only two places in Seoul
that regularly exhibit work from China's increasingly interesting contemporary art
scene: the other is Arario in Samcheongdong (see box below). The gallery moved to
trendy Seochon in 2013, and its basement hall is perfect for larger-scale exhibitions,
which change every month or so.

Samcheongdong

삼청동

The youthful district of **Samcheongdong** is crammed with restaurants, cafés and
galleries, many of which have a contemporary appearance. For years a surprisingly
well-kept secret (given its location between two major palaces), the area's maze of tiny
streets is now regularly jam-packed with camera-toting youngsters – especially on warm
weekend afternoons. The area's charming main drag, **Samcheongdonggil** (삼청동길),
heads off from Gyeongbokgung's northeastern corner – a mere five-minute walk from
the palace's eastern exit. The district is also home to Korea's most important road in
artistic terms, **Samcheongno**, which runs along the eastern flank of the palace and
sports a number of excellent art galleries (see box below), as well as the city's new
National Museum of Modern and Contemporary Art.

National Museum of Modern and Contemporary Art

국립미술관 • Samcheongno 30 • Tues, Thurs, Fri & Sun 10am–6pm, Wed & Sat 10am–9pm; closed Mon • W4000 • ⓦ mmca.go.kr •
Anguk subway (line 3); four daily shuttle buses run to their other location in Gwacheon (see p.101)

Opened in late 2013, this third wing of the **National Museum of Modern and
Contemporary Art** (see p.60 and p.101 for the other two) boasts an interesting history
– this site was, among other things, once home to the national Taoist temple, the
Gyeongbokgung library, the Joseon Office of Censors and the Office of Royal
Genealogy. The main building, now renovated, was erected to house the Japanese

---

SAMCHEONGNO'S ART GALLERIES

Arario Seoul Bukchonno 5-gil 84 ⓦ ararioseoul
.com; Anguk subway (line 3). This large venue lends
itself to sculptures and large paintings, with artworks
from renowned artists. With a sister gallery in Shanghai,
the Arario is a great place to check out the latest
offerings from the increasingly interesting Chinese art
scene. Tues–Sun 11am–7pm; free.

Gallery Hyundai Samcheongno 14 ⓦ gallery
hyundai.com; Anguk subway (line 3). This large gallery
possesses the most esteemed collection in the area;
established in the 1960s, it's Korea's longest-running

commercial gallery. Its focus has long been on artists born
before 1930, though there's an ever-increasing emphasis
on newer trends. Tues–Sun 10am–6pm; free.

Kukje Gallery Samcheongno 54 ⓦ kukjegallery
.com; Anguk subway (line 3). The Kukje is one of
the most important players in the area, actively
promoting Korean artists abroad, and displaying a
wide, well-selected range of exhibits in its own space.
It's surrounded by excellent cafés, and there's an Italian
restaurant in the same building. Mon–Sat 10am–6pm,
Sun 10am–5pm; free.

1

SEOUL'S QUIRKY MUSEUMS

Samcheongdong and Bukchon are home to countless tiny museums, and while none is exactly a must-see, it can be worth popping into one or two on your way around the area – especially if the weather is inclement.

Gahoe Museum 가회박물관 Gahoedong 11-103; Anguk subway (line 3). Housed in one of Bukchon's many wooden *hanok* abodes, the folk art here is suitably traditional. The friendly curators also offer regular hands-on craft programmes. Wed–Sat 10am–6pm; W3000.

Owl Art & Craft Museum 부엉이박물관 Samcheongdong 27-21; Anguk subway (line 3). The result of its founder's quirky (and slightly scary) obsession, this small museum is stuffed to the gills with anything and everything pertaining to owls.

There's a small tearoom-cum-café in which you can purchase strigiform trinkets of your very own. Wed–Sat 10am–7pm; W5000.

World Jewellery Museum 세계장신구박물관 Hwadong 75-3, ⓦ wjmuseum.com; Anguk subway (line 3). With a name that's as coldly descriptive as they come, it may come as a surprise that this museum is the most rewarding in the area, with the pieces on display offering great subtlety and variety. Wed–Sat 11am–5.30pm; W5000.

Defence Security Command during the occupation. Despite the building's history, the art on display today is most definitely modern and contemporary. There's no permanent display, but all the exhibitions (there's usually a new one every two weeks) are highly creative. Start your visit in the open-air Madang Gallery, a space inspired by the Turbine Hall in London's Tate Modern.

Cheongwadae

청와대 • Sejongno 1 • Guided tours Tues–Sat at 10am, 11am, 2pm & 3pm • Free, but must be booked at ⓦ english.president.go.kr at least three weeks in advance; bring your passport. Tickets can be collected at Gyeongbokgung • Gyeongbokgung or Anguk subway (both line 3)

What the White House is to Washington, **Cheongwadae** is to Seoul. Sitting directly behind Gyeongbokgung and surrounded by mountains, this official presidential residence is sometimes nicknamed the "Blue House" on account of the colour of its roof tiles. In Joseon times, blue roofs were reserved for kings, but the office of president is the nearest modern-day equivalent. This is not without its hazards: in 1968, there was an attempt here to **assassinate** then-President **Park Chung-hee** (see p.170). Security measures mean that it's only possible to visit Cheongwadae on a guided tour. Unfortunately, tours do not include any of the main buildings, so visitors will have to be content with strolling around the luscious gardens, and popping into the occasional shrine.

Note that even if you're not visiting Cheongwadae, the road bordering the palace is a high-security area; while you're unlikely to be accused of wanting to assassinate the incumbent head of state, those loitering or straying too close are likely to be questioned.

Samcheong Park

삼청공원 • Waryonggongwongil 41 • Daily 24hr • Free • Anguk subway (line 3)

At the top of Samcheongdonggil, **Samcheong Park** is a small but delightful spot that for some reason never finds itself overrun with visitors, even on the sunniest Sunday of the year. It was Korea's first-ever officially designated park, having been awarded said status in 1940, and its leafy, sheltered trails make for fantastic walking. The park can also be used as an entry point for the loftier trails of Bugaksan (see p.76).

Bukchon Hanok Village

북촌 한옥 마을

Although it has few actual sights, **Bukchon Hanok Village** is one of the city's most characterful areas and there's some delightful walking to be done among this web of quiet, hilly lanes, mopping up the odd café, picturesque view or traditional workshop (see box below) along the way. Despite being just across the road from Insadong and its teeming tourists, Bukchon feels a world apart, with its cascades of tiled rooftops, and a pleasing clutch of tearooms and traditional museums.

The area is characterized by its traditional wooden **hanok buildings** (see box, p.9), which have been saved from demolition by the city authorities, partly due to their proximity to the presidential abode, and partly because of protest movements led by locals; a few of the buildings have even been converted into guesthouses (see box, p.104). *Hanok* housing once covered the whole country, but most of those lucky enough to survive the Japanese occupation and civil war were torn down during the country's economic revolution, and replaced with rows of sterile fifteen-storey blocks – it's estimated that today more than seventy percent of the country's population lives in high-rise apartment buildings. Even in Bukchon, many of the *hanok* houses are far from traditional, with basement levels, garages, Western-style beds and other modern accoutrements.

Bukchon Hanok Ilgil

북촌 한옥 1길 • 24hr • Free • Anguk subway (line 3)

Many Bukchon visitors make a beeline to **Bukchon Hanok Ilgil**, a steep lane with a particularly good view of the *hanok* abodes. From the top of the lane, the high-rise architecture of the City Hall area is impossible to ignore – standing behind such wonderful original structures, this quintessential "tradition-meets-modernity" view certainly poses questions about how Korea might have looked had its progress been a little more gentle.

BUKCHON'S TRADITIONAL WORKSHOPS AND CLASSES

Bukchon boasts more than just architecture and tea – the area is riddled with workshops producing quintessential Korean products. Some also offer visitors a hands-on experience and a chance to learn some traditional crafts.

Bukchon Traditional Culture Center 북촌문화센터 Gyedong 105, ⓦbukchon.seoul .go.kr; Anguk subway (line 3). Just north of Anguk station, the Bukchon Traditional Culture Center hosts regular classes and workshops of traditional art and craft such as knot-making, calligraphy and tea ceremonies: it also functions as a small tourist information centre. Daily 10am–6pm; free.

Cheongwon Sanbang 청원산방 Bukchonno 6-gil; Anguk subway (line 3). Woodworking classes offered in a suitably pine-lined *hanok* space that's a wee bit tricky to find. Classes Thurs–Sun.

Dak Paper Doll Studio 닥종이 공방 Changdeo-kgung 4-gil 45-13; Anguk subway (line 3). A genuine doll-making workshop, though one geared towards allowing guests to create their own – there are hour-long classes most days. Tues–Sun 10.30am–5pm; free.

Donglim Knot Workshop 동림매듭공방 Gahoedong 11-7; Anguk subway (line 3). Small venue with assorted embroidered knots on display, and for sale. Have a go at making your own for W7000–10,000. Tues–Sun 10am–6pm; W1000.

Folk Painting Workshop 가회 민화공방 Bukchonno 12-gil 17; Anguk subway (line 3). A great place for children, though adults can also have fun making amulet stamps, roof-tile rubbings and painted bags. Tues–Sun 10am–6pm; W2000.

Hansangsoo Embroidery Workshop 한상수 자수 박물관 Gahoedong 11-32, ⓦhansangsoo .com; Anguk subway (line 3). Former embroidery workshop with a number of prized folk relics on display, as well as some made by the eponymous Han Sang Soo and his apprentices. Unfortunately, it's now more commonly used as a pretty backdrop for Asian tourists dressed up in Korean silks. Tues–Sun 10am–5pm; W2000.

Jeontong Cultural Center 전통 공예 체험관 Gahoedong 11-91; Anguk subway (line 3). Not exactly a workshop, but a cultural space offering visitors the chance to make all sorts of artefacts – gilded bookmarks, indigo-dyed handkerchiefs, paper dolls and *hanji* handmirrors. There are three courses a day, all costing W7000–15,000. Tues–Sun 10.30am–5pm.

1

Jungang High School

중앙고등학교 • Changdeokgunggil 164 • Daily 24hr; usually closed during class times • Free • Anguk subway (line 3)

While on a Bukchon stroll you may come across **Jungang High School**, built in the 1930s along vaguely Tudor architectural lines. The front gates have for years been fronted by stalls selling tat pertaining to soap opera king Bae Yeon-jun, and a T-shirt, cup or pair of socks with his countenance on it could make for a quirky souvenir. Parts of Bae's most famous drama, *Winter Sonata*, were filmed at the school, and as such both this and the *hanok* village in general are highly popular with visitors from Japan, where the actor's work was best received.

Changdeokgung

창덕궁 • Yulgongno 99 • Tues–Sun: Feb–Oct 9am–6pm; Nov–Jan 9am–5.30pm • Secret Garden by tour only, usually on the hour 10am–4pm • English-language palace tours at 10.30am & 2.30pm • Palace W3000; Secret Garden an additional W5000; both also on combination ticket (see box, p.39) • ⓦ eng.cdg.go.kr • Anguk subway (line 3)

Sumptuous **Changdeokgung** is, for many, the pick of Seoul's palaces, with immaculate paintwork and carpentry augmenting a palpable sense of history – home to royalty as recently as 1910, it's the best-preserved palace in the city. Its construction was completed in 1412, under the reign of King Taejong. Like Gyeongbokgung, it suffered heavy damage during the **Japanese invasions** of the 1590s; Gyeongbokgung was left to fester, but Changdeokgung was rebuilt and in 1618 usurped its older brother as the seat of the **royal family**, an honour it held until 1872. In its later years, the palace became a symbol of Korea's opening up to the rest of the world – King Heonjong (r.1834–49) added distinctively Chinese-style buildings to the complex, and his eventual successor King Sunjong (r.1907–10) was fond of driving Western cars around the grounds. Sunjong was, indeed, the last of Korea's long line of kings; Japanese annexation brought an end to his short rule, but he was allowed to live in Changdeokgung until his death in 1926. This regal lineage still continues today, though claims are contested and the "royals" have no regal rights, claims or titles.

The palace

The huge gate of **Donhwamun** is the first structure you'll come across – dating from 1609, this is the oldest extant palace gate in Seoul. Moving on, Changdeokgung's suitably impressive **throne room** is without doubt the most regal-looking of any Seoul palace – light from outside is filtered through paper doors and windows, bathing in a dim glow the elaborate wooden beam structure, as well as the throne and its folding-screen backdrop. Beyond here are a number of buildings pertaining to the various kings who occupied the palace, some of which still have the original furniture inside. One building even contains some of the vintage cars beloved of **King Sunjong**, the Daimler and Cadillac looking more than a little incongruous in their palatial setting. Further on you'll come to **Nakseonjae**, built during the reign of King Heonjong. The building's Qing-style latticed doors and arched pavilion reveal his taste for foreign cultures, and without the paint and decoration typical of Korean palace buildings, the colours of the bare wood are ignited with shades of gold and honey during sunset.

The Secret Garden

The palace's undoubted highlight is **Huwon** (후원), most popularly known as **The Secret Garden**. Approached via a suitably mysterious path, it is concealed by an arch of leaves and has a **lotus pond** at its centre. One of Seoul's most photographed sights, the pond comes alive with colourful flowers in late June or early July. A small building overlooking the pond served as a library and study room in imperial times, and the tiny gates blocking the entrance path were used as an interesting checking mechanism by the king – needing to crouch to pass through, he'd be reminded of his duty to be humble.

CHEONGGYECHEON AT NIGHT

Insadong and around

Insadong has long been Seoul's main tourist hub, and for good reason: here, there has been a concerted effort to maintain Korean culture, and the area's small alleyways are filled almost to bursting with rustic restaurants and secluded tearooms, as well as small shops selling trinkets, art supplies and traditional clothing. There are also umpteen galleries to visit, many of them displaying a fusion of old and contemporary styles very much in keeping with the atmosphere of the place. That said, Insadong's main appeal lies in simply strolling around and taking it all in; you could spend a whole day here, especially since the delights of the palace district (see p.36) are within easy walking distance to the north.

2

BEST OF INSADONG AND AROUND

Shopping All over Insadong, you'll find some great souvenir shops, with dozens in the Ssamziegil complex alone. See p.133

Galleries It's hard to imagine how a city district could be more crowded with art galleries than Insadong – there's almost one on every corner. See box, p.52

Jongmyo An ancestral shrine holding the "spirit tables" of the Joseon kings, this complex doubles as some incongruously central Seoul woodland. See p.50

Cheonggyecheon Despite controversial beginnings, the banks of this gorgeous little stream make a lovely place to take a stroll. See p.53

Traditional food Seoul may be heavily Westernized, but the dining options around Insadong are almost exclusively Korean – pop into any one you see, and you can't go wrong. See p.110

Taking tea Insadong has a decent number of teahouses serving distinctive and fantastic-tasting Korean brews. See p.121

The area isn't all about consumption and paintings – there are a fair few bona fide sights to take in too. At the southern end of **Insadonggil**, a road which courses through Insadong, you'll be able to take what's likely to be a well-earned rest at tiny **Tapgol Park**, home to an ancient pagoda. East of Insadonggil are two regal sights: **Jongmyo**, a shrine where ancient ancestral ceremonies are still performed; and the lesser-known palace of **Unhyeongung**. Heading west instead will bring you to

SEOUL'S PROTEST CULTURE

At certain times, visitors to central Seoul may be forgiven for wondering if they've landed in a police state. The focal point of both city and nation, and home to their leaders, the small area around Insadong is ground zero for **street protests**. Those mounted against the national or city government tend to converge around Gwanghwamun or City Hall, and in the weeks (or even months) surrounding such events, main junctions are manned by police, military personnel and armoured buses. Mercifully, the tear gas that characterized protests through the 1970s and 1980s is no longer used by police – the result of a curious deal struck with protesters, who promised to stop using Molotov cocktails if the police would desist with their own chemical concoctions.

Recent protests have included the **anti-government demonstrations** which followed the sinking of the *Sewol* in 2014, when hundreds of schoolchildren lost their lives (see p.172) – the issue was hi-jacked by opposition parties keen to inflict damage on the incumbent president Park Geun-hye. The **US beef protests of 2008** centred on the decision of president Lee Myung-bak to allow American beef back into the Korean market, after trade ceased in the wake of the 2003 BSE crisis. The decision led to clashes between police and civilians, and resulted in a slew of burnt-out armoured vehicles, as well as one death by self-immolation (one more than the number of Koreans killed by contaminated American beef). These protests fed off a pool of anti-American sentiment building since 2002, when two schoolgirls were run over by an American army tank.

Tapgol Park (see p.52) was the venue for a **Declaration of Independence** against Japanese rule on 1 March, 1919, drawn up by students in a nearby restaurant. A large crowd gathered during the speech, and the ensuing demonstration was countered in brutal fashion by the Japanese, who killed hundreds of Koreans, and arrested thousands more. The independence movement went little further, but in commemoration of the student declaration, March 1 is now a national holiday.

While anti-American protests have subsided, those against the Japanese continue. Each Wednesday at noon a dwindling number of elderly Korean women protest outside the Japanese embassy – these are the "**comfort women**" who were forced into sexual slavery during the Japanese occupation of Korea, and are still seeking compensation, or even an apology. "Say you're sorry!" and "You know you did wrong!" are the most popular chants, and with younger protesters joining the cause, the demonstrations seem likely to continue until Tokyo issues an official apology.

Jogyesa, Seoul's most visited temple. Underlining them all is **Cheonggyecheon**, a below-street-level paradise for pedestrians and joggers, though possessive of a curious history and an element of controversy.

Insadonggil
인사동길

Insadong's action is centred on **Insadonggil**, the area's main thoroughfare, and sadly still open to traffic for much of the day despite its teeming masses of people. The road is lined with galleries, traditional shops, tearooms and restaurants, with more of the same in the side-alleys which sprout off at regular intervals; one of the most notable buildings here is **Ssamziegil** shopping complex, a paradise for souvenir-hunters (see p.133). Towards the road's southern end, it becomes more westernized, including a controversial *Starbucks*: due to protests when it first opened, the company made a slight concession by having its name spelt in *hangeul* – the first time the chain had ever represented itself in non-Roman text.

2

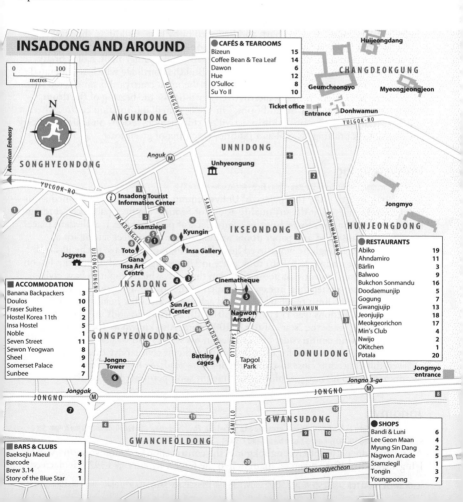

INSADONG AND AROUND

CAFÉS & TEAROOMS	
Bizeun	15
Coffee Bean & Tea Leaf	14
Dawon	6
Hue	12
O'Sulloc	8
Su Yo Il	10

● RESTAURANTS	
Abiko	19
Ahndamiro	11
Bärlin	3
Balwoo	9
Bukchon Sonmandu	16
Doodaemunjip	5
Gogung	7
Gwangjujip	13
Jeonjujip	18
Meokgeorichon	17
Min's Club	4
Nwijo	2
OKitchen	1
Potala	20

■ ACCOMMODATION	
Banana Backpackers	3
Doulos	10
Fraser Suites	6
Hostel Korea 11th	2
Insa Hostel	5
Noble	1
Seven Street	11
Sewon Yeogwan	8
Sheel	9
Somerset Palace	4
Sunbee	7

■ BARS & CLUBS	
Baekseju Maeul	4
Barcode	3
Brew 3.14	2
Story of the Blue Star	1

● SHOPS	
Bandi & Luni	6
Lee Geon Maan	4
Myung Sin Dang	2
Nagwon Arcade	5
Ssamziegil	1
Tongin	3
Youngpoong	7

2

ON THE BUDDHIST TRAIL IN SEOUL

There's no need for the Buddhist experience to stop with Jogyesa. Indeed, there are a number of Buddhist diversions right outside the temple entrance – here you'll find Buddhist clothing, jewellery, incense and assorted trinkets on sale at dozens of small shops. On the other side of the road is the huge **Templestay Center** (ⓦeng.templestay.com), where you can book nights at temples across the land – a great chance to get away from city life, though would-be monks should note that a typical temple day starts at around 3am. On an upper floor of the same complex, *Balwoo* (see p.111) is a restaurant that serves immaculately prepared Buddhist temple food. Those who have a little more time on their hands can take a Zen meditation session at the **Ahnkook Zen Centre** (see p.29) north of Anguk station, or head to two wonderful **temples** on Seoul's periphery – Gilsangsa, up in the Seongbukdong district (see p.74), and Bomunsa, which stares over the sea on the island of Seongmodo (see p.154).

Jogyesa

조계사 · Gyeonjidong 45 · Tues–Sun 9am–6pm · Free; Buddhist activities W10,000 · Jonggak station (line 1)

Just west of Insadonggil's northern end is **Jogyesa**, the only major temple in this part of Seoul, and headquarters of the **Jogye sect** – Korea's largest Buddhist denomination. Built in 1910, fronted by a car park and hemmed in by large buildings, the temple has neither history nor beauty to its credit, but for some visitors to Seoul it may represent the only chance to see a Korean temple of such size, and its huge main hall is pretty spectacular. The best time to visit Jogyesa is on Buddha's birthday which is celebrated with the Lotus Lantern festival (see p.26), when the main courtyard is smothered with a kaleidoscope of paper lanterns; alternatively, turn up for the beating of the drum, which takes place daily at 6am and 6pm. On site is a small information centre, where you can arrange a session of Buddhist activities; this includes lessons on lantern-making and woodblock printing, as well as a traditional serving of green tea.

Unhyeongung

운현궁 · Unnidong 114-10 · Tues–Sun 9am–7pm · Free · Anguk subway (line 3)

East of Insadonggil is the tiny palace of **Unhyeongung**. Never having functioned as an official royal residence, it doesn't qualify as one of Seoul's "big five" palaces; accordingly, it's less showy than the others, but the relative lack of people makes it a pleasant place to visit – the bare wood and paper doors would provide the perfect setting for a Japanese *anime*. Though he never lived here, King Gojong's marriage to the ill-fated Princess Myeongseong (see p.166) took place in Unhyeongung, and during the Joseon period it was also the centre of neo-Confucian thought, which sought to base civil progress on merit rather than lineage: for much of the Joseon dynasty, each Korean was born with a specific limit to what they could achieve in life. One man who railed against such restrictions was Yi Hwang (1501–70), a chap who ends up in most visitors' pockets – he's the "star" of the W1000 note. Also known as Toegye, he was born in the Korean countryside, but excelled in his studies and was brought to Seoul aged 23, in order to prepare for the notoriously difficult civil service exams. He received this education close to Unhyeongung (the academy has long since disappeared), and his anti-establishment thought soon permeated the palace.

Jongmyo

종묘 · Hunjeongdong 1 · Sun & Wed–Fri only accessible on a guided tour; English-language tours at 10am, noon, 2pm & 4pm; Sat 9am–6pm free access · W1000 · Jongno 3-ga subway (lines 1, 3 & 5)

Along with the palace of Gyeongbokgung, the construction of **Jongmyo shrine** was on King Taejo's manifesto when he inaugurated the Joseon dynasty in 1392. He decreed

2

INSADONG'S ART GALLERIES

Gana Insa Art Centre 인사동길 가나 인사 아트 센터 Gwanhundong 188, ⓦinsaartcenter.com; Jonggak (line 1), Jongno 3-ga (lines 1, 3 & 5) or Anguk (line 3) subways. This interesting building's seven floors of exhibitions could keep you busy for some time – the acres of wall-space display a wide range of modern styles, with exhibits changed every week to make room for new works. Usually open daily 10am–7pm; closes early on Tues and opens late Wed; free.

Insa Gallery 인사 갤러리 Gwanhundong 29-23, ⓦinsagallery.net; Jonggak (line 1), Jongno 3-ga (lines 1, 3 & 5) or Anguk (line 3) subways. This three-floored gallery's collection features some of the most interesting Korean artists of recent times. Its exploration of modern themes and styles is renowned in this competitive neighbourhood, and the twice-monthly change-around system keeps things fresh. Daily 10am–6.30pm; free.

Kyungin Museum of Fine Art 경인 미술관 Insadong 10-gil 11-4, ⓦkyunginart.co.kr; Jonggak (line 1), Jongno 3-ga (lines 1, 3 & 5) or Anguk (line 3) subways. Exhibitions are rarely poor at this long-time local favourite, whose traditional-with-a-twist style

fuses the conventional with the contemporary. Its four pleasant and spacious rooms are centred around a leafy courtyard that's also home to *Dawon*, a decent tearoom (see p.121). Daily 10am–6pm; free.

Sun Art Center 선 아트 센터 Insadong 5-gil 8, ⓦsungallery.co.kr; Jonggak (line 1), Jongno 3-ga (lines 1, 3 & 5) or Anguk (line 3) subways. Spoken about in hushed tones by curators at other Insadong galleries, this houses probably the most renowned collection in the area. It mainly consists of early twentieth-century paintings, and shows that modern art in Korea goes back way before the country's growth into an economic power – look for pieces by Kim Sou, who had a Rubens-like obsession with flesh, or the floral works of Kim Chong Hak. Tues–Sun 10am–6pm; free.

Toto 토토 Gwanhundong 169-2; Jonggak (line 1), Jongno 3-ga (lines 1, 3 & 5) or Anguk (line 3) subways. Is it a gallery, a museum or a shop? Toto is filled with toy planes, trains and automobiles, as well as action figures of characters who wear their underpants on the outside. Some pieces are rare, but you can buy the cheaper ones as quirky souvenirs. Daily 10am–6pm; W1000.

that dead kings and queens would be honoured here in true Confucian style, with a series of ancestral rites. These ceremonies were performed five times a year – once each season, with an extra one on the winter solstice – when the ruling king would pay his respects to those who died before him by bowing profusely, and explaining pertinent national issues to their **spirit tablets**. These wooden blocks, in which deceased royalty were believed to reside, are still stored in two large wooden buildings that were said to be the biggest in Asia at the time of their construction. Jeongjeon (정전) was the first, but such was the span of the Joseon dynasty that another building, Yeongnyeongjeon (영녕전), had to be added. Though the courtyards are open – take the opportunity to walk on the raised paths that were once reserved for kings – the buildings themselves remain locked for most of the year; the one exception is the **Jongmyo Daeje** day in May (see p.25), a long, solemn ceremony followed by traditional court dances, and an absolute must-see if you're in Seoul at the time. If possible, try and visit the shrine on a Saturday when you have free rein to wander around the wooded complex.

On exiting the shrine, you'll find yourself in tiny **Jongmyo Park**. Though not a "park" in the true sense of the word, it nevertheless manages to be one of the most atmospheric places in the capital – on warm days, and even most of the cold ones, it's full of old men selling calligraphy, drinking *soju* and playing *baduk* (바둑), a Korean board game. Find a spot to sit, close your eyes and listen to the wooden clack of a thousand game pieces.

Tapgol Park

탑골공원 • Jongno 2-ga 38-1 • Daily 9am–6pm • Free • Jonggak subway (line 1)

At the southern end of Insadonggil, **Tapgol Park** is a small patch of land containing as much concrete as it does grass. Its main claim to fame is as the venue for 1919's declaration of independence against Japanese rule (see box, p.48), and it's also home to a huge, stunning Joseon-era **stone pagoda**, which sits resplendent at the park's northern end. Grandly titled official "National Treasure Number Two", the pagoda has actually been the de facto number one since the burning down of Sungnyemun (see box, p.61), but sadly the beauty of its ancient design has been diluted by the ugly glass box placed around it for protection.

While not terribly attractive in itself, the park does function as a rather interesting window on local society. Groups of old men play chess, drink *soju* and hold lengthy discussions, while office workers and students from the many neighbouring language academies flit in and out on extended cigarette breaks. In addition, the pavement outside the western wall is usually dotted with tent-like booths used by fortune-tellers, still an integral part of Korean society. A less heralded social facet is the gay area to the north and east of the park – homosexuality is still taboo in conservative Korea, but this area is relatively liberal, and gay males both young and old congregate here (see p.126 for more on gay Seoul).

Jongno

종로

A major east–west road, **Jongno** has been one of Seoul's most important travel arteries since the dawn of the Joseon dynasty. The name literally means "Bell Street", and there is indeed a bell in **Bosingak** belfry, off its southern side – during dynastic times, this chimed 33 times at 4am and 10pm each day, to announce the opening and closing of the city gates. Today, it is only used to ring in the New Year. As recently as the early twentieth century, Jongno was essentially for foot traffic only; wonderful pictures of that time were taken by colonial-era European travellers, showing white-robed chaps striding along in horsehair hats. Jongno also lends its name to the surrounding area, an earthy district filled with often-grimy alleyways both north and south of the road (see box below).

Jongno Tower

종로 타워 • Jongno 1-ga 1 • 24hr • Free • Jonggak subway (line 1)

Rising just north of Jongno, the unmistakable **Jongno Tower** is one of Seoul's most striking buildings. In 1994 Rafael Viñoly architects added three latticed metal columns to the original tower block, topping them with a storey far divorced from the main building; suspended in mid-air, this oval chunk of metal is now home to the aptly named *Top Cloud* restaurant-cum-bar.

Cheonggyecheon

청계천 • 24hr • Free • Accessible from many stations, including Gwanghwamun (line 5) and Jonggak (line 1)

One of central Seoul's most popular spots with locals and visitors alike is **Cheonggyecheon**, a small waterway whose bankside paths make great strolling territory.

AVOID-THE-HORSE ALLEY

For the average man or woman in dynastic-era Seoul, the appearance of a horse-drawn carriage meant dropping whatever they were doing, and prostrating to proffer Confucian-style respect to whoever was inside – either a member of the Joseon royalty, or the *yangban* aristocracy. These regular obligations to bow understandably annoyed many people, and as a result small alleyways were created either side of Jongno – those who couldn't see the horses did not need to bow, and could go about their daily business in peace. Known as *pimatgol* (피맛골), or "**avoid-the-horse alley**", some of these lanes are still in existence; the one heading north of Jongno, and west of Insadonggil, is the most visited, though the one to the south of Jongno is far atmospheric, and home to the *Jeonjulip* restaurant (see p.112).

2

CHEONGGYECHEON'S CHEQUERED HISTORY

Taking a walk along Cheonggyecheon, it's hard to imagine what this small strip of Seoul has been through, even within living memory. The stream's first significant use was as a channel for **royal waste**, after King Taejo built Gyeongbokgung palace in 1394. Taejo's wife, Queen Sindeok, was to become part of Cheonggyecheon in a most curious way: King Taejong (r.1400–18), Taejo's son and successor, was said to have used stones from her tomb to construct **Gwangtonggyo**, the first pedestrian bridge you'll come across if walking along Cheonggyecheon from the west.

Now rebuilt, this bridge was knocked down shortly after the Korean War (see p.168), the first stage of a process that saw Cheonggyecheon covered entirely with concrete and used as a road. The riverbanks were, at that time, home to one of Seoul's largest **shanty towns** – pictures from the postwar era show a level of poverty almost unimaginable today, only eradicated in the late 1970s under the economic reforms of Park Chung-hee (see p.170). True to form, Park favoured progress over tradition, and Cheonggyecheon's concrete covering was topped with an **elevated expressway**.

In 2003, **Lee Myung-bak** – then Mayor of Seoul, later President of Korea – announced his plan to tear down the expressway and beautify the stream, only to be met with outrage from Korea's hugely influential press, and a public angry at the near-$1bn cost of the project – years of neglect had run the stream almost dry, meaning that all water needed to be pumped in. The renovations went ahead, despite some heads rolling on corruption charges in the course of the project (Lee had strong links to the construction industry), and since being completed in 2005 it has become one of Seoul's most popular spots with locals and visitors alike.

Until recently, Cheonggyecheon was a mucky stream running beneath an elevated highway, but in 2003 the decision was made to ditch the road and beautify the creek – a far more controversial project than it may sound (see box above). Since completion in 2005 it has served as one of Seoul's most popular **pedestrian thoroughfares**: on descending you'll notice that the capital's ceaseless cacophony has been diluted, and largely replaced by the sound of rushing water; streamside features include **sculptures** and **fountains**, while regular chains of **stepping stones** make it possible to cross from one side to the other. On sunny days, local children (and the young at heart) can't resist the urge to jump in and have a splash around; the water quality is okay (it's all pumped in) but subject to the inevitable sullying when so many people are around, so you may prefer simply to bathe your feet.

Running parallel to Jongno for almost the entire course of the road, Cheonggyecheon starts just southeast of Gwanghwamun Plaza (see p.57), at a point marked by a curious piece of **modern art** designed to resemble a snail (though many locals call it a curly turd) by American husband-and-wife sculptors Claes Oldenburg and Coosje van Bruggen. Most visitors limit their visit to this area, but this is one of the few good chances for a long stroll that Seoul has to offer: the 3km walk east to Dongdaemun market (see p.69) is extremely pleasant, with the paths continuing for a further 7km beyond, joining the Hangang near Oksu station – a stretch used almost exclusively by local joggers, cyclists and power-walkers.

DEOKSUGUNG PALACE

Gwanghwamun and City Hall

Looking north from Gwanghwamun, the main gate of Gyeongbokgung palace, one can see little but cascading palace roofs, and the mountains beyond. Turn south instead, and the contrast is almost unbelievably stark – looming up behind Gwanghwamun Plaza are the ranked masses of high-rise blocks that announce Seoul's main business district, its walkways teeming with black-suited businessfolk and civil servants pouring in and out of the grand new City Hall. However, there's more of interest than you might expect in this balli-balli (Korean for "quickly, quickly!") area, including two palaces, a few major museums and art galleries, some fine examples of colonial architecture, and Jeongdonggil, one of Seoul's most charming roads.

> ## BEST OF GWANGHWAMUN AND CITY HALL
> **Colonial architecture** Several buildings built during the Japanese occupation survive today, and provide a pleasant contrast to the pervasive high-rise. See box opposite
> **National Museum of Korean Contemporary History** One of Seoul's newest museums, and a decent place to chart Korea's fascinating recent history. See opposite
> **Gyeonghuigung** The runt of the litter, as far as Seoul's palaces go, but it's still a charming and beautiful place – and the one to pick if you'd like to be away from the crowds. See opposite
> **Jeongdonggil** Ginkgo-lined street that's up there with the most romantic in town. See p.58
> **Deoksugung** A wonderful palace which houses one of the city's best art museums. See p.60
> **Namdaemun market** Seoul's most atmospheric market is a great place to eat and drink. See p.61

Though public transport in this area is excellent, you'll find it easy to get everywhere on foot. Two of Seoul's five royal palaces sit in the centre of this business district, and are both worth hunting out: at the western edge of the district is **Gyeonghuigung**, Seoul's "forgotten" palace, with the large **Museum of History** just outside its northern wall. From here, it's a short walk east to **Deoksugung**, a palace notable for a couple of

Western-style buildings, one of which houses the **National Museum for Contemporary Art**. Linking the two palaces is **Jeongdonggil**, a pleasant, ginkgo-tree-lined road with a number of interesting sights on its fringes, including the fantastic **Seoul Museum of Art**.

Gwanghwamun Plaza

광화문 프라자

Named after the southern gate of Gyeongbokgung (see p.37), **Gwanghwamun Plaza** is a large expanse of concrete renovated at enormous expense in 2009. There's not that much to see here, save a couple of statues, including a seated likeness of **King Sejong**, creator of the Korean alphabet (see box, p.180), and national hero **Admiral Yi Sun-shin**, a fourteenth-century naval commander who stands proudly at the plaza's southern end. There are several notable buildings around the plaza: to the west is the **Sejong Center**, famed for its performances (see p.130), while on the eastern flank you'll find the giant **Kyobo Building**, the relatively small **Bigak** pavilion, the fortified-to-the-hilt **US Embassy**, and the **National Museum of Korean Contemporary History**.

National Museum of Korean Contemporary History

대한민국 역사박물관 · Sejongno 82-1 · Tues, Thurs, Fri & Sun 9am–6pm, Wed & Sat 9am–9pm · Free · ⓦ much.go.kr · Gyeongbokgung subway (line 3)

Opened in 2012, the **National Museum of Korean Contemporary History** focuses on Korean history post-1876, including plenty of material on the Japanese occupation and the Korean War. The displays here are less crassly nationalistic than in other museums around the country, and it pays heed to the foreign influence which ended said conflicts: in essence, however, it remains a feel-good exercise for Koreans – more of a primer in recent Korean history, rather than the full story. Of particular note is a spellbinding series of photographs from the occupation and war periods, as well as a re-created "street" from said times. In addition, from the upper level, or the on-site café, there are great views of Gyeongbokgung.

Gyeonghuigung

경희궁 · Saemunanno 45 · Tues–Sun 9am–6pm · Free · Gwanghwamun subway (line 5)

Humble **Gyeonghuigung** is the least visited of Seoul's five grand palaces – even locals may struggle to find it – but its simplicity tends to strike a chord with those who track it down. Built in 1616, Gyeonghuigung became a royal palace by default when Changdeokgung (see p.46) was burned down in 1624. Though a little forlorn,

---

COLONIAL ARCHITECTURE

Seoul's business district is home to the vast majority of its extant colonial architecture, built during the Japanese occupation of 1910–45. Although rather unpopular with locals on account of this historical pedigree, many visitors find these old colonial structures to be Seoul's most appealing architecture. Generally built along **Neoclassical** lines, though there are occasional splashes of Art Deco, these were intentionally designed to be the most dominant structures in what was then a wholly low-rise city; the survivors have been lent a new-found air of humility by the imposing skyscrapers of modern Seoul. Many colonial-era buildings have been destroyed since independence, including the colossal **Seoul Capitol** in Gyeongbokgung (see p.39), demolished in 1995. Others have avoided a similar fate on account of their listed status, including **City Hall** (see p.61), or given a second lease of life as museums or shopping malls. These include **Shinsegae** department store (see p.136) and **Myeongdong Theater**, as well as three notable museums – the **Seoul Museum of Art** off Jeongdonggil (see p.60), the **National Museum for Contemporary Art** inside Deoksugung palace (see p.60), and the **Bank of Korea Museum** opposite Shinsegae (see p.65).

it's a pretty place, and may be the palace for you if crowds, souvenir stands and false-bearded guards in faux period clothing aren't to your liking. Unlike other palaces, you can enter the throne room – bare but for the throne, but worth a look – before scrambling up to the halls of the upper level, which have a visually pleasing backdrop of grass and rock. Although the palace closes in the evening, its grassy **outer compound** is open all hours, and makes a good place to relax with a few drinks or some snacks.

Seoul Museum of History

서울 역사박물관 • Saemunanno 55 • Tues–Fri 9am–10pm, Sat & Sun 10am–7pm • Free; around W12,000 for big-name special exhibitions • ⓦ eng.museum.seoul.kr • Gwanghwamun subway (line 5)

A large building adjacent to Gyeonghuigung palace, the **Museum of History** has several halls which host **rotating exhibitions**, while the **permanent exhibition** is on the third floor and focuses on Joseon-era Seoul. Here you'll find lacquered boxes with mother-of-pearl inlay, porcelain bowls and vases thrown in gentle shapes, plus silk gowns with embroidered leaves and dragons; you may be surprised by how much "quintessentially" Japanese design actually started in Korea, or at least passed through here first on its way from China. Another room on the third floor fills its entire floorspace with a gigantic photographic image of Seoul.

Across the road from the museum, look out for an intriguing piece of art – a 22m-high **metal statue** of a man hammering. Intended by his sculptor, Jonathan Borofsky, to be a mute reminder that life's not all about work, he stands silently mocking the black-suited denizens of the surrounding business district.

Jeongdonggil

정동길

Jeongdonggil is a pretty, shaded side-street that bisects the easy-going neighbourhood of Jeongdong: its relative lack of traffic makes it feel a world removed from the bustle of the neighbouring business district. The road is lined with towering **ginkgo trees** (see box, p.96), each buzzing with cicadas in the summer, and illuminated at night by thousands of tiny lights, which makes it one of Seoul's most romantic places for a stroll. Ironically, this thoroughfare has long been eschewed by courting couples – Seoulites have historically held the superstition that those who walk here will soon break up, since the divorce courts were once present on this road. They have now relocated, and the road is slowly starting to attract camera-toting couples in matching T-shirts. However, Jeongdonggil is more than just strolling territory, as it links two of Seoul's five royal palaces, and features a few interesting sights of its own. It's also home to the **Chongdong Theatre** (see p.129), which puts on regular performances of *pansori* and other traditional Korean arts.

The former Russian legation

구러시아 공관부지 • Jeongdonggil 21-18 • Daily 24hr • Free • Gwanghwamun subway (line 5)

Though only its central tower remains, the **former Russian legation** is the most interesting of a few structures dotted nearby which prove that Japan was not the only imperial power taking an interest in the Korea of the late 1890s. The UK and Germany were among those to establish legations in Seoul, but Russia and Japan were the two empires with most to gain from Korea, and both vied for dominance. Japanese victory in the Russo-Japanese War of 1904–05 saw them take the upper hand, and the subsequent signing of a **Protectorate Treaty** in the nearby hall of **Jungmyeongjeon** (중면전) – also Russian-designed, and worth a look – ceded Korea's foreign policy-making to Tokyo, a prelude to full-scale annexation five years later.

Seoul Museum of Art

서울시립미술관 • Deoksugunggil 61 • Tues–Fri 10am–9pm, Sat & Sun 10am–6pm • Admission price depends on the exhibition; around ₩15,000 for major ones • ⓦ sema.seoul.go.kr • City Hall subway (lines 1 & 2)

The large, modern **Seoul Museum of Art** (SeMA) is more gallery than museum, and well worth popping in for a look at what are invariably high-quality exhibitions of art from around the world – Picasso, Monet, Van Gogh and Renoir have all found temporary homes here. In addition, there are always free secondary exhibitions to peruse, most commonly the work of local (or at least Asian) artists.

Deoksugung

덕수궁 • Sejongdaero 99 • Tues–Sun 9am–9pm • English-language tours Tues–Fri at 10.30am & at 1.40pm on either Sat or Sun; Changing of the Guard ceremonies Tues–Sun at 11am, 2pm & 3.30pm • ₩1000; also on combination ticket (see box, p.39) • ⓦ deoksugung.go.kr • City Hall subway (lines 1 & 2)

Located in the very centre of Seoul's business district, the **palace of Deoksugung** receives plenty of visitors, a volume amplified by the compound's relatively small size. The atmosphere here is somewhat different to that of the other royal palaces – Deoksugung's perimeter walls are surrounded by high-rise tower blocks, which if nothing else make for a pleasing contrast, as do the Western-style buildings found within the complex itself, one of which houses the **National Museum for Contemporary Art**.

Brief history

Deoksugung was the last palace of Seoul's big five to be built, and it became the country's seat of power almost by default in 1592 when the Japanese destroyed Gyeongbokgung (see p.37) and burned all the other palaces. Its reign was short, however, since only two kings – **Seonjo** (r.1567–1608) and **Gwanghaegun** (r.1608–23) – lived here before the seat of power was transferred to a newly rebuilt Changdeokgung (see p.46) in 1618. Deoksugung became the de facto royal residence again after the assassination of Empress Myeongseong in 1895 (see p.166); **King Gojong** fled here after the murder of his wife, then hid in the Russian legation for a short time before making a final return to the palace in 1897. Backed up by his new Russian comrades in the face of ever-increasing pressure from the Japanese, he declared the short-lived **Empire of Korea** here that same year. Despite having ceded control to Japan, Gojong remained in Deoksugung until his death in 1919.

The palace

The **palace** is entered through **Daehanmun** (대한문), a gate on the eastern side of the complex – this goes against the tenets of *feng shui*, which usually result in south-facing palace entrances. It's outside this gate that the **Changing of the Guard** ceremonies take place, the procession eventually heading up Jeongdonggil at a slow pace, usually backed up by a few unwanted cars. Back inside the palace walls, most visitors make a beeline to the main hall, **Junghwajeon** (중화전), whose ceiling sports a pair of immaculate carved dragons. Be sure to check out **Jeonggwanheon** (정관헌), a pavilion used for **coffee-drinking** by King Gojong, who developed something of a taste for said beverage while sequestered at the Russian legation (see p.58) in 1895. Indeed, he almost certainly became the first-ever Korean coffee addict, since even a century later the country had almost no decent cafés: today, however, there's a nice little one in the grounds of the palace itself. Jeonggwanheon features an intriguing mix of contemporary Western and Korean styles, Gojong having commissioned his Russian architect friend **Aleksey Seredin-Sabatin** to design it.

National Museum of Modern and Contemporary Art

국립미술관 • Tues, Thurs, Fri & Sun 10am–7pm, Wed & Sat 10am–9pm • Admission price depends on the exhibition; usually ₩3000–10,000, plus the palace entrance fee (see above) • ⓦ mmca.go.kr

Deoksugung contains a couple of other **Western-style buildings**, dating back to when the "Hermit Kingdom" of the latter part of the Joseon dynasty was being forcibly opened up to trade; these incongruous Neoclassical structures are the most notable in the complex. At the end of a gorgeous rose garden is **Seokjojeon** (석조전), which was designed by an English architect and built by the Japanese in 1910; the first Western-style building in the country, it was used as the royal home for a short time. It now houses the **National Museum for Contemporary Art**, whose exhibits are usually quality works from local artists, more often than not blending elements of traditional Korean styles with those of the modern day. The steps of the museum are a favourite photo-spot for graduating students – in June you may find yourself surrounded by grinning young doctors, accountants or nurses, all dressed up to the nines.

City Hall

시청 · Sejongdaero 110 · Daily 9am–9pm · Free · City Hall subway (lines 1 & 2)

Squatting by Seoul Plaza, Seoul's **City Hall** is, in fact, two buildings – one new, one old. Of more than symbolic and administrative importance to the city, the structures have lent their name to the entire area around them – indeed, when Seoulites say "Meet you in City Hall", they mean the area not the building – and each night (weekdays, in particular) a slew of suits pours into the surrounding bars and restaurants.

Seoul's **former City Hall**, which was built by the Japanese in 1926, sits just east of Deoksugung at the northern side of Seoul Plaza, a near-circular patch of grass that hosts free musical performances on summer evenings. Most locals would rather see this building torn down on account of its Japanese heritage; mercifully, it has been granted listed status, and was refurbished rather than demolished when the adjacent new building was constructed in 2012. Unfortunately, no attempts were made to integrate the two structures and Seoul's **new City Hall** squats in Seoul Plaza like some sort of grounded spaceship; the shape of the new chrome-and-glass building resembles a tsunami intent on wrecking the old. There's little for visitors to do here, bar take a lift to the upper levels of the new building for a nice view down over Seoul Plaza; there's a "sky gallery" on the eighth floor, and a café on the ninth.

Namdaemun market

남대문 시장 · Sections open daily, 24hr · Hoehyeon subway (line 4)

One of Seoul's most vaunted markets, **Namdaemun market** spreads across the area behind Shinsegae department store, with a dense collection of stalls, malls and restaurants. It's second only in size to Dongdaemun market out east (see p.69), and,

---

THE DEATH OF NATIONAL TREASURE NUMBER 1

Seoul's **Great South Gate**, the literal translation of Namdaemun, was built in 1398 by King Taejo as a means of glorifying and protecting his embryonic kingdom. This was by no means the only major project to come out of Taejo's first years of rule (see p.165), but random fires, Japanese invasions and civil war rubbed out the rest over the following centuries. Also known as Sungnyemun and feted as the country's official "**National Treasure Number One**" on account of its age, beauty and importance, Namdaemun was the sole survivor from the Taejo era, which made things all the more harrowing when after six centuries standing proudly over Seoul, it was destroyed in a matter of minutes by a lone arsonist, **Chae Jong-gi**. Chae had noticed that Namdaemun was guarded by nothing but a single set of motion sensors – not the best way to protect one of the oldest wooden structures in the land. Early in the morning on February 10, 2008, he mounted the gate armed with a few bottles of paint thinner – hours later, images of weeping Seoulites were being beamed around the world, all bemoaning the loss of their smouldering city icon. However, Korea's incendiary history means that it has substantial experience of reconstructing its treasures, and renovation of Namdaemun was completed in 2013.

like Dongdaemun, its name is taken from that of a hefty **city gate**, which stood here from the 1390s until it was destroyed by an arsonist in 2008 (see box, p.61). You'll essentially find the same things on offer here as at Dongdaemun, but Namdaemun is particularly known as a source of two handy products – cheap **spectacles**, and used **camera equipment**. There's also a pleasing line of **outdoor snack stands** just outside exit 5 of Hoehyeon subway station (see map, p.56), which make a good place to chow down and meet the locals.

3

GWANGJANG MARKET

Myeongdong and Dongdaemun

To Koreans, and a whole generation of travellers from other Asian countries, the words Myeongdong and Dongdaemun mean one thing and one thing alone – shopping. Many visitors from China, Japan, Thailand and Taiwan pin their Korean travel plans on these two areas alone, and never venture beyond their wider perimeter – a pity, for sure, but testament to the zone's ever-increasing international reputation. Myeongdong's tightly packed web of streets features literally hundreds of shops selling clothing, cosmetics and street snacks, while Dongdaemun is the market-place equivalent, and of more interest to those buying fabric or knock-off handbags. However, it's not all about consumption – Myeongdong Cathedral is up there with Korea's prettiest Christian places of worship, while just to the south rises Namsan, Seoul's own mini-mountain.

MYEONGDONG AND DONGDAEMUN

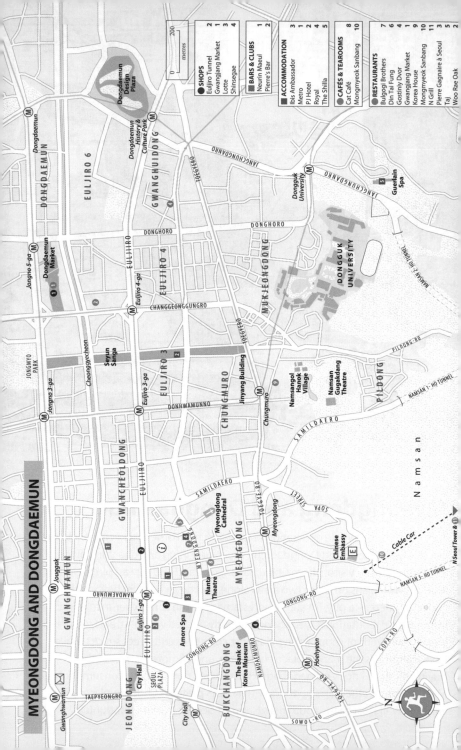

SHOPS
Euljiro Tunnel	2
Gwangjang Market	1
Lotte	3
Shinsegae	4

BARS & CLUBS
Neurin Maeul	1
Pierre's Bar	2

ACCOMMODATION
Ibis Ambassador	3
Metro	1
PJ Hotel	2
Royal	4
The Shilla	5

CAFÉS & TEAROOMS
Cat Café	8
Mongmyeok Sanbang	10

RESTAURANTS
Bulgogi Brothers	7
Din Tai Fung	6
Gostiniy Dvor	4
Gwangjang Market	9
Korea House	10
Mongmyeok Sanbang	11
N Grill	3
Pierre Gagnaire à Seoul	5
Taj	2
Woo Rae Oak	1

BEST OF MYEONGDONG AND DONGDAEMUN

Myeongdong Cathedral Seoul's largest Christian place of worship, and a good place to get a handle on the nation's recent religious conversion. See below
Chungmuro The old-fashioned alleys south of Chungmuro are quite absorbing – the sound and smell of the printing presses and budget eateries seem far from central Seoul. See p.66
Namsangol Hanok Village Check out the pretty traditional buildings here, arrayed next to a stretch of parkland. See p.66
Namsan Get great views of Seoul from this easily climbable peak, rising just south of the city centre. See p.66
Gwangjang Market Not so much a must-see as a must-do – if you leave Seoul without having enjoyed a night out at Gwangjang, you haven't really been at all. See p.69
Russiatown Though it's home to more Uzbek, Kazakh and Mongolian businesses, you'll find Cyrillic text all over this area, as well as restaurants serving tasty Russian food. See p.68

Myeongdong

명동

With a justifiable claim to being Korea's most popular shopping area, and particularly favoured by Chinese visitors, **Myeongdong** is home to an intricate lattice of streets, running from the east–west thoroughfare of Euljiro to the northern slopes of Namsan peak. Though those visiting Myeongdong tend to be primarily concerned with shopping or eating, there are a couple of worthwhile sights in the area.

4

The Bank of Korea Museum

한국은행 화폐금융 박물관 • Namdaemunno 3-ga 110 • Tues–Sun 10am–5pm • Free • City Hall (lines 1 & 2) or Myeongdong subway (line 4)

The **Bank of Korea Museum** was designed and built by the Japanese in the first years of their occupation (see box, p.57), and once served as the headquarters of the now-defunct **Bank of Choson**. A contemporary competitor, the former **Choson Savings Bank**, sits almost directly opposite, alongside the old wing of **Shinsegae** department store (신세계), another colonial structure. The exhibitions inside the museum are less interesting than the building housing them, with an array of notes and coins from around the world on display, as well as plenty of Korean currency from down the ages.

Myeongdong Cathedral

명동성당 • Myeongdonggil 74 • Daily 9am–7pm; Mass daily at 6.30am & 6pm; English-language Mass Sun at 9am • Free • Euljiro 1-ga subway (line 2)

The hub of Korea's large – and growing – Catholic community, **Myeongdong Cathedral** stands proudly over the surrounding shopping area, and is the best-known non-Buddhist religious building in the country. The cathedral was designed in Gothic style by **French missionaries**, and the elegant lines of its red-brick exterior are a breath of fresh air in the business district's maze of concrete cuboids. It was completed in 1898 at the bequest of King Gojong, who wanted to make up for persecutions witnessed under his predecessors: the site on which the cathedral stands had previously been home to a Catholic faith community, many of whom were executed during the **purges** of 1866 (see p.86). In the 1970s, during the dictatorial rule of Park Chung-hee, the cathedral and its auxiliary buildings were used as a refuge for **political dissidents**, since the police refused to enter this place of worship – a recourse still taken today by occasional fugitives. On the road outside the cathedral, you may come across one of Myeongdong's most famous characters: a zealous gentleman bearing a sandwich board stating "Lord Jesus Heaven, No Jesus Hell!" (although further questioning reveals that Protestants will also go to hell). On the same stretch, you'll often hear locals reading from the Bible through megaphones, and the occasional hymn from a choir – all in all, this is by far the best place to witness Korea's recent religious conversion (see p.175).

BACK IN TIME ON THE SEYUN–EULJIRO CROSSROADS

Rising up from Chungmuro station, the **Jinyang Building** (진양빌딩) was one of Seoul's first high-rise buildings, erected in the late 1960s. Together with most of its surrounding area, it has long been slated for demolition, but until this happens it should be possible to sneak to the top for one of the best views of Seoul – it's high enough to see the palace and business districts in full, but close enough to feel part of the city. Looking north from the top, you can make out the **Seyun Sanga**, a line of buildings of similar vintage, sketching a perfect tangent all the way to Jongmyo (see p.50), over 1km away. In the late 1960s, this was one of the largest development projects of its time and prime real estate; today, of course, it's small fry and much of the lower levels are taken up with eerily empty market space – heaven for photographers, or those making a B-movie.

At one point, the Seyun Sanga passes over the pedestrianized **Euljiro tunnel**, which runs beneath Euljiro (을지로), one of Seoul's most important thoroughfares, for a whopping 4km – it's possible to walk from City Hall all the way to Dongdaemun Design Plaza, a journey of around forty minutes, without having to rise above the surface. The tunnel was a popular shopping area during the 1970s, and it's still a good place to shop for some unique clothing, including the trilbies, linen shirts and rhinestone-studded ties popular with elderly local gentlemen, or the lurid floral blouses sported by their female counterparts – great party costumes, at the very least.

Chungmuro

충무로

Just east of Myeongdong, **Chungmuro** is a fascinating area that mixes the youthful exuberance of local university students with old-fashioned pleasures more suited to their grandparents. The students cluster in a dense area of cafés and cheap restaurants that spreads southeast from Chungmuro subway station to Donggook University. North of Chungmuro station, you'll see the **Jinyang Building**, erected in the late 1960s and the northernmost outcrop of one of Seoul's first major modern-day building projects (see box above). The tiny maze-like **side-streets** surrounding this chain of bizarre buildings are a joy to get lost in, with their clutches of cheap restaurants, as well as a fair number of *dabang* – coffee bars popular in the 1970s, but almost extinct in most parts of town. Adding to the area's worn mystique are literally hundreds of **printing presses**, many of which operate late into the night, when their hissing steam and whirring machinery exude a decades-old charm.

Namsangol Hanok Village

남산골 · Toegyero 34-gil 28 · Daily: April–Oct 9am–9pm, Nov–March 9am–8pm · Free · Chungmuro subway (lines 3 & 4)

South of Chungmuro station, **Namsangol** is a small re-created **folk village** of *hanok* housing. There's not that much to do here, though the area is pretty and quite photogenic, while children may enjoy playing a few of the traditional games and watching the occasional displays of dance and music. Other than this, the centrepiece of the surrounding park is a giant **time capsule**, buried in 1994 and due to be reopened in 2394. Computer displays indicate what must have been a very hurried filling of the vault – future Seoulites are set to be wowed by an underwhelming collection of twentieth-century memorabilia including bags of rice, documents pertaining to the sewage system and subway tickets.

Namsan

남산 · Cable car daily 10am–11pm · W6000 one-way, W8000 return · Buses (#2 from Chungmuro, #3 from Seoul station and Itaewon, #5 from Myeongdong and Chungmuro) run every 15–20min

South of Myeongdong station the roads rise up, eventually coming to a stop at the foot of **Namsan**, a 265m-high mini-mountain in the centre of Seoul. Namsan once marked the natural boundary of a city that has long since swelled over the edges and across the

NAMSAN: SEOUL'S GIANT MESSENGER

Hunt around next to the N Seoul Tower, just above the upper terminal of the cable car, and you may be able to discern five curious brick chimneys – these are the remains of the **fire beacons** that, during the Joseon dynasty, used to relay warnings across the country. If just one flame was lit, all was well; the remaining four would be flared up to signify varying degrees of unrest, with the message repeated along chains of beacons that stretched across the whole Korean peninsula.

Today, Namsan's peak is used to relay messages of a different kind. Clustered around the tower, you'll see thousands of **padlocks** which are placed here by the many young couples who scale Namsan for the romance of the views. The done thing is to scrawl your names or initials on the padlock (preferably inside a love heart), secure it to the railing, then dispose of the key – everlasting love, guaranteed.

river – some restored sections of the old city wall can still be seen on the mountain, as can the remains of **fire beacons** that once formed part of an ingenious pan-national communication system (see box above).

Most visitors reach the top by **cable car**, whose base is a stiff fifteen-minute climb uphill from Myeongdong subway station; you can avoid much of the climb by taking the lift that runs from near exit 4 of the station (go straight on, then turn left at the first major road). Alternatively, you can take a bus (see above), or walk the whole way up from Myeongdong, Seoul station or Itaewon (approx thirty minutes). However you arrive, there are **spectacular views** of the city from the peak, and yet more from N Seoul Tower, a giant hypodermic needle sitting at the summit. There are other great paths on Namsan, including one which wraps around much of its northern midriff; pick it up just above the lower cable-car station.

N Seoul Tower

N서울타워 • Observatory Mon–Fri 10am–11pm, Sat & Sun 10am–midnight • W9000 • ⓦ nseoultower.net

N Seoul Tower sits proudly on Namsan's crown, the most recent incarnation of Seoul Tower, whose name was clearly not trendy enough to pass the consultancy test that followed the redesigning of its interior in 2005. The five levels of the upper section are now home to a viewing platform, and assorted cafés and restaurants, best of which is *N.Grill* (see p.114). For many, the free views from the tower's base are good enough, and coming here to see the **sunset** is recommended, when the grey mass of daytime Seoul turns into a pulsating neon spectacle.

Dongdaemun

동대문

A famed market area that spreads over both sides of Cheonggyecheon creek, **Dongdaemun** was named after the gigantic **ornamental gate** that still stands here (*dong* means "east", *dae* means "great" and *mun* "gate"). Originally built in 1396, this was once the eastern entrance to a much smaller Seoul, a counterpart to Namdaemun, way to the southwest (see box, p.61). This was yet another of the structures added by the incredibly ambitious King Taejo in the 1390s (see p.165), at the dawn of his Joseon dynasty; fires and warfare have taken their inevitable toll, however, and the present structure dates from 1869.

Dongdaemun is now best known for its colossal **market**, by far the largest in the country, sprawling as it does across several city blocks: Seoul's tourist offices (see p.35) can provide a map of the market, and point out the areas to aim for if you are looking for something specific. Just to the south of the market is the new **Dongdaemun Design Plaza**, one of Seoul's most ambitious pieces of modern architecture: further south again is an intriguing district, known as "**Russiatown**" to the few expats aware of its presence.

This small area is home to tradespeople and businessmen from Central Asia, particularly Uzbekistan and Mongolia, and you'll see occasional shops, offices and hotels marked with Cyrillic text. There are also a couple of restaurants, such as *Gostiniy Dvor* (see p.113), serving delicious Russian food.

Dongdaemun market
동대문 시장 • 24hr • Dongdaemun subway (lines 1 & 4)

Hectic **Dongdaemun market** is Korea's largest, spread out both open-air and indoors in various locations along the prettified Cheonggyecheon creek (see p.53). It would be impossible to list the whole range of things on sale here – you'll find yourself walking past anything from herbs to *hanbok* (traditional clothing) to paper lanterns, usually on sale for reasonable prices.

Though each section of the market has its own opening and closing times, the complex as a whole never shuts, so at least part of it will be open whenever you decide to visit. Night-time is when the market is at its most atmospheric, with clothes stores pumping out music into the street at ear-splitting volume, and the air filled with the smell of freshly made food sizzling at street-side stalls. Though some of the fare on offer is utterly unrecognizable to many foreign visitors, it pays to be adventurous and try some of the mouthwatering – or just downright curious – dishes on offer.

Gwangjang market
광장 시장 • Jongno 5-ga subway (line 1)

One section of Dongdaemun that is particularly popular with foreigners is **Gwangjang market**, a salty offshoot to the northwest, and one of Seoul's most idiosyncratic places to eat in the evening (see p.69) – most people favour mung-bean pancakes and rice beer, but there's all sorts of weird stuff available too, so just look for something tasty (or gross) and point. During the daytime, it's also the best place in Seoul to buy **second-hand clothes** (see p.135).

Dongdaemun Design Plaza
동대문 디자인 플라자 • Complex open 24hr • Most exhibitions around W8000 • Museum daily 9am–6pm • Free • ⓦ ddp.or.kr • Dongdaemun History & Culture Park subway station (lines 2, 4 & 5)

The newest and most notable sight in the Dongdaemun area is the **Dongdaemun Design Plaza**, a collection of futuristic buildings and grassy walking areas. Opened in 2014 and colloquially referred to as the "DDP", this gargantuan city project aimed to give Seoul a new, futuristic look, and provide some much-needed parkland to its citizens. It sits on the site of the former **Dongdaemun Stadium**, which was built in 1926 and hosted major football and baseball matches, including the first-ever Korean league games for both sports. It also saw some action during the Olympic Games in 1988, but this event (as well as the World Cup in 2002) saw Korea building larger and better facilities elsewhere, and the stadium fell into disrepair. Following the turn of the millennium, it was used as a flea market, selling mostly army surplus clothing, secondhand T-shirts and Chinese sex toys, and was finally torn down in 2008 to make way for the DDP.

Iraq-born architect **Zaha Hadid** won the tender for the new plaza with a design said to echo plumes of smoke – it was then altered slightly to its present shape, which resembles a high-heeled shoe. The reason for this change was the discovery of thousands of dynastic relics found in the earth; construction was delayed for more than a year, and a small **museum** was added to display some of the excavated treasures. In addition, there's a café or two and a couple of gallery and exhibition spaces, though overall the complex seems a little overlarge and underused – perhaps, with more ambition, it will become a place of genuine tourist interest.

Northern Seoul

North of Gyeongbokgung, Seoul appears to come to a rather abrupt end, with lofty mountains rearing up immediately behind the palace. The city did, indeed, once peter out here, but the "economic miracle" of the 1970s saw its population mushroom, and consequently Seoul's urban sprawl pushed around the mountainsides. Development was, however, not as rampant as in other parts of the city, and Seoul's northern quarters maintain a relatively secluded air, with some excellent walking paths stringing together many of the district's temples, cafés, mountainsides and other sights.

5

BEST OF NORTHERN SEOUL

Walking trails Many sights in northern Seoul can be reached on a newly improved series of walking trails, which are steep but easy to follow. See box, p.73

Daehangno Seoul's lively student area has long been popular with backpackers for its buzzing atmosphere, prolific bars and cheap food. See below

Changgyeonggung More natural in feel than Seoul's other palaces, with some delightful grassy areas – and an intriguing history, involving Japanese desecration and a royal murder. See below

Gilsangsa One of Seoul's nicest temples, tucked up in the Seongbukdong area. See p.74

Buamdong This peaceful neighbourhood makes a pleasant half-day trip from the centre, and is a great place for lunch or a coffee. See p.76

Bugaksan Peer down on Gyeongbokgung from this mountain, whose lovely paths conceal a fascinating recent history. See p.76

Bukhansan National Park Many cities would love to have a national park right on their doorstep – in Seoul, a short subway ride gets you to the base of these spectacular mountains. See p.77

To the northeast of Gyeongbokgung are a couple of intriguing areas – the buzzing student district of **Daehangno**, and **Seongbukdong**, with its traditional garden, secluded temple and enchanting tearoom. Seongbukdong lies on the eastern slopes of **Bugaksan**, a mountain whose trails provide some superb views of Seoul. Beyond here, Seoul's undulating northwestern districts have a lower population density, and a calmer atmosphere, than the northeast, with the quiet, hilly area of **Buamdong** becoming increasingly popular thanks to its assorted clothing boutiques and swanky restaurants, as well as a couple of superb galleries. Finally, the peaks of **Bukhansan**, within the world's most visited national park, boast a range of historical sites and some excellent hiking paths.

Daehangno

대학로

With an artily sophisticated ambience, a near-total dearth of camera-toting tourists, and some of the cheapest guesthouses in Seoul (see p.106), studenty **Daehangno** has become very popular with backpackers in the know. Literally meaning "university street", it's actually the name of the road that heads north from Dongdaemun market, but most of the action takes place in a tightly packed area around Hyehwa subway station, meaning that it's also a good starting point for a trip to **Changgyeonggung**, one of Seoul's nicest palaces.

The area has been one of the city's main student zones ever since the opening of Seoul National University in 1946; while this has since moved south of the river, the presence of at least four more educational institutions keeps this place buzzing. It's almost choked with bars, games rooms and cheap restaurants but has more recently attained national fame for its youthful **theatre scene**. Over thirty establishments big and small can be found dotting the side-streets east of Hyehwa station, but be warned that very few performances are in English. There are, however, regular free shows in the paved expanse of **Marronnier Park** (마로니에 공원), a short walk along the road from Hyehwa station's exit two. Here performers take their first tentative steps to stardom, seeking to drum up custom for later performances or showcase their talents, and you can often catch short bursts of magic, music, comedy or mime, all going on at the same time.

Changgyeonggung

창경궁 • Changgyeonggungno 185 • Wed–Mon 9am–5pm; free tours at 11.30am & 4pm • W1000; also on combination ticket (see box, p.39) • 15min walk from Hyehwa subway (line 4), 30min walk from Insadong, or bus #150 or #171 from Anguk station

Separated from Changdeokgung (see p.46) to the west by a perimeter wall, **Changgyeonggung** may have little to actually see, but its history and the

5

relatively natural beauty of its grounds make it possibly one of Seoul's most pleasant palaces.

Changgyeonggung was built by **King Sejong** in 1418 as a resting place for his father, the recently abdicated King Taejong. In its heyday the palace had a far greater number of buildings than are visible today, but these suffered badly from fires and the damage inflicted during the Japanese invasions. Almost the whole of the complex burned down during the Japanese attacks of 1592, and then again during a devastating inferno in 1830. In 1762 the palace was the site of the grisly murder of a crown prince by his father (see box opposite). When the Japanese returned in 1907, they turned much of the palace into Korea's first **amusement park**, which included a botanical garden and zoo, as well as a museum – the red-brick exterior and pointed steel roof were very much in keeping with the Japanese style of the time, and pictures of this era can still be seen around the palace entrance. Almost all the Japanese-built features were tolerated by the local

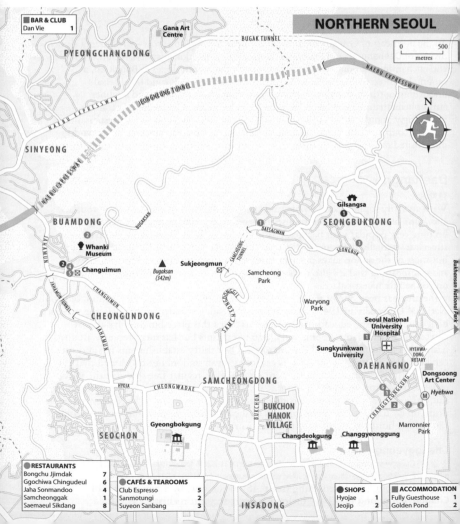

5

WALKING PATHS AROUND NORTHERN SEOUL

Many of Northern Seoul's sights are accessible on a series of splendid **walking paths**, which can be tackled in sections, or you can complete the lot in one day. To do this you'll need decent footwear, water and snacks, though the path does veer into civilization from time to time, so you'll be able to stock up at mini-markets. Also remember to bring your passport (or other photo ID) for the Bugaksan section.

The best place to start is at **Dongdaemun** station (lines 1 & 4); come out of exit 1, turn back on yourself along the main road, then turn right at the major crossroads. To your right you'll spot a small path – this is the start of the uphill slog along Seoul's old city wall, which has been restored along this section. Follow this along and you'll soon be in **Naksan Park**, a pleasant place with several good viewpoints overlooking the Daehangno area (see p.71). From here, press north again until you reach the main road near **Hansung University** station (line 4), another good place to start the walk. From here, you'll have to use your own initiative to find the fastest, most pleasant way to the back of **Sunkyungkwan University**, where the forested path starts again – the easiest method is to head west down the main road to the Hyehwa Rotary roundabout, turn right, then walk for 1km or so.

Waryong Park starts just to the west of the university buildings, and constitutes the eastern entrance of **Bugaksan** mountain (see p.76), the most challenging part of the walk (though it's not really too tricky). This is where you'll need your passport or other photo ID. The path drops you down in **Buamdong** (see p.76), a good place for lunch – grab coffee and a slice of cake at *Sanmotungi* café (see p.120), or some dumplings at *Jaha Sonmandoo* (see p.114). The old city wall continues over the other side of the main road in Buamdong, and those with more energy can follow this to reach the peaks of **Inwangsan** (see p.83), eventually dropping down somewhere near Dongnimmun station (line 3).

government for well over half a century, until 1983 when pretty much everything was finally ripped down – though the **botanical garden** still remains today (access included on palace ticket).

The palace

Considering its turbulent history, the palace is a relaxed place to wander around. The buildings themselves are nowhere near as polished as those in the Gyeongbok or Changdeok palaces, though some people feel that they look more authentic as a result; the history of each structure is chronicled on information boards. Be sure to look for **Myeongjeongjeon** (명정전), the oldest main hall of any of Seoul's palaces – it was built in 1616, and somehow escaped the fires that followed. From here, a number of lovely, herb-scented paths wind their way to a pond at the north of the complex. Near the pond are a couple of dedicated **herb gardens**, while also visible are the white-painted lattices of the Japanese-built botanical garden.

THE MURDER OF CROWN PRINCE SADO

In 1762, a sinister event occurred in the grounds of Changgyeonggung, one whose story is, for some reason, omitted from the information boards that dot the palace grounds – a **royal murder**. A young prince named **Sado** was heir to the throne of **King Yeongjo**, but occasionally abused his position of power, as evidenced by the apparently groundless murder of several servants. Fearing dire consequences if the nation's power were placed into his son's hands, Yeongjo escorted Sado to Seonninmun, a gate on the eastern side of the palace, and ordered him to climb into a rice casket; his son obeyed, was locked in, and starved to death. Sado's wife, Hyegyong, held the secret until after Yeongjo's death in 1776, at which point she spilled the beans in a book named *Hanjungnok* (published in English as *The Memoirs of Lady Hyegyong*). Sado's son **Jeongjo** became king on the death of Yeongjo, and built Hwaseong fortress in Suwon (see p.154) to house his father's remains. Jeongjo went on to become one of Korea's most respected rulers.

5 Seongbukdong
성북동

Home to much of Seoul's diplomatic corps, the hilly district of **Seongbukdong** has a secluded air with some low-key attractions, but it's a pleasant place to spend a half-day, and the steep roads will give your calf muscles some definition. Chief among the sights are the Zen temple of **Gilsangsa** and the entertainment and dining complex known as **Samcheonggak**.

Gilsangsa
길상사 • Seongbukdong 323 • 24hr • Free • ⓦ kilsangsa.info • Templestay W50,000; book in advance at ⓦ eng.templestay.com • Hansung University subway (line 4), then take the shuttle bus, or it's a 20min walk through a labyrinthine network of roads – the dearth of signage means that it's best to ask for directions

Uphill from Seongnagwon, the wonderful **Zen temple** of **Gilsangsa** was once one of Seoul's most famous *gisaeng* houses of entertainment (see box below), but was converted into a Seon (the Korean word for Zen) temple in 1997; it now makes one of the most convenient places for visitors to Seoul to experience a **templestay**, though it's only possible on the third Saturday of each month. Gilsangsa's coloration is notably bland compared to most Korean temples, and as a result it looks at its best under a thin blanket of winter snow; this is also the best time to take advantage of the little tearoom on the complex. Almost directly opposite the temple entrance, *Hyojae* is a tiny store selling superb Korean handicrafts (see p.133).

Samcheonggak
삼청각 • Daesagwanno 3 • Daily 10am–10pm • Free shuttle bus (hourly 10am–9pm) from outside Youngpoong bookstore (see p.134) near Jonggak, or Gyeongbokgung east gate; alternatively, it's a short taxi-ride from Hansung University station, Samcheongdong or Gyeongbokgung

Nestling in the foothills of Bugaksan (see p.76) are the pleasing wooden buildings of the **Samcheonggak** complex. This was built surprisingly recently – 1972, to be exact – and in the decades following its opening served as a place of entertainment for

---

MEMOIRS OF A GISAENG

Many Westerners are familiar with the concept of the Japanese geisha, but few are aware that Korea once had something very similar. **Gisaeng** were female courtesans trained to entertain the rich and powerful from the Goryeo dynasty onwards (see p.164). Girls chosen to be *gisaeng* received artistic instruction from the age of eight or nine, and though most found themselves retired after their late teens, some went on to become noted experts in dance, music or poetry. *Gisaeng* were employed by the state, and as such were also required to entertain the few foreign dignitaries or businessmen who entered the "Hermit Kingdom". Most were based in Seoul or Pyongyang, cities that were also home to the most reputable *gisaeng* schools, while others found work in regional centres or at inns along major travel arteries.

Despite their frequent interaction with members of the elite, *gisaeng* were technically at the very bottom of the Joseon dynasty's Confucian social ladder, their rank no higher than that of slaves. One of the few opportunities for advancement was to be taken as a **concubine** by a customer, but very few made it this far since *gisaeng* had to be purchased from the government at exorbitant prices. Over the centuries, however, more and more *gisaeng* came under the financial protection of patrons known as **gibu**. During the colonial period, almost all *gisaeng* were under the sponsorship of a *gibu*, but the Korean War and the economic boom which followed took their toll. Though the practice trickled on through the 1970s, it has since all but disappeared.

Among the most famous *gisaeng* was **Hwang Jin-i**, born in sixteenth-century Kaeson in what is now part of North Korea. Hwang was an entertainer of remarkable beauty and intellect who, in her spare time, created wistful poetry in the Korean style known as *sijo*. To date she has spawned one film, one TV series, and an eponymous novel; the latter is of particular note, having become the first North Korean publication to achieve critical success in the South.

5

politicians, businessmen and other folk from the upper echelons of Seoul society. Here they would wine and dine in style, entertained all the while by *gisaeng* (see box, p.74). The complex was restored in 2000, and now features a teahouse and rather expensive restaurant (see p.114).

Buamdong
부암동

Hidden from central Seoul by the mountain of Bugaksan, **Buamdong** is one of the capital's quaintest and calmest corners. Recent years have seen its popularity explode, its fame propelled by modern Korea's number one cultural catalyst, the television drama – ever since the picturesque café *Sanmotungi* (see p.120) was used as a set in hit drama *The Coffee Prince*, young Seoulites have been heading to the area in crowds, joined by the odd curious foreigner.

Despite its new-found fame, Buamdong retains a tranquillity that's almost impossible to find in other parts of Seoul, as well as a smattering of galleries and excellent places to eat and drink. The area is perhaps most notable for its lack of high-rise structures, as well as what may be Seoul's greatest concentration of **hangeul typography** – much of what you'll see has changed little since the 1970s, predating the current mania for Roman text. The most famous example by far, and the subject of countless photographs, is the logo of the Hanyang Ricecake Shop, starkly emblazoned in paint on a newly whitewashed brick wall; you'll come across it on the way to the superb **Whanki Museum**.

ARRIVAL AND DEPARTURE
BUAMDONG

By bus Buamdong is not accessible by subway (which may be the main factor behind its relaxed air), but regular buses run here from the Gyeongbokgung area. The best is bus #1020, which heads to Buamdong from a stop just up the road from exit 2 of Gwanghwamun subway station. There's also a shuttle bus, which departs from Insadong's Gana Insa

Art Center (see p.52) on the hour, stopping at various galleries on its way to the Gana Art Center (see opposite). Alternatively, the area is a 20min uphill walk from Gyeongbokgung station – follow the road flanking the palace's western wall, and keep going straight.

Whanki Museum
환기 미술관 • Jahamunno 40-gil 63 • Tues–Sun 10am–6pm • W7000 • ⓦ whankimuseum.org

The little-visited **Whanki Museum** is a shrine of sorts to the unfortunately-named Kim Whanki, one of Korea's first modern artists. In the 1940s, Kim proved a conduit between east and west, mopping up ideas from the Paris avant-garde movement while disseminating Asian techniques to a curious Europe. You may have to ask around to get to it – it's located down a small slope from the main road.

Bugaksan
북악산 • Hiking route open daily 9am–5pm; last entry 3pm • Free • Bring your passport, or some other form of photo ID, to register at entrance • Photography is not permitted at certain points on the trail • The park's western entrance is at Changuimun gate in Buamdong. The eastern entrance is at Waryong Park, a taxi-ride or a 25min walk from Anguk station: it's also accessible on local bus #8 from Hyehwa station

Rising up directly behind the palace of Gyeongbokgung (see p.37), **Bugaksan** is one of the most significant mountains in Seoul. It provides some of the most glorious views of the capital, but for decades only soldiers were able to take them in, the mountain trails having been off limits thanks to the important building nestling on its southern slopes – **Cheongwadae**, official home of the country's president (see p.44). These protective measures were not without foundation, as in 1968 Bugaksan was the scene of an assassination attempt, when a squad of North Korean commandos descended from the mountain to try and assassinate then-president Park Chung-hee (see p.170). Near the mountain's eastern entrance, beside the gate of **Sukjeongmun**, you can still see

5

a tree riddled with bullet holes – evidence of the shoot-out that occurred when the would-be assassins were sprung. The mountain reopened to the public in 2006, but there's still a substantial military presence here, and those wishing to take a hike must register with officials on arrival.

The **hiking route** across Bugaksan is 3.8km long, and though it gets rather steep at times almost anyone can tackle it. On the way you'll see remnants of Seoul's fortress wall, which once circled what was then a much smaller city. The first fortifications were built in 1395, at the outset of the Joseon dynasty just after the completion of Gyeongbokgung and Jongmyo, with the aim of protecting the new national capital. Most of the wall has now been destroyed, and this is one of the few places that you can still see it.

Pyeongchangdong

평창동

Just north of Buamdong is **Pyeongchangdong**, a low-rise district with a high-class air, having served as Seoul's high-roller residential area of choice during the economic boom of the 1970s and 1980s. Most have now upped sticks and moved south of the river to Gangnam, Apgujeong and Jamsil (see Chapter 00), but those who favoured tradition over modernity stayed put, and have now been joined by hundreds of writers and artists. Indeed, it's the endeavours of the area's artistic fraternity that now form its main tourist draw, with dozens of excellent **galleries** to choose from, including the colossal **Gana Art Center**. Art aside, Pyeongchangdong's hilly lanes make for excellent strolling territory, giving the few foreigners who make it here a chance to savour a relaxed atmosphere, with low-rise luxury houses, tree-clad hills, and the majestic, ever-present vista of Bukhansan National Park (see below).

Gana Insa Art Center

가나 아트 갤러리 · Pyeongchangdong 97 · Daily 10am–7pm · W3000 · ⑩ ganaart.com · Bus #1020 or #1711 from Gyongbokgung subway (line 3), or take the free shuttle bus (see opposite) which leaves from Insadong's Gana Insa Art Center on the hour

Korea's largest art gallery, the **Gana Insa Art Center** nestles in relative obscurity, way up on the Pyongchangdong slopes. Designed by French architect Jean-Michel Wilmotte (who also designed Incheon Airport), it's a fabulous treasure-trove of modern art, with a delightful sculpture garden out back. The displays here include the works of notable international artists (which have, in the past, included Jean Miró and Roy Lichtenstein), as well as Korean artists from the early twentieth century.

Bukhansan National Park

북한산 국립공원

Few major cities can claim to have a national park right on their doorstep, but looming over central Seoul, and forming a natural northern boundary to the city, are the peaks of **BUKHANSAN NATIONAL PARK**, spears and spines of off-white granite that burst out of the undulating pine forests. Despite the park's relatively small size at just 80 square kilometres, its proximity to one of the Earth's most populated cities makes it the **world's most visited** national park, drawing in upwards of five million visitors per year. While an undeniably beautiful place, its popularity means that the trails are often very busy indeed – especially on warm weekends – and some can be as crowded as shopping mall aisles, with hikers having to queue up to reach the peaks.

The national park can be split into north and south areas. The southern section – **Bukhansan** proper – overlooks Seoul and is home to the fortress ruins, while 10km to the north is **Dobongsan**, a similar maze of stony peaks and hiking trails. Both offer good day-trip routes which are easy enough to be tackled by most visitors, but still enough of a challenge to provide a good work-out.

5

HIKING INFORMATION

BUKHANSAN NATIONAL PARK

Maps are available at all entrances, and larger signboard versions can be seen at various points en route. Most local hikers choose to wear proper boots, but unless it's rainy a sturdy pair of trainers should suffice.

Eating and drinking You'll have no problem finding a meal after a hike: all the entrances have plenty of restaurants, with *pajeon*, a savoury pancake, and *makgeolli*, rice beer (see p.125), the favoured post-hike combo for Koreans.

Southern Bukhansan

Gupabal station (line 3), then bus #704 to Sanseong park entrance (10min)

The southern half of Bukhansan is best accessed through **Sanseong**, an entry point on the western side of the park. On the short walk to the clutch of restaurants that surround the entrance, you'll see the park's principal peaks soaring above; unless you're visiting at a weekend, the hustle and bustle of downtown Seoul will already feel a world away.

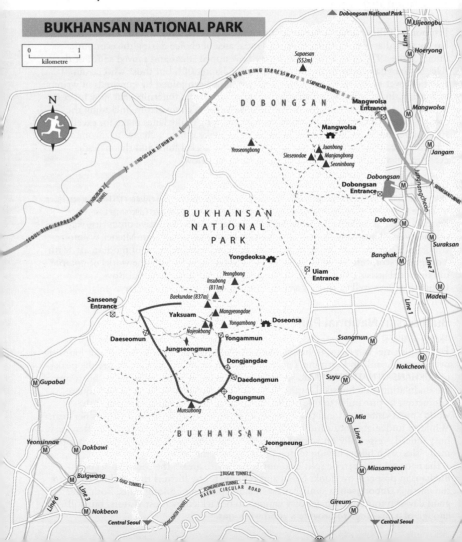

It's around two hours from the entrance to **Baekundae** (백운대), the highest peak in the park at 837m: routes are closed off in rotation to allow them time to regenerate – bilingual signs point the way. Around ten minutes into your walk you'll find yourself at **Daeseomun** (대서문), one of the main gates of the fortress wall. From here, it's a long slog up to Baekundae; once you've reached **Yaksuam** (약수암), a lofty hermitage, you're almost there (and will doubtless be grateful for the presence of spring-water drinking fountains). Continuing on, the route becomes more precipitous, necessitating the use of steel stairways and fences. Having finally scaled the peak itself, you'll be able to kick off your boots awhile and enjoy the wonderful panoramic views.

From Baekundae, the easiest route back to the park entrance is along the same path, though there are other options. One trail heads south, squeezing between some neighbouring peaks to Yongammun, another fortress gate. From here – depending on which paths are open – you can head downhill towards Jungseongmun, then follow the pretty stream to the park entrance, or take a half-hour detour along a ridge further south to Daedongmun gate. Those seeking a sterner challenge can head yet further southwest of Daedongmun to **Munsubong** peak (문수봉), then take the punishing up-and-down route back to the park entrance – from the entrance, the round trip via Baekundae and Munsubong will be a full-day hike.

It's also possible to exit the park at different locations – from Baekundae, a two-hour route heads east to Uiam entrance via the temple of **Yongdeoksa**; while from Yongammun, a trail heads downhill to **Doseonsa**, the park's principal temple; and from Bogungmun – a gate just south of Daedongmun – a path drops down the **Jeongneung** valley to the entrance of the same name.

Northern Bukhansan

Mangwolsa and Dobongsan subway (both line 1), then an uphill walk of around 20min to the park entrances

The scenery in the **Dobongsan** area is much the same as around Baekundae to the south – trees, intriguing rock formations and wonderful views at every turn – though the hiking options are less numerous. Most choose to scale the main peak (740m) on a C-shaped route that curls uphill and down between **Mangwolsa** and **Dobongsan** subway stations (each around 30min from Jongno 3-ga). It's hard to say which direction is better, but most people start from Dobongsan. From this station, cross the main road, then go left along the perimeter of a dense network of ramshackle snack bars, then right up the main road. Whichever way you go, it takes just over two hours up to the gathering of peaks at the top; like Baekundae to the south of the park, the upper reaches of the trail are patches of bare rock, and you'll be grateful for the steel ropes on which you can haul yourself up or down. Coming back down, you can take a rest at **Mangwolsa** (망월사), a small but rather beautiful temple originally built here in 639, before heading back into Seoul. Mangwolsa roughly translates as "Moon-viewing temple", and was likely used for such purposes by the kings of the Joseon period from the late fourteenth century.

SEOUL'S GUARDIAN MOUNTAIN

With its position overlooking Seoul, Bukhansan has played a significant role in protecting the city. In the second century a **fortress** was built during the capital's earliest days as the hub of the Baekje dynasty. Sizeable fortifications were constructed during the rule of **King Sukjong** (r.1674–1720), a leader notable for his peacemaking abilities in a time of national and international strife: not only did he pacify the warring factions that threatened to tear the peninsula apart, but he also negotiated with the Chinese Qing dynasty to define the borders between the two countries as the Yalu and Tumen rivers. These borders remain in place today, albeit under the control of Pyongyang, rather than Seoul, and it was while the two halves of Korea were jostling for control of the peninsula during the Korean War that much of Bukhansan's fortress was destroyed. Remnants of the wall can still be found, including much of the section that stretched down from the mountains to connect with Seoul's city wall (see box, p.73).

PARK, SEONYUDO ISLAND

Western Seoul

Western Seoul is best known for the huge university area which spreads north from the Hangang River: it's a hectic and noisy district, with more than 100,000 students squeezed into a tight band of land. Some studying gets done, of course, but the area is better known for its extracurricular activities – the streets here are stuffed to the gills with bars, nightclubs, karaoke rooms and cheap restaurants, and the action continues all night. The focus of attention is the area around Hongik University, known as Hongdae – by day this is a pleasantly artsy district, which morphs each evening into Korea's most hectic nightlife zone.

BEST OF WESTERN SEOUL

Seodaemun Prison One of Seoul's most thought-provoking sights, this prison was used to house separatists during the Japanese occupation period – and local dissenters during the first decades of South Korean rule. See below

Inwangsan Head up this small mountain to visit Seoul's most important Shamanist site, and do a spot of hiking. See p.83

Hongdae nightlife Korea's best nightlife, bar none, can be found in the wider Hongdae area. See p.124

Hanging along the Hangang The banks of the Hangang are where Seoulites go to relax – and they provide a fascinating window into contemporary life in the city. See box, p.87

Seonyudo Formerly a waste treatment site, this little islet in the Hangang has been gentrified, and now makes for great strolling territory. See p.88

Noryangjin The city's main fish market is as fascinating as it is smelly – very, in other words. See p.88

6

To the northeast of Hongdae, the unprepossessing **Seodaemun** district is home to two contrasting sights – the eponymous **prison** which hosted immunerable atrocities during the Japanese occupation, and **Inwangsan**, a small mountain with a spider's web of fantastic walking trails. South of Hongdae flows the mighty **Hangang River**, along whose banks Seoulites jog, cycle, picnic or simply chill, while **Yeouido** island is one of Seoul's main business hubs as well as housing Korea's National Assembly.

Seodaemun

서대문

Those who've seen the gates of Namdaemun and Dongdaemun may have some idea what to expect of **Seodaemun** – its name means western gate and, unsurprisingly, it is the site of Seoul's old western entrance. The city has now, of course, expanded much further west, and the gate itself is long gone – there is still one gate-like structure visible in the area, near Dongnimmun subway station, though this is a mere independence monument. The main reason to visit the district, however, is to see the notorious **Seodaemun Prison**, or to wander round the trails and temples of **Inwangsan**, a mountain rising up just to the north.

Seodaemun Prison

서대문 형무소 역사관 • Tonggillo 251 • Tues–Sun 9.30am–6pm • W3000 • Dongnimmun subway (line 3)

During the occupation of Korea (1910–45), umpteen prisons were built across the land to house thousands of activists and those otherwise opposed to Japanese rule (see box, p.83), of which **Seodaemun Prison** was by far the most notorious. The prison became a symbol of the power of the Japanese, whose brutality during occupation ensured the Korean resistance movement rarely blossomed into anything more than strikes and street protests, though on March 1, 1919, the Declaration of Independence was read out at Tapgol Park (see p.52), an event that achieved nothing concrete but kept the Korean spirit of independence alive.

Today, the red-brick wings of the prison's main barracks have been reopened as a "history hall", with photos of the prison during occupation filling its rooms and corridors, together with written material from the period, and some televised documentaries. Few of these exhibits are in English, but the eerie vibe of the buildings themselves needs no translation, from the tiny vertical booths used for "coffin" torture to the lonely outpost where executions were conducted. The **execution area** has one particularly poignant feature, a pair of **poplar trees**, one inside the compound wall, and one just outside. The latter – termed the "wailing tree", on account of the number of prisoners who clung to it as a last means of resistance – is a large, healthy specimen, as

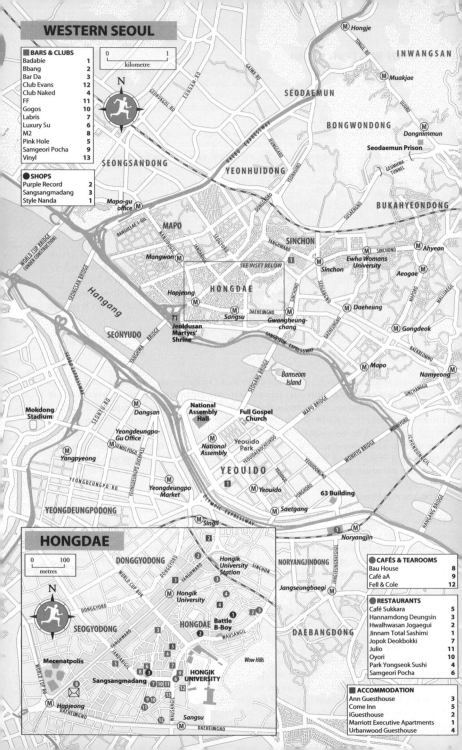

6

JAPANESE OCCUPATION

If you've done any sightseeing in Seoul, you'll no doubt have come across information boards telling you when, or how often, certain buildings were burnt down or destroyed by the Japanese. The two countries have been at loggerheads for centuries, but the **1910–45 occupation period** caused most of the tension that can still be felt today. In this age of empire, Asian territory from Beijing to Borneo suffered systematic rape and torture at the hands of Japanese forces, but only Korea experienced a full-scale assault on its **national identity**. Koreans were forced to use Japanese names and money, books written in *hangeul* text were burnt and the Japanese language was taught in schools. These were merely the most blatant measures of the many employed by the Japanese – others were barely perceptible, and used as subliminal attacks on the Korean psyche. One example was the almost surgical removal of the tallest trees in Korean cities, which were ostensibly chopped down for their wood: straight and strong, they were said to symbolize the Korean mind, and were replaced with willows, which drifted with the wind in a manner more befitting the programme. The most contentious issue remains the use of over 100,000 **comfort women**, who were forced into slave-like prostitution to sate the sexual needs of Japanese soldiers, and are yet to receive compensation or an official apology (see box, p.48).

---

opposed to the tree inside the compound, which is apparently kept short and stunted by the souls of those departed.

One piece of information not conveyed on any signboards, in any language, is the fact that the prison was not only used by the Japanese: though independent, South Korea only became democratic in the late 1980s, and until then the prison was used to hold political activists and other enemies of the state. It was finally closed in 1987, immediately after the first fully democratic elections. Also kept off the information boards is the role played by local collaborators during resistance, or any details of how independence was actually achieved: it was simply part of the package in Japan's surrender to the United States (see p.167).

Inwangsan

인왕산 • 24hr • Free • Dongnimmun subway (line 3), then it's a 15min walk uphill to Guksadang

Just north of Seodaemun Prison rise the craggy peaks of **Inwangsan**. While Inwangsan is less visited than the crowded Bukhansan range (see p.77), it contains more of tourist interest, including a number of **temples**, some **Shamanist shrines**, and one of the longest sections of Seoul's old **fortress wall**. The main sight here is the shrine of **Guksadang** (국사당), a boulder-surrounded prayer hall that hosts at least three Shamanist ceremonies known as *gut* (굿) each day, giving visitors a convenient opportunity to take in this lesser-known facet of Korea's religious make-up.

The **peak** of Inwangsan (338m) lies a further 1km hike uphill from the shrine, and from here the massif's spider's web of routes continues further north. As with other mountain routes in Seoul, everything is well signposted and it's almost impossible to get lost; the military base near the top can, however, get in the way at times. In dry weather, a sturdy pair of trainers should suffice to reach the peak.

The university district

Within a few square kilometres of western Seoul, the universities of Hongik, Yonsei, Ehwa and Sogang lie at the peripheries of the areas most commonly known as **Hongdae**, **Sinchon** and **Edae** – and each district has its own distinctive atmosphere. Hongdae and Edae are the colloquial terms for Hongik and Ehwa universities – the Korean tendency is to take the first syllable of the name and add the *dae* from *daehakkyo*, which means university – and it's these names that you're most likely to

6

HIDDEN SEOUL

Seoul presents an almost relentlessly modern face to the world, and though the progress of both the city and Korea as a whole has been admirably uniform in international terms, certain pockets of poverty still stand out. One such place is **Gaemi Maeul** (개미 마을), a district little changed in decades, despite its fairly central location. While not quite a shanty town, as some locals like to describe it, the dilapidated, semi-rural atmosphere of this small residential area forms an almost shockingly stark contrast with the rest of the city. In recent years, it has started to draw young, camera-toting Seoulites curious to see this odd facet of their city, and some of the buildings have been pimped with funky paintings. Gaemi Maeul sits on the western flank of Inwangsan (see p.83), and can be accessed by a path from the mountain; however, it's far easier to walk or take local bus #7 there from Hongje subway (line 3).

---

hear. Though there are precious few tourist sights as such, there's nowhere better to get an understanding of what really makes Korea tick.

Hongdae

홍대 • Hongik University subway (line 2), or Sangsu subway (line 6)

Hongdae is one of the edgiest districts in the whole country, teeming with young and trendy people at almost every hour. The area only truly comes into its own after dark, its hundreds of bars and clubs buzzing with activity every night of the week (see p.124). During the daytime, it's fun to explore the streets lined with small shops selling stylish and secondhand clothing, and there are quirky cafés on every corner. Hongdae University itself specializes in the **arts**, a fact that'll be most evident to the visitor in **Nolita Park** (놀이터공원) – actually a triangular wedge of ground with almost no greenery – which plays host to anything and everything from Beatles impersonators to choreographed hip-hop dancing. At weekends, the park is home to an interesting **flea market**, where local students sell handmade earrings, bangles and other such trinkets.

Sinchon

신촌 • Sinchon subway (line 2)

The atmosphere in the university district of **Sinchon** (pronounced "Shin-chon") is a little earthier than in neighbouring Hongdae. It's is best visited at night, when the surrounding side-streets are splashed with neon and filled with barbecue smoke – restaurants here can be incredibly cheap, and since one building in every four seems to house a bar, it makes for an interesting night out. Sinchon is also the centre of Seoul's small **lesbian** community (see p.126), most likely due to the presence of Ehwa Women's University a few hundred metres to the east (see below).

Edae

이대 • Ehwa Women's University subway (line 2)

The 20,000-plus students at Ehwa Women's University, more commonly referred to as "**Edae**", make this the world's largest institution of female learning. It is also Korea's oldest female-only university, and broke ground by providing Korea's first female doctor and lawyer. The **main campus** itself is also worth a look for its mishmash of **architectural styles** – there are a couple of Gothic-style buildings, augmented by a new wing designed by French architect Dominique Perrault. This wing is largely underground, its open-air access path delving below surface level to reveal floor upon floor of study halls, as well as the odd shop, restaurant and café. Outside the south gate, the area is packed not so much with bars and clubs, as is the case with most universities, but with hundreds of cheap shops selling clothes, shoes, make-up and fashion accessories.

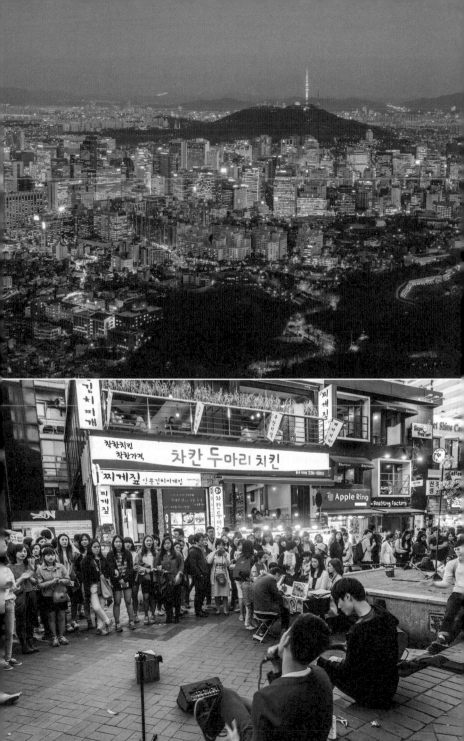

Jeoldusan Martyrs' Shrine

절두산 순교성지 • 24hr • Free • Hapjeong subway (lines 2 & 6)

On a small hill overlooking the Hangang, the **Jeoldusan Martyrs Shrine** commemorates the many Catholic Koreans who lost their lives because of their faith. Despite the staggering number of neon crosses searing the night skies of present-day Seoul, the country has not always been so tolerant of Christians – in 1866 there was a royally sanctioned purge of thousands of Korean Catholics, who had started to proliferate thanks to the efforts of European missionaries (some of whom were also murdered). Pope John Paul II visited the shrine in 1984 and canonized 103 of the martyrs; Mother Teresa visited the following year, and in 2014 Pope Francis beatified a further 123 victims of the slaughter.

Yeouido and around

From its source in the Geumgang mountains of North Korea, the Han River – known in Korean as the **Hangang** – moseys along for over 500km before emptying into the West Sea. Close to its end it passes through Seoul, and cleaves this great city almost perfectly in two. The south bank of the Hangang's central stretch contains some notable sights, clustered around the island of **Yeouido**. This forms one of Seoul's main business districts, and as such has some of its largest towers, including the magnificent 63 Building. Just to the south is **Noryangjin** and its atmospheric **fish market**, while west along the Hangang is the recently redeveloped islet **Seonyudo**, a popular draw for Seoulites wishing to stroll or cycle.

Yeouido

여의도

An island in the Hangang may sound nice, but you'd do well to banish any romantic visions before arriving in **Yeouido**. Meaning something akin to "useless land", it lay barren for years before finally undergoing development during Park Chung-hee's economic reforms in the 1970s. Progress came fast, and little "Sweet Potato Island", as it's nicknamed on account of its shape, is now one of Korea's most important **business districts**, not to mention the home of its National Assembly and the **63 Building**, formerly the tallest structure in Asia. However, as Yeouido is manifestly a place to work, rather than live or go out, at weekends and in the evenings it has some of the quietest roads in the city. Most of the northern fringe is now a **riverside park**, which is a favourite picnicking place for families at weekends and on warm evenings, while

---

THE HANGANG

Despite being the major waterway of one of the world's largest cities, the **Hangang** (한강) is almost entirely devoid of traffic, with nary a vessel to be seen. The reason for this is that part of the river delta, west of Seoul, belongs to North Korea – any vessel attempting to make the voyage out to sea would likely be blown to smithereens. In central Seoul, however, the river continues to play an integral part in daily city life. Despite being a kilometre wide, it's crossed by an astonishing number of **bridges** – 28 and counting in Seoul alone. None is of any historical interest, since in June 1950, at the beginning of the Korean War, the few bridges that existed were blown up in an attempt to stymie the North Korean advance. No warning was given, and hundreds of evacuating soldiers and refugees were killed as a result. Most of the bridges seen today were built in the 1970s and 1980s during Seoul's rapid economic and geographic expansion; one unfortunate side effect is that both river banks – rare pieces of flat, usable land in congested, mountainous Seoul – are now home to colossal **elevated highways**. This may sound like the stuff of urban nightmares, but beneath the concrete and hulking lattices of steel lurks the very heart of Seoul, where many of the city's residents spend their evenings and leisure time (see box opposite).

6

HANGING ALONG THE HANGANG

The banks of the Hangang are a hive of activity, and proof of Seoul's open-all-hours nature: at any time of day or night, you'll see locals riding their bikes, puffing and panting on exercise equipment, going for a run, or having a picnic. However, the river and its banks also offer up a whole raft of other possibilities, the best of which are detailed below.

Coffee and cocktails Six bridges now have stylish cafés at their northern and southern ends, providing great views of the river and the teeming bridge traffic. They're a little tricky to get to, and are best approached by taxi; all are open daily from 10am to around 2am, making them equally good spots for an evening cocktail. The Dongjak and Hannam bridges (see map, p.91) are particularly recommended, since they provide great views of the Banpo bridge fountain shows (see below).

Cycling The Hangang is the most popular spot for cycling in Seoul, and a scoot along the grassy river banks constitutes one of the city's most pleasurable and picturesque activities. The main route runs for a whopping 21km between World Cup Stadium to the west (see below), and Olympic Park in the east (see p.98). Bikes can be rented from various points along the river, including several in Yeouido Park for around W3000 an hour.

Fountain shows Banpo bridge, located between the Seobinggo and Express Bus Terminal subway stations, plays host to some eye-catching fountain shows from April–Oct. Jets of water burst from the bridge for ten minutes at noon, 2pm, 4pm, 8pm and 9pm (more shows at weekends); the night-time shows are particularly recommended, since the fountains are illuminated in eye-catching colours.

Picnicking On balmy summer evenings in Seoul, the Hangang's banks are packed with locals barbecuing meat, throwing back beer and supping *soju* on mats known as *dotjari* (돗자리). These mats, and disposable barbecue sets, are sold for a pittance at most convenience stores close to the river, then you can simply pop into a local butcher for some meat. Alternatively, amble along the river looking curious and you may well get an invite to a *dotjari* party.

Swimming There are seven open-air swimming pools along the Hangang, with those on Yeouido easiest to reach for foreign visitors (see map, p.82). All are open 9am–8pm from June–Aug, and entry costs W5000; note that they may be closed during bad weather.

cycling is fun here at any time of year (see above). There's also a great **open-air swimming pool** (see above) here in the summer.

63 Building

63 빌딩 • 63-ro 50 • **Sky Art observation deck** daily 10am–11pm • W13,000 • **Seaworld** daily 10am–10pm • W19,000 • **Wax Museum** daily 10am–10pm • W15,000 • ⓦ 63.co.kr • Yeouinaru (line 5) or Yeouido subway (lines 5 & 9)

A short walk south of Wonhyo bridge, the **63 Building** is one of the largest and most notable of Seoul's innumerable towers. A distinctive golden monolith 249m in height, it was the tallest structure in Asia when completed in 1985, though had already lost the title by the time the Olympics rolled into town three years later, and is today struggling to stay in the national top ten. Right at the top of the building, the sixtieth-floor **observation deck** provides predictably good views of Seoul, while the basement houses the **Seaworld** aquarium that's home to over twenty thousand sea creatures (there's also a reptile hall). Also in the basement, the **Wax Museum** – like all similar places worldwide – is full of celebrity effigies.

The Full Gospel Church

순복음 교회 • Yeouidodong 11-2 • Services most days; check website for details • ⓦ english.fgtv.com • National Assembly subway (line 9)

With a membership exceeding one million people, the almost sinfully ugly **Full Gospel Church** is by some measures the largest church on earth. Obviously, not all the congregation comes along for prayers at the same time, but to meet the needs of Seoul's huge Protestant population there are no fewer than seven separate Sunday services, translated into sixteen languages in a dedicated foreigners' section. This is quite a trip, whatever your denomination, since most Sunday services see more than ten thousand people pack into the building, creating something of a football crowd atmosphere on the way in. On occasion half of the congregation ends up in tears, as Korean pastors have a habit of ratcheting up the rhetoric, better to exploit the national tendency towards melodrama.

Noryangjin fish market

노량진 • Nodeullo 688 • Daily 24hr; auctions 4–6am • Noryangjin subway (lines 1 & 9)

Just south of Yeouido, the mind-boggling **Noryangjin fish market** is the place to come for seafood, though it remains well off the radar for most foreign visitors. During the evening the place is particularly picturesque – under strings of bright lights, you can wander around whole soggy acres of shells, seaworms, spider crabs and other salty fare. Much of the goods on offer will be unfamiliar to the average Western traveller, but fortune favours the brave; unless you have suitable cooking skills and a home to repair to, bag up your goodies and take them up to one of the second-floor restaurants, whose chefs will do the necessary preparations for a surprisingly reasonable price. Prime time at Noryangjin market is early morning, when noisy **fish auctions** are held.

Seonyudo

선유도 • Daily 24hr • Free • Seonyudo subway (line 9), or walkable from Hongdae and Hapjeong over Yanghwa bridge

A tiny island just west of Yeouido, **Seonyudo** was, until recently, the site of a gargantuan water treatment plant. The city authorities felt that the land could be put to better use, and in 2009 a gentrified Seonyudo began a new lease of life as a strolling and picnicking place. It has since become extremely popular, especially at weekends, when you'll see Seoulites arriving in their hundreds for a spot of cycling, rollerblading, or a family meal; stay until evening time to see **Yanghwa Bridge**, which links Seonyudo to the north and south banks of the Hangang, lit up in pretty colours.

TEN-STOREY PAGODA, NATIONAL MUSEUM OF KOREA

Itaewon and Yongsan

One of Seoul's best-known districts, Itaewon is something of an enigma. It has long been frequented by American soldiers stationed at the nearby Dragon Hill military garrison, with expat businessmen and visiting foreigners following suit – indeed, until English teachers started pouring into Korea by the planeload this was one of the few places in the country in which "Western" items such as leather jackets, deodorant, tampons or Hershey's Kisses could be found. Times are changing, however, and the gradual withdrawal of American troops has coincided with the opening of an ever more cosmopolitan array of hip restaurants. The district also heaves with clubbers at weekends, while "Hooker Hill", where the American soldiers sought good-time girls, has sprouted a new district, "Homo Hill", Korea's most prominent gay area.

BEST OF ITAEWON AND YONGSAN

Leeum Museum of Art One of Korea's most highly regarded galleries, hosting exhibitions by some of the top international names in the art world. See below

Itaewon's craft beers Sample some of Korea's best craft beers where they are made, in Itaewon's burgeoning microbreweries. See p.92

National Museum of Korea Seoul's grandest museum is a repository of dynastic and pre-dynastic artefacts from around the land. See p.92

Cosmopolitan restaurants Bulgarian, Brazilian, Japanese, Nigerian and French cuisines are just some of the international cuisines you could be sampling in Itaewon. See p.117

Tailored clothing Prices for tailored suits and shirts are still surprisingly low in Itaewon – get measured up on arrival, then pick up your goodies before leaving Korea. See p.135

Dragon Hill Spa Take some time out from the hectic city at Seoul's biggest spa by far. See p.141

However, Itaewon also has its cultural side, being home to the **Leeum Museum of Art**, the city's most vaunted gallery space. Nearby, in the neighbouring high-rise area of **Yongsan**, you'll find the **War Memorial Museum**, crammed with planes, choppers and smaller items pertaining to the Korean War, and the vast **National Museum of Korea**.

Itaewon

이태원

Since **Itaewon** has long been Seoul's main base for foreigners, it comes as no surprise that it's also home to the country's most cosmopolitan array of restaurants (see p.117), and some pretty kicking nightlife (see p.124). However, in recent years prices have been rising, and the prevailing demographic has become older, more affluent and more Korean – no bad thing, though present-day Itaewon certainly lacks the seedy bite of old. The effect has been magnified by the fact that the area of interest has grown larger – Greater Itaewon now encompasses **Hannamdong** to the east, and the conjoined area of **Gyeongnidang** and **Haebangchon** to the west; all three boast funky bars and restaurants, and a relatively mellow nightlife.

Leeum Museum of Art

리움미술관 · Hannamdong 747-18 · Tues–Sun 10.30am–6pm · W10,000, plus W7000 for special exhibitions · Ⓦ leeum.samsung foundation.org · Hangangjin or Itaewon (both line 6)

The excellent **Leeum Museum of Art** is not so much a museum as one of the most esteemed galleries in the country. It's split into several halls, each with a distinctive and original design; one, built in black concrete, was designed by acclaimed Dutch architect Rem Koolhaas, who has since worked on the fantastic CCTV headquarters in Beijing. The permanent collection here includes a traditional section displaying objects such as pottery and calligraphic scrolls, while the modern art section features paintings from Korean and international artists. The museum also hosts the occasional special exhibition of world-famous artists, both past and present – works by the likes of Mark Rothko and Damien Hirst have been displayed here.

Yongsan

용산

Perhaps best known to travellers on account of the eponymous train station and electronics market, the **Yongsan** district is one of the more affluent on the north side of the river, and home to some particularly tall residential blocks. There are more high-rises on the way, with the area earmarked for development by the city authorities. It's also home to a couple of interesting museums – the **War Memorial Museum** and the **National Museum of Korea**.

War Memorial of Korea

전쟁기념관 • Itaewonno 29 • Tues– Sun 9.30am–5.30pm • Free • ⓦ warmemo.or.kr • Samgakji subway (lines 4 & 6)

The huge **War Memorial Museum** charts the history of Korean warfare from ancient stones and arrows to more modern machinery. You don't need a ticket to see the larger sights, as the museum's park-like periphery is riddled with B-52 bombers and other flying machines – you can even clamber up ladders to cockpit windows for a look inside some of them. Before entering the main building itself, look for the names written on the outer wall: these are the names of every known member of the Allied forces who died in the Korean War, and the list seems to go on forever. This is particularly heart-wrenching when you consider the fact that a far greater number of people, unmarked here, died on the Chinese and North Korean side – in total, the war

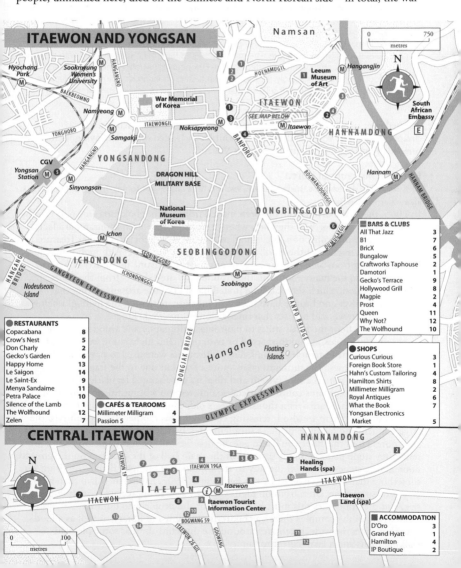

SEOUL'S CRAFT BEER SCENE

It's safe to say that **Korean beer** has a poor reputation – indeed, many a traveller has claimed that it's the worst they've ever tasted. One reason for this is that, until recently, the country's beer market was dominated by two gigantic breweries: Hite-Jinro and Oriental Brewers, whose three main brands – Hite, Cass and OB – were ubiquitous across the land. None of them tasted very nice, largely due to the dubious preservatives used to lengthen the drinks' lifespan – something in the same chemical family as formaldehyde. Other than familiarity with the major brands, the lack of competition was exacerbated by government regulation prohibiting beer sales by firms producing less than a million litres per year – so small-scale breweries simply couldn't enter the market.

Things all changed in 2010, when the government relaxed its ridiculous – and rather suspicious – beer-production laws. The scene was set for the birth of a domestic **craft beer industry**, with **microbreweries** soon proliferating in Itaewon – the most notable are Craftworks, Magpie and The Booth (see p.125). All three ventures were started off by beer-loving expats, though most of the demand for craft beer in the Itaewon area is actually from Koreans; said demand is now outstripping supply, especially since bars in other Korean cities have started to sell the brews. The major breweries have been spooked, too, with the labelling of some brands altered to effect a more European appearance, and slight changes to the flavour. Even more pleasingly, it looks like craft beer production is not just a local fad, but here to stay – something that deserves three cheers from any visitor or expat interested in ale.

claimed over two million people. After all this, the main hall itself is a little disappointing, but you'll find plenty of exhibits and video displays relaying incredibly one-sided information about the Korean War.

National Museum of Korea

국립 중앙 박물관 • Seobinggoro 137 • Tues, Thurs & Fri 9am–6pm, Wed & Sat 9am–9pm, Sun 9am–7pm • Free • ⓦ museum.go.kr Ichon subway (line 4 & Jungang line)

In 2005, the **National Museum of Korea** moved from Gyeongbokgung (see p.37) to this huge building just north of the Han, where it houses over eleven thousand artefacts from the museum's collection, including an incredible 94 official National Treasures, though only a fraction of these will be on show at any one time. Although it may look like something from *Star Trek*, it's a Seoul must-see for anyone interested in Korean history. Among the many rooms on the ground level are exhibits from the **Three Kingdoms** period, which showcase the incredible skill of the artisans during that time – gold, silver and bronze have been cast into ornate shapes, the highlight being a fifth-century crown and belt set that once belonged to a Silla king.

Moving up a floor the focus shifts to paintings, calligraphy and wooden art, and there's usually a colossal **Buddhist scroll** or two, over 10m high; some were hung behind the Buddha statue in temples' main halls, while others were used to pray for rain and other such purposes. The museum owns quite a few, but due to the fragility of the material, they're put on a rota system and displays are changed regularly. The uppermost floor contains countless metal sculptures and a beautiful assortment of pots – some of these are over a thousand years old, though they look as if they were made yesterday. There are also interesting collections from other Asian countries, the large Chinese and Japanese displays supplemented by relics from Turkestan, Sri Lanka and more. From this floor you'll also get the best view of the museum's pride and joy, a ten-storey stone **pagoda** that is situated in the main hall of the museum on the ground floor, and stretches almost all the way to the top floor. It's in remarkable condition for something that was taken apart by the Japanese in 1907, hauled to Tokyo then all the way back some years later; from on high, you'll be able to appreciate more fully its true size, and the difficulties this must have posed for the people who built it.

Elsewhere in the complex there's a **children's museum** and library, as well as a food court and café; the wide, green area around the museum also has some pleasant walking paths and a lake – great for a picnic.

BONGUENSA TEMPLE, GANGNAM

Southern Seoul

The Korean capital is a city of two distinct halves. Seoul proper once stopped north of the Hangang, so almost all its historical sights are located there. Development then spilled over the river during the heady days of the 1970s, giving rise to an almost entirely new part of town. The area immediately south of the Hangang is known as Gangnam, which since that era of economic expansion has become the wealthiest area in the land, and indeed one of the richest urban zones in the whole of Asia. Seoulites have relocated here in their millions, creating a distinct north-south divide: northerners tend to find those from the south money-obsessed and self-centred, while southerners find the north relatively lacking in modern sophistication.

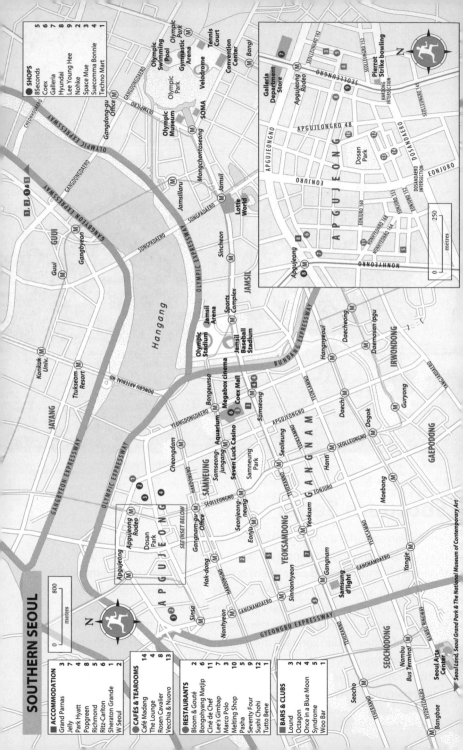

BEST OF SOUTHERN SEOUL

Boutique hunting Grab a W10,000 latte from a trendy café, and you'll fit right into the fashionable area around Apgujeong's Dosan Park, home to boutiques galore. See p.135

Samsung d'light Check out the gadgets of the future – plus some retro ones too – at Samsung's impressive electronics showroom. See p.97

Samneung Park Visit the burial mounds of three Korean royals in this pretty park, surrounded by woodland and walking paths. See p.97

Bongeunsa One of the most appealing temples in Seoul, despite its incongruous setting just north of the Coex Mall. See p.98

Olympic Park Created for the 1988 Summer Games, this park is home to some interesting Brutalist architecture. See p.98

Seoul Grand Park This large expanse of greenery makes for a great day out of the city with its neat zoo, theme park, and excellent modern art museum. See p.101

While the north wins hands-down in sightseeing terms, there's still a fair amount to see down south: **Bongeunsa** is the most enchanting temple in central Seoul, while just down the road the **royal tombs** in **Samneung Park** are the grassy resting place of a few dynastic kings and queens. Moving into the modern day there's **Coex**, a large underground shopping mall, and **Lotte World**, a colossal theme park. The area also sheds light on Seoul's artistic scene, with several prominent galleries and performance halls, most notably those in and around the Seoul Arts Center; there are even a few in **Olympic Park**, an area that provides a glimpse into the Seoul of the 1980s. However, southern Seoul is perhaps best viewed as a window into **modern Korean society** – the teeming streets surrounding Gangnam station are simply pulsating with neon and noise, with innumerable tower blocks rising into the heavens. In addition, the restaurants, cafés and **boutique shops** of the classy **Apgujeong** district are without doubt the priciest and most exclusive in the land.

Apgujeong
압구정

Seoulites refer to **Apgujeong** as "Korea's Beverly Hills", and the comparison is not far off the mark – if Louis Vuitton bags are your thing, look no further. Boutique clothing stores (see p.135), chic restaurants and European-style outdoor cafés line streets frequented by a disproportionate number of Seoul's young and beautiful, but bear in mind that their good looks may not be entirely natural – this is also Korea's plastic surgery capital, and clinics are ubiquitous. Though there are no real sights as such, Apgujeong is one of the most interesting places in Seoul to sit down with a latte and people-watch.

The best restaurants (see p.118) huddle in a relaxed, leafy area outside the main entrance to **Dosan Park** (도산공원), a pleasant quadrant of grass and trees. Further north, beyond the clothes shops and plastic surgeons, the area's main road **Apgujeongno** is home to Korea's most exclusive clothes shops and department stores, including the huge, eye-catching **Galleria department store** (see p.136), whose west wing was remodelled in 2004 by Dutch design team UN Studios. Its exterior is cloaked with thousands of perspex discs, which are illuminated at night in a kaleidoscope of vivid colour.

Garosugil
가로수길 • Sinsa station (line 3)

West of Dosan Park, **Garosugil** is a trendy street studded with hip cafés and sharp designer boutiques – though rocketing rents have made it hard for aspiring new designers to open up here, and the chain stores are starting to move in. Its name

---

SEOUL'S GOLDEN GINKGO TREES

Growing up to 50m in height, the **ginkgo biloba** is one of East Asia's most characteristic species of tree. Since they can live for more than 2000 years, they have long been heralded as a symbol of longevity, and are often found on mountainsides and outside temples throughout Korea. They are known locally as *eunhaeng-namu* (은행나무) – *eunhaeng* means "bank", as *ginko* does in Japanese, on account of the magical golden hue the tree's leaves assume in autumn. Unfortunately, at this time the ginkgo also release their juicy seeds, which when trampled underfoot release a smell somewhat akin to dog excrement. However, if rescued pre-squish and roasted, they're quite delicious – keep an eye out for old ladies selling paper cupfuls of what look like green beads.

---

literally means "tree-lined street", bestowed on account of the roadside lines of gorgeous **ginkgo trees** (see box above), whose spectacular golden fall foliage makes Garosugil a superb place to stroll in Seoul's all-too-short autumn.

Gangnam

강남

Literally meaning "South of the River", **Gangnam** is the name for a huge swathe of land south of the Hangang, and an all-encompassing term for several distinct city districts. However, it's most commonly used to describe the area around **Gangnam subway station**, a relatively flat district almost entirely built since the 1970s. This zone is easy to get around, its grid of perfectly straight streets served by a number of bus and subway lines. While almost entirely devoid of traditional tourist sights, this is an absorbing place to walk around; these streets – especially to the northeast of the station – are hugely popular with young Koreans, and crammed full of cafés and cheap restaurants. Recent years have seen the local city district adding huge LED displays, full-building octaves of neon and all sorts of other technological gizmos to the roadsides, which, in addition to the massed ranks of high-rises, bring something of a

8

GANGNAM STYLE

In June 2012, YouTube's most-viewed-clip chart was dominated by American superstar singers, but the following month they'd all been beaten from the unlikeliest of places – an unassuming-looking Korean guy, and his light-hearted, Korean-language diatribe about an area of southern Seoul. Psy's **Gangnam Style** came from nowhere and went on to conquer the world, though few outside Korea knew on earth he was rapping about – the popularity of the song, of course, stemmed from its zany video and signature horse-style dance, one hurriedly mastered across the world by newspaper columnists, TV presenters, singers and even politicians. It remains the most-watched clip in YouTube history, with over **2.3 billion views** at the time of writing – double that of the video in second place.

For Koreans themselves, *Gangnam Style* was both something old and something new. Psy had already been a big name here since his 2002 hit *Champion*, which caused a bit of a stir with expats thanks to what sounded like repeated mentions of the N-word (the actual lyrics meant something completely different, though the accident may have been intentional). Unlike most K-pop success stories, Psy writes his own songs, choreographs his own videos, and dares to inject a little satire into his lyrics. With *Gangnam Style*, however, he went further, launching a musical assault on the hollowness of Korea's richest neighbourhood, and the phoniness of those who aspired to live there – watch the video carefully and you'll see apparent opulence continually dissolving away to something more modest (the beach becomes a sand-pit at a playground, the nightclub becomes a tour-bus, and so on). To the wider world, *Gangnam Style* may have been little more than a silly dance; for Koreans it was a bit of an eye-opener, though somewhat ironically it has now become a major source of national pride.

Blade Runner feel to the area. While sights are rather thin on the ground here, it's an important cultural hub, being home to the superb **Seoul Arts Centre** (see p.130) and the **National Center for Korean Traditional Performing Arts**.

Samsung d'light

삼성 딜라이트 • Seochodaero 74-gil 11 • Daily 10am–7pm • Free • Gangnam subway (line 2)

On the lower levels of Samsung Electronics' towering Gangnam headquarters, **Samsung d'light** is the company's sharply designed and highly appealing showroom where you can get a sneak preview of the gadgets that will be racing around the world in the near future. Samsung is the largest of Korea's *jaebeol* (see box below), and it's better known abroad than many of its Korean rivals, largely thanks to its success in the electronic goods market. Exhibitions at its showroom change as often as the products themselves, but there's a clear emphasis on nature – water trickles down some walls, while others are festooned with (fake) greenery, and there's a notable use of natural and ambient lighting, rather than the neon soaking the streets of Gangnam outside.

Samneung Park

삼릉공원 • Tues–Sun daily 6am–4.30pm • W1000 • Seolleung subway (line 2)

During the Three Kingdoms period and beyond, deceased Korean royalty were buried in highly distinctive grass mounds. While these are more numerous elsewhere in Korea, Seoul has a few of its own, with the easiest to visit being in **Samneung Park**, whose name means "Three Mounds". One was for **King Seongjong** (r.1469–94), an esteemed leader who (unusually) invited political opponents to have a say in national government. Two of his sons went on to rule; **Yeonsangun** (r.1494–1506) undid much of his father's hard work in a system of revenge-driven purges, and was overthrown to leave his half-brother **Jungjong** (r.1506–44) in control. Jungjong's mound can also be found in the park, as can one created to house one of Seongjong's wives.

8

JAEBEOL SOCIETY

Korean society is dominated by a string of colossal conglomerates known as the **jaebeol** (재벌), which permeate most spheres of local society. Many of these are also household names around the world, although poor international marketing means that few people realize that these companies hail from Korea. The largest and most famous is **Samsung**, which helped to revolutionize the global mobile phone market, while **Hyundai** cars are sold in more than one hundred countries, with **Daewoo** and **Kia** (the latter a Hyundai subsidiary) not far behind, and homes around the world feature electronic goods from **LG**. Consumer goods are just the tip of the iceberg, however – in the 1970s, for example, colossal **shipyards** built by Samsung and Daewoo sounded the death knell for such business in the UK, at that time the world leader. Korea now has 29 percent of the global shipping industry, second only to China; the whole of the EU, by comparison, accounts for around one percent.

In Korea itself, these businesses have their fingers in almost everything: construction, insurance, telecommunications, heavy industries and much more besides. Indeed, many locals feel that the president of Samsung, the largest of the *jaebeol*, is actually more powerful than the head of the country. Many of these companies have even meddled directly in politics – prominent company heads have, on occasion, successfully run for government roles, while in the late 1990s Hyundai was at the forefront of the **Sunshine Policy** (see p.171), a North–South thaw that saw business transferred across the North Korean border and the purchase of a whole chunk of land in the Geumgang mountains for South Korean tourist use. However, this led to allegations of money laundering and the suicide of the company founder's son: subsequent government investigations into widespread **corruption** led to yet more high-level suicides at other *jaebeol*, and the enforced break-up of Hyundai, Samsung and other large conglomerates into more easily manageable, policeable and taxable chunks. Smaller in size they may be, but the *jaebeol* remain a hugely influential element of modern Korean culture.

For all the history, it's the prettiness of the park itself that appeals to many visitors, a green refuge from grey Seoul crisscrossed by gorgeous tree-shaded **pathways**. The area is popular with workers from nearby offices as a lunch spot, many of whom come here to munch a sandwich or go for a jog. Its early opening times mean that you can visit at daybreak, an atmospheric time when dew sits on the grass and the morning mist occludes nearby buildings.

The Coex complex

코엑스 • Yeongdongdaero 513 • **Mall** Tues–Sun Daily 9.30am–10pm • ⓦ www.coexmall.com • **Aquarium** Daily 10am–8pm • W22,000 • ⓦ coexaqua.com. Samseong subway (line 2)

The **Coex complex** houses a huge assortment of shops, restaurants, cafés, offices and a couple of five-star hotels. One of the few sizeable covered spaces in the whole city, its large underground **mall** attracts Seoulites in their droves when the weather is inclement. The complex is also home to the **Coex Aquarium** (코엑스 아쿠아리엄), which has been designed with rare flair – it must be the only aquarium in the world to use toilets as goldfish tanks, though mercifully there are normal facilities for public use. Sharks, manta rays and colourful shoals of smaller fish are on display.

Bongeunsa

봉은사 • Bongeunsaro 531 • 24hr • Free • Samseong subway (line 2)

Despite its incongruous location amid a plethora of skyscrapers, **Bongeunsa** is the most appealing major Buddhist temple in Seoul. Like Jogyesa, its uglier sibling to the north of the river (see p.50), it's affiliated to the **Jogye sect**, the largest Buddhist denomination in Korea. There has been a temple here since the late eighth century, but assorted fires and invasions mean that all of its buildings are of fairly recent vintage; still, it's worth peeking at its gorgeous main hall and clutch of small yet appealing outer buildings.

Jamsil

잠실

Jamsil is primarily a residential area of 1980s vintage, whose lofty tower blocks fan out in ever-increasing semicircles from the main **Olympic Stadium**. The Olympic sites, including a large park studded with other stadia, are the area's major tourist attraction, though for Koreans it's the **Lotte World** theme park that's the big draw.

Lotte World

롯데월드 • Daily 9.30am–11pm • **Lotte World Adventure** W46,000; W26,000 after 4pm; W17,000 after 7pm • **Lotte Water Park** W35,000; W30,000 after 2pm • ⓦ lotteworld.com • Jamsil subway (line 2 & 8)

A local version of Disneyland, **Lotte World** is one of Korea's most popular attractions – the complex receives more than five million visitors a year, and it's hard to find a Korean child, or even an adult, who hasn't been here at some point. While it may not be quite what some are looking for on their visit to "The Land of Morning Calm", Lotte World can be a lot of fun, particularly for those travelling with children. It comprises two theme parks: the indoor section is known as **Lotte World Adventure**, which is connected by monorail to the outdoor **Lotte Water Park**, located in the middle of a lake, and also home to a spa. Also within the complex are a bowling alley, an overpriced ice rink, and a large swimming pool.

Olympic Park

올림픽공원 • Daily 24hr • Free • Bikes W3000 per hour • Olympic Park Mongcheontoseong (line 8) or Olympic Park subway (line 5)

Built for the 1988 Summer Olympics (see box, p.100), the large **Olympic Park** remains a popular picnicking place for Seoul families, and hosts a regular roster of small-scale

THE 1988 SUMMER OLYMPICS

Seoul's hosting of the **Olympic Games** in 1988 was a tremendous success, bringing pride not just to the city, but to the whole nation. In fact, it did much to make Korea the country that it is today, and has even been credited with bringing democracy to the nation. President **Park Chung-hee** had been first to toy with the idea of bidding for the games in the 1970s, seemingly wishing to win international approval for his authoritarian running of the country; he was assassinated in 1979, but the bid went ahead. However, large-scale protests against the government in the years running up to the games brought a hitherto unprecedented level of international scrutiny, and direct elections took place in 1987.

The games themselves were no less interesting, and produced several moments that have become part of sporting folklore. This is where American diver **Greg Louganis** won gold despite bloodying the pool by walloping his head on the dive-board, and where steroid use saw Canadian sprinter **Ben Johnson** stripped of first place and his 100m world record. A lesser-known tale is that of Canadian sailor **Lawrence Lemieux**, who sacrificed a probable medal to race to the aid of two Singaporean competitors who had been thrown into the water in treacherous conditions.

municipal festivals, with something on most weekends. The park is very large, around 2km square, but everything is well signposted, with the main concentration of sights running along the south of the park, so it's best to stick to these paths. Bikes can be rented at the two main park entrances. The **Olympic Stadium** itself is not actually in the park, but lies a few subway stops to the west.

Near the eastern entrance to the park are a number of facilities that remain from the games, including a couple of gymnasiums and an indoor swimming pool. Few of the facilities are open for public use, though the velodrome does host occasional races (see p.131). There's a general air of decay about the place, but it's all part of the appeal; the order of play from the Olympics is still in place outside the ground, and through the peeling paint you can see the routes that Miroslav Macir and Steffi Graf took to their gold medals. On the way into the park, you'll pass by buildings and sculptures displaying the rather Stalinist themes that were in vogue in 1980s Seoul – some of this would look quite at home in Pyongyang, and those with interests in art and architecture may find the area quite absorbing.

Seoul Olympic Museum of Art

소마미술관 • Bangidong 88-2 • Tues– Sun 10am–6pm • W3000 • ⓦ somamuseum.org • Mongcheontoseong subway station (line 8)

Near the southwestern corner of the park, the **Seoul Olympic Museum of Art**, or SOMA, is a small art centre. Its indoor gallery hosts temporary exhibitions, most of them revolving around nature as a central concept. To either side of the gallery is an outdoor sculpture garden, which makes for particularly good strolling on a sunny day.

Olympic Museum

올림픽 박물관 • 10am–5pm; closed Mon • W3000 • Mongcheontoseong subway station (line 8)

The **Olympic Museum** will appeal to sports buffs with its collection of Olympic torches from various games, as well as an exhibit showing just how terrifying Olympic mascots have been through the years – two examples are Atlanta's "Izzy", a repulsive character of indeterminate species, and Barcelona's "Cobi", a cubist Catalan sheepdog. Outside the museum, flags from the 159 countries that competed in the games stand in a semicircle; though several countries have since merged, split or changed their flags, the authorities have decided to leave the originals as a symbol of what the world was like at the time – the Soviet and Yugoslav flags remain, but there's no South Africa, the country at that time having been banned from competing.

Gwacheon

과천

Although it's actually located in Gyeonggi province, the commuter-belt town of
Gwacheon sits just south of Seoul proper and has two main sights that are popular with
visiting Seoulites. **Seoul Grand Park** is a delightfully green area with a neat zoo, while
Seoul Land is one of Korea's most popular theme parks.

Seoul Grand Park

서울대공원 • Daegongwongwangjangno 102 • **Park** Daily 9.30am–9pm • Free • **Zoo** Daily 9am–6pm • W3000; dolphin shows W1500 •
ⓦ grandpark.seoul.go.kr • Seoul Grand Park subway (line 4)

Seoul Grand Park is one of the largest expanses of greenery in Seoul, and one of the best
places to take children for a fun day out. Its highlight is the **zoo**, where a pleasingly
diverse variety of animals from around the world live in conditions that are
considerably better than most such venues in Asia. It puts on special dolphin shows at
least four times a day, as well as other animal performances. In 2005, six elephants
escaped during one of these events, and were only caught hours later after trashing a
restaurant and wading through a nearby resident's garden; needless to say, security has
since been tightened, and a repeat performance is unlikely.

Seoul Land

서울랜드 • Daily 9am–6pm, later in peak season • Entry W20,000; day-pass for rides W36,000 • ⓦ eng.seoulland.co.kr • Seoul Grand
Park subway (line 4), then it's 15min walk, or take a tram train (W1000) from the Grand Park entrance

One of the main attractions in the Grand Park area is **Seoul Land**, a large amusement
park with an abundance of roller coasters and spinning rides – around forty in all, at
the last count. Along with Lotte World (see p.98), this is one of the most popular
places in the country for domestic tourists – with an average of almost three million
visitors a year, it's hard to find a Korean who hasn't been here at least once.

National Museum of Modern and Contemporary Art

국립미술관 • March–Oct Mon–Fri 10am–6pm, Sat & Sun 10am–9pm; Nov–Feb Tues–Fri 10am–5pm, Sat & Sun 10am–8pm •
Admission price varies by exhibition, usually W3000–10,000 • ⓦ mmca.go.kr • Seoul Grand Park subway (line 4); then it's a 15min walk,
or take a tram train (W1000)

Also within the confines of the Grand Park, the **National Museum of Modern and
Contemporary Art** houses an excellent collection of works by some of the biggest
movers and shakers in the Korean modern art scene. It's affiliated to the museum of the
same name in central Seoul (see p.60), though here the focus is on visual arts other
than painting and sculpture – with architecture, design and crafts all represented here.

8

RAKKOJAE HANOK

Accommodation

Seoul boasts a wide range of accommodation, with everything from five-star hotels to cheap-and-cheerful hostels. Those seeking high-quality accommodation have a great wealth of places to choose from, particularly around Myeongdong and City Hall north of the river, and Gangnam to the south, while budget travellers will find an increasing number of backpacker guesthouses. One interesting option popular with foreign travellers is to stay in one of the traditional wooden guesthouses north of Anguk station (see box, p.104). Motels too can form a cheap alternative to official tourist hotels, sometimes having rooms of comparable size and quality.

Almost all the big **hotel** chains have a presence in Seoul and, along with independent local establishments, offer all the usual creature comforts, though rooms can be rather small by international standards. Although **motels** are often used by local couples seeking private time, most have perfectly comfortable rooms with everything one could need – cable TV, hairdryers, shampoo, drinking water, 24-hour hot water in the bathrooms, free wi-fi, sachets of instant coffee, and, occasionally, complimentary condoms. Needless to say, Korean motels won't appeal to everybody, but any seaminess is kept behind closed doors, and even for lone women most are acceptable places to stay – indeed, those that can put up with the decor will find them Korea's best-value accommodation option. **Guesthouses** known as *yeogwan* (여관) are more or less the same as motels, but older and less stylish; some have been given new leases of life as boutique hotels, though these tend to be poor value.

The city also has a huge number of **hostels**, which tend to be clustered in the areas that backpackers find most interesting – Hongdae, for drinking; Insadong, for sightseeing; and Daehangno, for those on a budget. Most hostels offer a choice of dormitories or private rooms, some en-suite, others with shared facilities. Free wi-fi is now the norm, and a simple breakfast is usually included too. Lastly, Seoul has a range of **serviced residences**, which are particularly popular with business visitors: all offer daily rates, though there are considerable savings for those staying for a month or more.

ESSENTIALS

Booking sites The main international booking sites often give substantial discounts: try ⓦ trivago.com for hotels, and ⓦ hostelworld.com for hostels. Sadly, the properties advertised in Seoul on ⓦ airbnb.com tend to be overpriced, with many of the cheaper ones merely shoebox rooms in basic student accommodation. Seoul city operates a decent website listing some of the more modern, boutiquey guesthouses (ⓦ stay.visitseoul.net). Most motels don't take advance bookings – just turn up at the door and see what you get.

Prices In general, motels in Seoul cost W30,000–60,000 for a double room, while a dorm bed in one of the city's hostels will set you back around W20,000. For hotels, the sky's the limit, with most top places charging a W450,000-plus rack rate for their cheapest doubles, and cheaper places starting

---

KNOW YOUR NEIGHBOURHOOD: WHERE TO STAY IN SEOUL

Seoul is a big city with a tremendously diverse range of accommodation spread across its various neighbourhoods – to find the ideal place to stay it's wise to consider your budget, and what exactly you'd like to do in the city.

Gyeongbokgung and around There aren't too many places to stay in the area surrounding the palaces, bar a couple of boutiques in the Seochon neighbourhood, and the traditional wooden guesthouses of Bukchon Hanok Village (see box, p.44).

Insadong and around Despite Insadong's status as a tourist magnet, accommodation here is firmly in the cheap-to-midrange bracket – good value, and an excellent location for sightseeing.

Gwanghwamun and City Hall A number of five-star hotels can be found around Seoul Plaza and City Hall, near Deoksugung palace; it's also convenient for the shopping area.

Myeongdong and Dongdaemun Myeongdong is Seoul's busy shopping area, and has a wide range of accommodation, from flophouses to five-star luxury. Pickings are slimmer around Dongdaemun.

Northern Seoul The only place with any notable accommodation in Northern Seoul is Daehangno, which

has a number of decent hostels.

Western Seoul Hotels and motels in the two student areas of Hongdae and Sinchon are horrendously overpriced, though Hongdae does boast some new hostels and boutiques – it's now Seoul's main backpacker area. Though unlikely to be a venue of choice for the casual visitor, Yeouido has a few hotels that cater predominantly for its population of travelling businessmen.

Itaewon Given the area's popularity with foreigners, and its excellent nightlife scene, it's surprising that there aren't that many places to stay in Itaewon, other than a couple of higher-end venues, and some seedy-as-hell guesthouses which are best avoided.

Southern Seoul There are a great number of places to stay in Gangnam, including five-star hotels and a few motels, though you'll be far from most of Seoul's sights here. Apgujeong, Seoul's fashion capital, has surprisingly few places to stay, and those that exist tend to be overpriced.

9

HANOK GUESTHOUSES

In Bukchon Hanok Village, a tranquil city sector north of Anguk subway station, you'll find some of Seoul's most interesting places to stay – here you can spend the night in traditional Korean housing known as **hanok** (한옥). These are wooden buildings with tiled roofs, set around a dirt courtyard – a style that once blanketed the nation, but is rarely seen in today's high-rise Korea (see box, p.9). The generally bed-less rooms – you sleep Korean-style in a sandwich of blankets – are kept deliberately rustic and heated in the winter with the underfloor *ondol* system; most, however, provide modern indoor toilets and free wi-fi. There are also a few "proper" guesthouses dotted around (see "Gyeongbokgung and around" reviews, below), as well as some charming homestay options bookable through the district authorities (**⑩**homestay.jongno.go.kr); the latter cost in the region of W50,000 per room.

at around W90,000, though you can haggle these down at most times of year. When booking, bear in mind that the ten percent tax levied on hotel rooms is not always included in the quoted prices; in higher-end establishments, you're also likely to be hit with an additional ten percent service charge. The prices given for the accommodation listed below are for the cheapest double room in high season unless otherwise stated: breakfast is not included at motels and rarely at hotels. For dormitory accommodation, we have quoted the price per person.

Wi-fi Almost everywhere has wi-fi these days, bar the cheapest motels. However, some upper-end hotels levy a ridiculous daily charge of around W20,000 for wi-fi access – a problem that, perversely, gets worse the higher one climbs up the price ladder. Motels, on the other hand, often have free computer terminals for you to use.

GYEONGBOKGUNG AND AROUND

Aroma Motel 아로마 모텔 Chebudong 9 **☎**02 735 8641; Gyeongbokgung subway; map p.38. Motel that's seedy but cheap, and a good place to sleep if you've been over-drinking in the adjacent Seochon area. Some rooms can be full of flies in the summer. **W30,000**

Bukchon Guesthouse 북촌 게스트하우스 Gyedong 72 **☎**010 6711 6717, **⑩**bukchon72.com; Anguk subway; map p.38. Simple yet comfortable rooms set around a pleasingly authentic *hanok* courtyard, within easy walking distance of two palaces and Insadonggil. The friendly owners will even pick you up at nearby Anguk subway station, if you phone ahead. **W80,000**

★**Bukchon Maru** 북촌 마루 Gyedong 2-164 **☎**02 744 8571, **⑩**bukchonmaru.com; Anguk subway; map p.38. Presided over by a delightful, English-speaking local couple, this is a homely affair, with granny whipping up breakfast, and guests encouraged to get to know each other. A lovely choice. **W90,000**

Haemil Guesthouse 해밀 게스트하우스 Gwonnong-dong 152-2 **☎**070 8950 1546, **⑩**haemilguesthouse.com; Anguk subway; map p.38. A touch more expensive than most *hanok* guesthouses in the area, though just about worth the extra expense on account of a wonderful location facing Jongmyo shrine (see p.50), and rooms decorated with even more attention to detail. **W115,000**

★**Hide & Seek Guesthouse** 하이덴식 게스트하우스 Tonguidong 35-68 **☎**02 6925 5916, **⑩**hidenseek.co.kr; Anguk subway; map p.38. Set in a building dating from the Japanese occupation period, this is a truly charming place – the family who runs it makes every effort to please, especially with their yummy breakfasts. The rooms are cosy, and there are sunloungers on the wide patio area, which is grand for an evening drink, too. **W60,000**

★**Rakkojae** 락고재 Gahoedong 218 **☎**02 742 3410, **⑩**rkj.co.kr; Anguk subway; map p.38. The most authentic of Bukchon's *hanoks*, character-wise. Not only is it an 1870s original, but the owners serve traditional food for dinner – a little like a Japanese *ryokan*. Studded with maple and pine trees, the courtyard is divine, with precious few concessions to the modern day; it's best appreciated at night, when soft light pours through the paper doors. **W275,000**

★**Sopoong Guesthouse** 소풍 게스트하우스 Gyedong 140-17 **☎**010 8998 9159; Anguk subway; map p.38. A tiny place with only three rooms, this relatively recent addition to the Bukchon area's *hanok* list has proven a real winner with international guests. The owner will do everything possible to ensure that guests are happy – the breakfasts are particularly nice. **W85,000**

INSADONG AND AROUND

Banana Backpackers 바나나 백크패커스 Ikseondong 63 **☎**02 3672 1972; Anguk subway; map p.49. One of the oldest hostels in the city, this is an easy walk from Insadonggil; it has free internet, laundry and cooking facilities, and a common area that's great for making new mates. There's bread and jam to tuck into in the morning, as well as free tea and coffee throughout the day. Dorm beds **W23,000**

★**Doulos** 돌로스 호텔 Gwansudong 112 ☎02 2266 2244, ⓦdouloshotel.com; Jongno 3-ga subway; map p.49. Excellent value, comfy rooms, friendly staff and a convenient location... this mid-range hotel ticks all the boxes, even if it's a little tricky to find: take a few steps south of Jongno and you should be able to make out its sign. Usually gives discounts if booking online. $\overline{W120,000}$

★**Fraser Suites** 프레이저 스위츠 Insadong 4-gil 18 ☎02 6262 8888, ⓦseoul.frasershospitality.com; Jongno 3-ga subway; map p.49. The plushest serviced residence in Seoul, with rack rates starting at W7,000,000 per month for a single room. Also on site are a gym and swimming pool, as well as a rooftop driving range for golfers. The location, just off Insadonggil, is hard to beat. $\overline{W330,000}$

Hostel Korea 11th 호스텔 코리아 11th Waryong-dong 140 ☎070 4705 1900, ⓦcdg.hostelkorea.com; Anguk subway; map p.49. High-rise hostel just down the road from the palace of Changdeokgung (see p.46). It's a trendy place with a café-like lobby area, and is often full on account of its popularity with tourists from other Asian countries. Dorm beds $\overline{W26,000}$

Insa Hostel 인사 호스텔 Insadong 14-gil 48 ☎02 714 0644, ⓦinsahostel.co.kr; Anguk subway; map p.49. Hostel in the very thick of the Insadong action. Though it could occasionally benefit from more attentive service, the rooms are fine enough. Dorm beds $\overline{W26,000}$

Noble 노블 관광 호텔 Yulgongno 6-gil 13-3 ☎02 742 4025, ⓦnoblehotel.co.kr; Anguk subway; map p.49. One of the least seedy options in this convenient, highly atmospheric area – unlike many of its neighbours, rooms here are not rentable by the hour. Some are rather small, but they're quiet and kept at the right temperature. $\overline{W60,000}$

Seven Street 세븐스트리트 호텔 Cheonggye-cheonno 117 ☎02 2260 6300; Jongno 3-ga subway; map p.49. One of precious few hotels overlooking the Cheonggyecheon creek (see p.53), this has passed through several owners of late – at the time of writing, the *Sutton Hotel* signs were still in place. Only twin rooms face the stream, and these are the hotel's best in any case. Book online for discounts. $\overline{W185,000}$

Sewon Yeogwan 세원 여관 Jongno 3-ga 166-2 ☎02 2265 2127; Jongno 3-ga subway; map p.49. This old-fashioned *yeogwan* has some of the cheapest private rooms in the area – if you can find it, for it's secreted away down a slightly terrifying alley. $\overline{W25,000}$

Sheel 쉴 모텔 Gwansudong 137 ☎02 2278 9993; Jongno 3-ga subway; map p.49. Something of a "high-end" love motel, filling its rooms with all sorts of interesting quirks. Lace curtains billow from the ceilings, projectors fill whole walls with computer or televisual output, and some bathrooms are decked out in the style of a sauna; there's free coffee and popcorn at reception. You can usually cut the price in half if checking in after 9pm. $\overline{W100,000}$

Somerset Palace 서머셋 팰리스 Yulgongno 2-gil 7 ☎02 6730 8888, ⓦsomersetpalace.co.kr; Anguk subway; map p.49. Venue of choice for long-term expats, thanks to its impeccable service and wonderful on-site facilities. Some rooms have views of Gyeongbokgung (see p.37), though you'll be paying a premium; rack rates start at W4,600,000 per month. $\overline{W380,000}$

Sunbee 호텔 썬비 Gwanhundong 198-11 ☎02 730 3451, ⓦhotelsunbee.com; Anguk subway; map p.49. Tucked into a side-street near Insadonggil, this hotel has benefited from a recent renovation, and remains good value despite the doubling of prices. Professional staff will lead your way from the fancy lobby, which features a pleasant café; the rooms themselves can be quite large, and some have views of Inwangsan (see p.83). $\overline{W100,000}$

GWANGHWAMUN AND CITY HALL

The Plaza 더 플라자 Sogongno 119 ☎02 771 2200, ⓦhoteltheplaza.com; City Hall subway; map p.56. Directly facing City Hall and adjacent to Deoksugung, you could hardly wish for a more central location. In addition, a thorough overhaul in 2010 made its interior one of the most attractive in the city, with immaculate rooms and superb on-site restaurants – even the corridors exude a sleek beauty. Try to grab a room on one of the north-facing upper floors for some wonderfully Manhattanesque views. $\overline{W360,000}$

★**Westin Chosun** 웨스틴 조선 Sogongno 106 ☎02 771 0500, ⓦechosunhotel.com; City Hall subway; map p.56. Serious effort has been put into making this the most appealing hotel in central Seoul, with one of Korea's best swimming pools. An energetic group of knowledgeable staff preside over rooms that eschew the typical Korean concrete blockiness for splashes of lime, plush carpets and curved sofas – even the bathrooms are graced with modern art, and a free mobile phone will be yours for the duration of your stay. Prices often fall to W250,000 off-season. $\overline{W420,000}$

MYEONGDONG AND DONGDAEMUN

Ibis Ambassador 이비스 앰배서더 Namdaemunno 78 ☎02 3454 1101, ⓦibishotel.com; Euljiro 1-ga subway; map p.64. Mid-range hotel right in the centre of Myeongdong, with clean and presentable rooms. Staff make a concerted effort, and are particularly adept at dispensing advice to those fresh off the plane: handy, since the airport bus stops right outside. $\overline{W240,000}$

★**Metro** 메트로 호텔 Myeongdong 2-gil 14 ☎02 752 1112, ⓦmetrohotel.co.kr; Euljiro 1-ga subway; map p.64. A modern, squeaky-clean hotel away from the

---

SEOUL'S TOP TEN PLACES TO STAY

Best wooden guesthouse *Rakkojae* (see p.104)

Best rooftop sunbathing *Hide & Seek* (see p.104)

Best swimming pool *Westin Chosun* (see p.105)

Best for traditional Korean style *The Shilla* (see p.106)

Best love motel *Jelly* (see p.107)

Best for wild design *W Seoul* (see p.108)

Best views (and bathrooms) *Park Hyatt* (see p.107)

Best on a budget *Come Inn* (see p.106)

Best serviced residence *Fraser Suites* (see p.105)

Best morning coffee *Urbanwood* (see p.106)

---

bustling Myeongdong main roads, where the staff are friendly and breakfast is included. Rooms are fresh and have free wi-fi, though views are generally poor – ask to see a few. W140,000

PJ Hotel PJ호텔 Mareunnaero 71 **☎**02 2280 7070, **ⓦ**eng.hotelpj.co.kr; Euljiro 3-ga station; map p.64. This mid-range hotel is the only modern link in a bizarre chain of 1960s structures that stretches all the way from Chungmuro to Jongmyo (see box, p.66). Rooms here are larger than at most competing hotels, and though facilities are as modern as they come, the surrounding area provides a fascinating peek into 1960s Seoul. W260,000

Royal 로얄 호텔 Myeongdong 1-ga 6 **☎**02 756 1112, **ⓦ**seoulroyal.co.kr; Euljiro 3-ga subway; map p.64. Golden hues and comfy beds make the cosy rooms rather

appealing at this towering hotel, which rises near the cathedral at the centre of Myeongdong's sprawling shopping district. The grill and buffet bars on the 21st floor are great places to eat, and there are free shuttle buses to and from the airport. W220,000

★**The Shilla** 더 신라 Donghoro 249 **☎**02 2233 3131, **ⓦ**shilla.net; Dongguk University subway; map p.64. Tucked away in a quiet area on the eastern access road to Namsan, this hotel is characterized by the traditional style of its rooms and exterior. The lobby and restaurants are a luscious shade of brown, as if they've been dunked in tea, though the common areas can often be a little busy – this is one of Seoul's most popular conference venues. The rooms themselves are five-star quality, if a little overpriced, and feature genuine Joseon-era antiques. W480,000

NORTHERN SEOUL

Fully Guesthouse 풀리 게스트하우스 Myeongnuyn 3-ga 5 **☎**010 3266 4721; Hyehwa subway; map p.72. A bit of a trek from central Daehangno, but worth the extra effort – this is the most welcoming of the area's many hostels. The English-speaking owner encourages guests to bond, and often leads pub-crawls himself. In addition, it's one of the cheapest hostels in Seoul, with a further W2000 knocked off the price on weekdays. Dorm beds W17,000

Golden Pond 골든 폰드 Changgyeonggungno 240-15 **☎**02 741 5621, **ⓦ**goldenpond.co.kr; Hyehwa subway; map p.72. Highly popular with Western backpackers and those seeking work in Seoul, this is the cleanest and most secure guesthouse in the area. Set around a *hanok*-style building, it's small and very often full. Dorm beds W20,000

WESTERN SEOUL

Ann Guesthouse 안 게스트하우스 Yanghwaro 157 **☎**070 8279 0835, **ⓦ**annguesthouse.co.kr; Hongik University subway; map p.82. Terrific location, peering over Hongdae subway station. Despite being in the centre of Seoul's nightlife, it's a quiet and relaxed place, presided over by a friendly couple. Free laundry service. Dorm beds W20,000

★**Come Inn** 컴인 Seogyodong 358-91 **☎**070 8958 7279, **ⓦ**comeinnkorea.com; Hongik University subway; map p.82. A winner for its dorms and private rooms alike, this guesthouse draws a real mixed bag of travellers – most emerge feeling as though they've been staying at a local's home, such is the welcome afforded here. The place is spick and span, which seems a little odd when the country's biggest nightlife area lies just outside. Dorm beds W15,000, doubles W58,000

★**iGuesthouse** 아이 게스트하우스 Donggyodong 10-14 **☎**070 8779 6161, **ⓦ**seouliguesthouse.com; Hongik University subway; map p.82. While Apple Corp probably wouldn't be too happy about the name, guests usually come away more than satisfied with this hostel, which is the best of a glut in this residential part of Hongdae. Dorms are more spacious and better-appointed than most of the competition, and staff keep abreast of the area's goings-on. Dorm beds W20,000

Marriott Executive Apartments 메리어트 아파트 Yeouidaero 8 **☎**02 2090 8000, **ⓦ**marriott.com; Yeouido subway; map p.82. A good choice for those who have business to do in Yeouido, with immaculate rooms and a decent on-site restaurant. Rates go down for those staying longer than one month. W200,000

★**Urbanwood Guesthouse** 어번우드 게스트하우스

Seogyodong 333-30 ☎010 8320 0833, ⓦurbanwood
.co.kr; Hongik University subway; map p.82. Run by an
affable, English-speaking local who whips up a mean cup
of coffee in the morning, this is the most pleasant of the

Hongdae area's many new boutique-style operations. Its few
rooms are decorated along seasonal colour schemes; only the
triple, though, is en-suite. The rooftop is a grand place for
evening drinks. W̲8̲0̲,̲0̲0̲0̲

ITAEWON

★**D'Oro** 호텔 디오로 Itaewondong 124-3 ☎02 749
6525; Itaewon subway; map p.91. Highly recommended
mid-range establishment just uphill from Itaewon's main
drag, and rare value for money in a notoriously poor area
for accommodation. Free wi-fi and minibar, and standards
of service more akin to a hotel. W̲9̲0̲,̲0̲0̲0̲

Grand Hyatt 그랜드 하얏트 Sowollo 322 ☎02 797
1234, ⓦseoul.grand.hyatt.com; Noksapyeong subway;
map p.91. A favourite of visiting dignitaries, this is one of
Seoul's top hotels in more ways than one – perched on a
hill overlooking Itaewon, almost every room has a fantastic
view through floor-to-ceiling windows. There's a fitness
centre, an ice rink and squash courts, as well as swimming
pools, indoors and out. W̲3̲9̲0̲,̲0̲0̲0̲

Hamilton 해밀톤 호텔 Itaewondong 119-25 ☎02

794 0171, ⓦhamilton.co.kr; Itaewon subway; map
p.91. More of an Itaewon landmark than a decent place to
stay, but countless foreigners make this their Seoul home
in any case. The rooms are a wee bit dated, but staff are
professional, and guests can make use of an outdoor pool
in warmer months. W̲1̲4̲5̲,̲0̲0̲0̲

IP Boutique IP부티크 Hannamdong 737-32 ☎02
3702 8000, ⓦipboutiquehotel.com; Itaewon subway;
map p.91. Korea's first genuine stab at the boutique hotel
concept, though sadly a little flawed. The rooms have all
been individually decorated, with different colour schemes
for each floor, and are mercifully a lot better than the
nightmarish lobby, which looks something like a giant
handbag with a few swing-chairs and medieval statues.
W̲2̲6̲0̲,̲0̲0̲0̲

SOUTHERN SEOUL

Grand Parnas 그랜드 파르나스 Teheranno 521
☎02 555 5656, ⓦihg.com; Samseong subway; map
p.94. Designed with exceptional attention to detail, this
Intercontinental hotel belies its age with regular overhauls.
The rooms are fresh and tastefully decorated in pleasing
tones, with modern furniture. Some great restaurants can
be found on the lower floors, and guests have access to a
gym and indoor swimming pool. W̲4̲5̲0̲,̲0̲0̲0̲

★**Jelly** 젤리 호텔 Yeoksamdong 648-7 ☎02 553
4737, ⓦjellyhotel.co.kr; Yeoksam subway; map p.94.
A hip and extremely interesting love hotel that has
achieved cult status with young Seoulites, some of whom

come to couple up (a "rest" is half the price of a night's stay),
others to party with a group of friends. The hotel is possibly
home to the most idiosyncratic rooms in the city – some
contain pool tables, jacuzzis or karaoke systems, making
them popular with young groups wanting a night out.
W̲1̲0̲0̲,̲0̲0̲0̲

★**Park Hyatt** 파크 하얏트 Teheranno 606 ☎02 2016
1234, ⓦseoul.park.hyatt.com; Samseong subway;
map p.94. First things first: this is Seoul's best hotel.
Designed in its entirety by Japanese firm Super Potato, its
class will already be evident by the time you've entered the
lobby, which is actually on the top floor. Rooms employ an

SEOUL'S CHEAPEST SLEEPS

For the most budget-friendly accommodation in Seoul, you just try to find a cheap hostel, right?
Wrong. The city's cheapest sleeps are in spa-like venues known as **jjimjilbang** (찜질방), which are
also among the most uniquely Korean places to spend a night. Almost entirely devoid of the
seedy reputations that may dog similar facilities abroad, *jjimjilbang* are large, round-the-clock
establishments primarily used by families escaping their homes for the night, businessmen who've
worked or partied beyond their last trains, or teenage groups having a safe night out together.
They typically cost W8000 or so in Seoul, and consist of a shower and pool area, a sauna or steam
room, and a large playschool-style quiet room or two for communal napping; most also have
snack bars and internet terminals. Upon entry, guests are given a locker key for their shoes,
another for their clothes, and matching T-shirts and shorts to change into – outside clothes are
not allowed to be worn inside the complex, though it's OK to wear underwear beneath your robe.
All must be sacrificed on entry to the pools, which are segregated by gender. The common rooms
are uniformly clean but vary in style; some have TVs and hi-tech recliner chairs, others invite you to
roll out a mini-mattress, but all will have a floorful of snoring Koreans. You're never far from a
jjimjilbang, but the two most popular with foreigners are **Dragon Hill**, a huge facility just outside
Yongsan station (see p.141), and **Itaewon Land**, a homelier place in Itaewon (see map, p.91).

almost Zen-like use of space, and the hewed-granite bathrooms were voted "Asia's best place to be naked" by *Time* magazine. Staff are experts at making themselves available only when needed, and those on a repeat visit will find their preferred room temperature, TV channels and light level all ready and waiting. Bliss. W520,000

Popgreen 호텔 팝그린 Sinsadong 614-1 ☎02 5446 6237; Apgujeong subway; map p.94. Mid-range hotel located on trendy Apgujeongno, a mere stroll from dozens of brand-name showrooms. The rooms are a little on the small side, though, and bathroom goings-on are sometimes a little too visible through the frosted glass – better not share with someone you don't know intimately. W125,000

Richmond 호텔 리치몬드 Yeoksamdong 605-17 ☎02 562 2151, ⓦhotel-richmond.co.kr; Sinnonhyeon subway; map p.94. A fantastic lower-budget option in an area whose establishments usually pride themselves on valet parking and other five-star facilities. Rooms come with free internet access and large TVs, and the more expensive ones are at least as big as those in the nearby *Ritz*. W65,000

Ritz-Carlton 리츠 칼튼 Bongeunsaro 120 ☎02 3451 8000, ⓦritzcarltonseoul.com; Sinnonhyeon subway; map p.94. Service here is as professional as you'd expect from the chain, and no effort has been spared to make this one of Seoul's top hotels. The on-site bakery and restaurants are excellent (including a leafy outdoor area for warmer months), and though the rooms aren't terribly spacious, there are wonderful views from those that face north. W430,000

Sheraton Grande 쉐라톤 그란드 Walkerhillo 177 ☎02 455 5000, ⓦsheratonwalkerhill.co.kr; Gwangnaru subway; map pp.6–7. With scented, plush-carpeted corridors and muted-tone rooms, this immaculately designed establishment is one of the best hotels in the land – a pity about the inconvenient location. There are some wonderful restaurants within the complex, which also features the most expensive rooms in the country – up to a colossal W15,000,000 per night. W480,000

★**W Seoul** W서울 Walkerhillo 177 ☎02 465 2222, ⓦstarwoodhotels.com; Gwangnaru subway; map pp.6–7. The *W* is the most distinctive hotel in Korea. With artfully designed furniture in its rooms, neon gym rings in the elevators, sharp-suited staff and a loungey beat pulsing through the lobby, every centimetre of it is achingly trendy – not to everyone's tastes. Particularly popular with Korean honeymooners, the rooms range in style – many have their own whirlpool and views over the river – while there's also a gym, a juice bar and a great swimming pool within the complex. On-site restaurants are excellent, as is the *Woo Bar* (see p.126), where the city's nouveaux riches come to slurp pricey cocktails. W520,000

TRADITIONAL KOREAN MEAL WITH SIDE DISHES

Eating

Food is one of the highlights of a trip to Seoul – despite a recent increase in global popularity, much of Korea's wonderful cuisine may be unfamiliar to first-time visitors, and those brave enough to dive in headlong are in for a treat. Dining is a more communal experience than you may be used to, and single travellers may quickly discover that Korean meals are usually for sharing; it's possible to take solace in one of the many cheap fast-food chains, which are also perfect for those on a budget. Whether you're eating at a snack shack or high-class restaurant, almost all Korean meals come with free water and side dishes known as banchan (반찬). *Kimchi* and pickled radish are all you'll get at the lower end of the scale, while at more salubrious venues there may be over a dozen plates, largely centred on roots and vegetables.

Restaurants

Seoul's excellent choice of **restaurants** is growing more cosmopolitan each year. They run the gamut from super-polished establishments in five-star hotels to local eateries where stomachs can be filled for just a few thousand won; even in the cheapest places, you may be surprised by the quality of the food. Many parts of the city have their own particular culinary flavour. Most popular with tourists are the streets around **Insadonggil**, where restaurants serve traditional Korean food in a suitably fitting atmosphere. At the other end of the scale is **Itaewon**, where local restaurants are outnumbered by those serving Indian, Japanese, Thai or Italian food, among others. Student areas such as **Hongdae**, **Sinchon** and **Daehangno** are filled with cheap restaurants, and the establishments of trendy **Apgujeong** cater to the fashionistas.

ESSENTIALS

Menus English-language menus are quite common, though the romanization is woefully inconsistent. For example, *gimchi jjigae* can be rendered as *kimchi zzigae* and *gimchee chigea*, and other versions besides. The official system of transliteration has been used in this guide (see box, p.182); one exception is *kimchi*, now in international usage but properly romanized as *gimchi*.

Opening times Seoul eateries are likely to be open whenever you'd want them to be – they start early and finish late, few of them take a day off, and many are even 24-hour operations. In fact, New Year and Chuseok (see box, p.34) are often the only times when you may have to turn more than a few street corners for a meal.

Reservations and tipping These are unheard of at all but the classiest places, which tend to tack a ten percent service charge onto the bill.

GYEONGBOKGUNG AND AROUND

★**Blacksmith Pizza** 대장장이 화덕 피자집 Gahoedong 62-1 ☎02 765 4298; Anguk subway; map p.38. Regularly deemed the "best pizzas in Seoul" by expats, this restaurant is run by genuine blacksmiths, who crafted the metalwork you'll see around the place; their pizzas (W16,000 and up) are just as lovingly prepared, and the place is usually rammed to the gills. Daily noon–10pm.

Cheonjin Poja 천진포자 Yulgongno 1-gil ☎02 3210 1122; Anguk subway; map p.38. Almost permanently packed, this small, steamy restaurant is so popular that you may have to wait outside while the Chinese chef doles out portion after portion of his famed Tianjin dumplings (W6000) to hungry diners. Daily 10am–10pm.

Solmoe Maeul 솔뫼마을 Samcheongdong 62-17 ☎02 720 0995; Anguk subway; map p.38. A neat place to eat if you're strolling Samcheongdonggil – traditional *ssambap* meals, consisting of side dishes and with leaves to wrap them in, go from W11,000. Try to nab one of the window tables if you don't fancy sitting Korean-style on the floor. Daily 10am–10pm.

★**Tongin Market** 통인 시장 Tongindong 6; Gyeongbokgung subway; map p.38. Hugely popular with local youngsters, this is perhaps the most user-friendly of Seoul's many markets. They've an intriguing payment system in place: first you pay W5000 for a batch of ten tokens shaped like ancient Korean coins, and then hand these over in exchange for food at the market's many stalls. Spicy rice-cake is the favourite with locals, though foreigners may prefer the slightly more nuanced taste of tempura-like *twigim*. Mon–Fri 9am–6pm, Sat 9am–1pm.

★**Tosokchon** 토속촌 Chebudong 85-1 85 ☎02 737 7444; Gyeongbokgung subway; map p.38. The grandest and most famous place in town for *samgyetang* (삼계탕), a delicious soup comprising chicken stuffed with ginseng, jujube and other healthy ingredients (W15,000). Fame and size aside, the food really does taste fantastic – be prepared to queue. Daily 11.30am–11.30pm.

INSADONG AND AROUND

★**Abiko** 아비코 Gwancheoldong 13-12 ☎02 730 3236; Jongno 3-ga subway; map p.49. Perhaps the spiciest food in Seoul, and it's not even Korean – *donkkaseu* (돈까스) from Japan, is a breaded pork cutlet, often served with curry, on rice. There are five levels of spice here – see if you can handle the hottest one. Various toppings and additions available; it'll work out at around W11,000 per head, all in. Daily 11am–9.30pm.

Ahndamiro 안다미로 Gwanhundong 15-2 ☎02 730 5777; Anguk subway; map p.49. There's something rather romantic about this Italian restaurant, tucked into an Insadong side-alley. It's a great date spot, and if you're worried about paying for two then rock up before 3pm for the W10,000 pasta or pizza lunch specials – a bargain. Daily 10.30am–midnight.

Bärlin 바르린 Susongdong 85 ☎02 722 5622, ⓦ baerlin.co.kr; Anguk subway; map p.49. Those hankering for a bit of bratwurst or sauerkraut should hunt down this upmarket German restaurant. Schnitzels can be made in three different styles (all around W27,000), the

KOREAN FOOD

Korean food can be a little bit bewildering for the first-time visitor, but if you're going to enjoy the country to the full, you need to let go of any inhibitions and get stuck into its fine cuisine. Note that *kimchi*, the most renowned Korean dish, is actually a side dish – you'll get it for free with most of the meals listed here.

BARBECUED MEAT

A favourite with foreigners are **barbecue houses** known as *gogitjip* (고깃집), where you barbecue pork, beef or chicken at your own table. Emanating from charcoal briquettes or gas burners, the open flames would contravene safety regulations in most Western nations, but the sight, sound and smell of the juices fizzing away is one of Korea's richest experiences. Most opt for marinated rib-meat known as *galbi*, with a choice of beef (*so-galbi*; 소갈비), pork (*dwaeji-galbi*; 돼지갈비), or fattier pork belly roll (*samgyeopsal*; 삼겹살). Chicken *galbi* (*dak-galbi*; 닭갈비) is only available at dedicated restaurants, and prepared slightly differently in a large pan.

RICE DISHES

Rice dishes include *bibimbap* (비빔밥), rice topped with a mix of vegetables; bubbling broths known as *jjigae* (찌개); and either broiled beef (*bulgogi*; 불고기), spicy squid (*ojingeo*; 오징어) or curry (*kare*; 카레) served on rice (*deop-bap*; 덮밥). Also of note are seaweed-wrapped rice rolls known as *gimbap* (김밥), which come with a wide variety of fillings and can be made to take away. Broths known as *jjigae* (찌개) are also served with rice, and prefixed by tofu (*sundubu*; 순두부), *kimchi* (김치) or soybean paste (*doenjang*; 된장) to indicate their main component.

NOODLES AND DUMPLINGS

Noodle dishes tend to revolve around simple from-the-packet creations called *ramyeon* (라면), though some add cheese or rice-cake. Buckwheat noodles, known as *naengmyeon* and like a chewier version of Japanese soba, are served cold in a spicy sauce (*bibim-naengmyeon*; 비빔냉면) or in an icy, spicy soup (*mul-naengmyeon*; 물냉면). **Dumplings** known as *mandu* (만두) are popular with foreigners, either fried (*gun-mandu*; 군만두) or boiled with *kimchi* (김치) or processed meat (*gogi*; 고기) fillings.

VEGGIE FOOD

Vegetarians often have a hard time in Seoul: very few Koreans make this particular lifestyle choice, and the few meals that do not contain meat are unlikely to be prepared in a meat-free environment. In Insadong, a couple of restaurants serve **Buddhist temple food**, and a few others specialize in **dynastic cuisine** (*hanjeongsik*; 한정식); a couple of places have taken the traditional concept further, and lay on **royal sets** approximating those once eaten by Joseon-era kings and queens; meat dishes will be included, but most of the meal will be vegetarian. *Bibimbap* and *gimbap* (see above) can also usually be made without meat.

STREET FOOD AND MARKET FOOD

Those who favour something more rustic can go for some of Seoul's wide variety of tasty **street food**. Most prevalent are stalls serving *deokbokki* (떡볶이), which consists of rice-cake pieces in a thick, spicy sauce. Rice-cake tends to be a bit bland and textureless for foreign tastes, so many choose to have it made with noodles instead (*rabokki*; 라볶이). Battered, refried comestibles known as *twigim* (튀김) can be thrown into the same delicious sauce: sweet potato, dumplings and squid are among the items on offer. Wintertime sees similar booths doling out *hoddeok* (호떡), delicious sweet pancakes filled with cinnamon and melted brown sugar. Perhaps best of all, however, is the **market food**, available at places such as Namdaemun and Dongdaemun, and often eaten at tent-like shacks known as *pojangmacha* (포장마차) – with plastic chairs to sit on, tables littered with *soju* bottles, and a cackling *ajumma* serving you food, they're hugely atmospheric.

10

---

raw beef tartare on rye is delicious (W25,000) and there's herring on the menu – extremely rare in Korea. Daily 11.30am–11.30pm.

★**Balwoo** 발우 Ujeonggungno 56 ☎02 2031 2081,

ⓦbaru.or.kr; Anguk subway; map p.49. Overlooking Jogyesa temple (see p.50), this is one of the best places to eat in Seoul, particularly for vegetarians. The huge set meals are consummately prepared approximations of Buddhist temple

10

food, and the balance of colour, texture, shape and taste is beyond reproach. Mung-bean pancakes, acorn jelly, sweet pumpkin tofu and sticky rice with ginkgo nuts are among the dozens of items that may appear on your table. Sets go from W27,500; note that cheaper versions of the same are sold on a lower floor. Reservations recommended. Daily: lunch 11.40am–1.20pm & 1.30–3pm, dinner 6–9pm.

Bukchon Sonmandu 북촌 손만두 Insadong 3-gil 6 ☎02 735 1238; Jonggak subway; map p.49. Cheap and tasty, this dumpling restaurant always has several different batches on the go, with portions selectable from a picture menu for W3000–4500. Good noodles, too. Daily 11.30am–11.30pm.

Doodaemunjip 두대문집 Gwanhundong 64 ☎02 737 0538; Anguk subway; map p.49. Tucked into the Insadong alleys, this is perhaps the most attractive of the area's many traditional restaurants, with chandeliers lending elegance to the scene. The lunch sets are super-cheap (W6000–8000), and there's plenty of Korean booze to enjoy of an evening. Daily 10.30am–10pm.

Gogung 고궁 Gwanhundong 38 ☎02 736 3211; Anguk subway; map p.49. On the basement floor of the Ssamziegil complex, the decor here is accordingly quirky, with walls festooned with threads and tie-dye. The food is traditional Korean – best is the *Jeonju bibimbap* (W11,000), a tasty southwestern take on the Korean staple. Daily 10.30am–8.30pm.

★**Gwangjujip** 광주집 Donguidong 43 ☎02 764 3574; Jongno 3-ga subway; map p.49. You can get barbecued meat all across the city, but the little three-way junction just north of Jongno 3-ga subway exit 6 is perhaps the most atmospheric in town – dozens and dozens of diners munch away outside every single night, eating from what look like overturned oil drums. This little venue usually has the best meat – W11,000 for a 200g portion of succulent beef. Daily 3pm–midnight.

Jeonjujip 잔주집 Gwancheoldong 40 ☎02 2278 3311; Jongno 3-ga subway; map p.49. Want something indisputably local? Wend your way down the atmospherically steamy alley south of Jongno to find this rowdy little place, the best of a clutch selling *gul-bossam* (sliced pork belly with oysters; 굴보쌈), plus a bunch of side dishes; the pork is steamed outside in large vats infused with medicinal herbs, and the results are fantastic.

A W20,000 set will feed two. Daily 11am–11pm.

★**Meokgeorichon** 먹거리촌 Insadong, no phone; Jonggak subway; map p.49. Not a restaurant, but a whole clutch of ramshackle stands operating illegally (look at the floor: this is technically a car park) in what looks like an aircraft hangar. Tremendously atmospheric, this is one of Seoul's most enjoyable places to eat and drink – some menus are now in English, and you'll pay W10,000–15,000 per head to fill up. Daily 6pm–midnight.

Min's Club 민스클럽 Gyeongundong 66-7 ☎02 733 2966; Anguk subway; map p.49. This restaurant is a little piece of history: named after Queen Min (see box, p.40), it was built in the 1930s to house one of her descendants. While the place may look traditionally Korean, this was actually one of the country's earliest "modern" structures, and the first to have a flushing indoor toilet. The menu is largely French, though Korean dishes such as barbecued beef and pumpkin congee also make an appearance; figure on around W70,000 per main. In addition, the wine list is one of the best in Seoul. Daily noon–11pm.

Nwijo 뉘조 Gyeongundong 84-13 ☎02 730 9301; Anguk subway; map p.49. Charmingly low-key restaurant where chefs create rounds of lovingly prepared traditional cuisine. Come before 4pm and you can take advantage of the great-value lunch meals (W18,000); dinner sets are W27,500 and up. Daily 10.30am–10pm.

OKitchen 오킷친 Jongno 1-gil 50 ☎02 722 6420; Gwanghwamun subway; map p.49. All the veggies and most of the meat used in this basement restaurant come from the Okinawan chef's own patch of farmland, located near the North Korean border. It serves a mix of European, Japanese and Korean food, and dishes change both with the season and the whim of the chef. Three-course lunch sets are a bargain at W27,000, while mains cost around the same for dinner. Daily noon–3pm & 5–9pm.

★**Potala** 포탈라 Gwancheoldong 35-2 ☎02 318 0094; Jongno 3-ga subway; map p.49. Run by a Nepali–Korean couple and centred on a functional Tibetan prayer wheel, this charmingly decorated basement restaurant serves Himalayan specialities (W15,000 for most curries, W9000 for Tibetan momo dumplings). Highly recommended is the *samosa chat* – three large samosas served with chopped green onion, chickpeas, curry sauce and sour cream (W11,000). Daily 10am–10pm.

GWANGHWAMUN AND CITY HALL

Gildeulyeo Jigi 길들여지기 Jeongdong 8-11 ☎02 319 7083; City Hall subway; map p.56. The name is a quote from the Korean translation of *The Little Prince*, and the decoration here is accordingly esoteric. Diners often call in here on their way out of Chongdong Theatre (see p.129) underneath, to feast on spaghetti or grilled meat. Alternatively, the salmon with herb pepper sauce is particularly recommended. Mains from W20,000. Daily

11am–10pm.

The Place 더 플레이스 Sinmunanno 103 ☎02 722 1300; Gwanghwamun subway; map p.56. Swanky Western-oriented place popular with staff from the local banks and embassies. Pasta meals go from W16,000, while waffles and cakes are available for dessert, and there are plenty of styles of coffee to choose from. Daily 8.30am–10pm.

10

KOREAN FAST-FOOD CHAINS

Seoulites live their lives at such a pace that many find it impossible to spare time for a leisurely meal, so it's no surprise that the city's streets are packed with fast-food outlets. The food may be fast, but the local offerings are far healthier than their Western equivalents – you could eat them every day and never get fat. However, few of these cheap places are used to dealing with foreigners, so don't expect English-language menus or service. Below is a selection of the chains you're most likely to come across as you explore the city – there'll be one of each within walking distance, wherever you are.

Gimbap Cheonguk 김밥천국. In Seoul street-space terms, this ubiquitous orange-fronted franchise is rivalled only by internet bars and the more prominent convenience store chains. The concept is pretty miraculous – almost all basic Korean meals are served here for around W5000 per dish, and despite the variety on offer you'll usually be eating within minutes of sitting down. They also do *gimbap* from W1500, and these can be made to go – perfect if you're off on a hike. Other similar chains include *Gimbap Nara* and *Jongno Gimbap*; you'll never be more than a minute's walk from one.

Isaac Toast 이삭토스트. Toast, but not as you know it. The Korean variety is made on a huge hotplate – first your square bread will be fried and smeared with kiwi jam, then joined by perfect squares of spam and/or fried egg (or even a burger), and the whole lot injected with two sauces, one spicy and one brown. No, it's not healthy, but it makes a tasty breakfast; prices start at W2000.

Kim Ga Ne 김家네. A slightly more upmarket version of *Gimbap Cheonguk* (see above), serving more or less the same things with a few snazzy "fusion" additions. Most branches have their menu on the walls in pictorial form, handy if you don't speak Korean. Dishes W3000–7000.

Lotteria 롯데리아. Unlike the similar, omnipresent *McDonald's* outlets, at least this is a Korean burger chain, a fact made evident by the local take on the simple Big Mac: witness the delicious *bulgogi* burger (W4500), made with marinated beef (at least in theory), or the meatless *kimchi* one served between two slabs of rice, rather than a bun.

Paris Baguette 파리바게트 and **Tous Les Jours** 뚜레쥬르. A pair of near-identical bakery chains, whose offerings may satisfy those who need something devoid of spice or rice for breakfast; many branches are also able to whip up a passable coffee. Baked goods start at around W1500, but note that in Korea, even the savoury-looking ones are usually extremely sugary. You'll find branches all over the place; harder to spot is *Paris Croissant*, a slightly more upmarket version, one of which is inside Anguk station near Insadong-gil.

Yu Ga Ne 유가네. This chain serves tasty barbecued meat, cooked at your table by an apron-wearing attendant. Unlike most barbecue joints, there are dishes for those dining alone, such as the delectable *dak-galbi bokkeumbap*, which is something like a chicken kebab fried up with rice. W10,000 should get you a bellyful.

MYEONGDONG AND DONGDAEMUN

Bulgogi Brothers 불고기 브라더스 Myeongdong 1-ga 7-1 ☎02 319 3351; Myeongdong subway; map p.64. The barbecuing of raw meat at your table is one of the quintessential Korean experiences, but new arrivals can find it hard to jump straight in at the deep end. This elegant venue is a good place to learn the ropes, and the meat is always of exceptional quality. Around W30,000 per person, including side dishes and drinks. Daily 11am–10pm.

Din Tai Fung 딘타이펑 Myeongdong 1-ga 59-1 ☎02 3789 2778; Euljiro 1-ga subway; map p.64. The Seoul outlet of this Taiwanese chain may be milking a decades-old magazine review, but it still makes darn good dumplings. It's W6500 for a round of their famed *xiaolongbao*, or try the shimp and wonton noodles (W10,000). Daily 11am–10pm.

★**Gostiniy Dvor** 가스티니드보르 Daehoro 34-gil 22 ☎02 2275 7501; map p.64; Dongdaemun History & Culture Park subway. Still the best restaurant in Dongdaemun's curious little Russiatown. Although its

owners are Uzbek, the food is typically Russian, including meaty mains (W10,000), filling soups (W6000) and delicious salads (W5000). The total lack of any sort of Korean atmosphere (and Koreans) can come as quite a surprise if you've been in Seoul a while, and the Russian beer (W5000) goes down nicely. Daily noon–2am.

★**Gwangjang Market** 광장시장 Off Jongno; Jongno 5-ga subway; map p.64. If you haven't had a meal at Gwangjang (see p.69), you haven't really been to Seoul. It's a beguiling place with all manner of indoor and outdoor places to eat; best is a *bindaeddeok* (mung-bean pancake; 빈대떡) in the central crossroads, though at lunchtime you should track down the alley selling *yukhoe* (raw beef tartare; 육회). Daily noon–2am.

Korea House 한국의집 Toegyero 10 ☎02 2266 9101; ⓦ koreahouse.or.kr; Chungmuro subway; map p.64. Modelled on the court cuisine enjoyed by the kings of the Joseon dynasty, dinner sets here start at W68,000 (small lunch sets from W18,000), and are made up of at least

10

SEOUL'S TOP TEN PLACES TO EAT

Best pizza *Blacksmith Pizza* (see p.110)
Best noodles *Woo Rae Oak* (see p.114)
Best atmosphere *Meokgeorichon* (see p.112)
Best barbecued meat *Gwangjujip* (see p.112)
Best concept *Oyori* (see p.116)
Best dumplings *Jaha Sonmandoo* (see p.114)

Best veggie food *Balwoo* (see p.111)
Best bibimbap *Mongmyeok Sanbang* (see p.114)
Best soup *Tosokchon* (see p.110)
Best desserts *Second Best Place in Seoul* (see p.121)

thirteen separate components, usually including broiled eel, ginseng in honey, grilled sliced beef and a royal hotpot. For W50,000 extra you'll be able to enjoy a performance of traditional song and dance after dinner (see p.130). Reservations recommended. Daily: lunch noon–2pm, dinner 5.30–6.30pm & 7.30–8.30pm.

★**Mongmyeok Sanbang** 목멱산방 Namsan ☎02 318 4790; Myeongdong subway; map p.64. On the Namsan walking track, a short walk uphill from the lower cable-car terminus, this traditionally styled venue is one of the most enchanting places to eat in Seoul – and also a great place for tea (see p.121). They sell three types of *bibimbap*: normal (W8000), with *bulgogi* beef on top (W9000), or with raw beef (W11,000), and it's beautifully presented. Eat outside, under the maple trees. Daily 11.30am–9pm.

N Grill N그릴 Namsan ☎02 3455 9298, ⓦnseoul tower.net; map p.64. Expensive steakhouse perched atop the N Seoul Tower (see p.68). You won't get much change from W100,000 per person, but the steaks are top-class, and there are few better views of Seoul. Daily 11am–11pm.

Pierre Gagnaire à Seoul 피에르가지에르 Euljiro 30 ☎02 317 7181, ⓦpierregagnaire.co.kr; Euljiro 1-ga subway; map p.64. Molecular gastronomy hits Seoul:

the unique creations of Michelin-starred French megachef Pierre Gagnaire are tickling tastebuds atop the otherwise awful *Lotte Hotel*. The menu has a discernible Korean twist, with ingredients such as ginger, sesame leaves and "five-flavoured" *omija* berries letting off little flavour bombs in certain dishes. Lunch menu W85,000, dinner from W170,000; reservations essential. Daily noon–3pm & 5–11pm.

Taj 타지 Myeongdong 1-ga 1-3 ☎02 776 0677; Euljiro 1-ga subway; map p.64. One of the best and most attractive Indian restaurants in Seoul, just downhill from Myeongdong Cathedral (see p.65). Curries start at W17,000 and dinner sets are around double that, though from noon–3pm on weekdays there are bargain lunch deals for just W11,000. Daily noon–3pm & 6–10pm.

★**Woo Rae Oak** 우래옥 Jugyodong 118 ☎02 2265 0151; Euljiro 4-ga subway; map p.64. This meat-house and its elegant, hotel lobby-like atrium have been here since 1946 – just one year less than Korea itself. The customer base seems to have changed little in decades, and the sight of septuagenarians munching away in their Sunday best is rather charming. Most are here for the meat (W25,000 or so per head), though they also serve superb *naengmyeon*, cold buckwheat noodles similar to Japanese *soba* (W12,000). Daily 11am–10.30pm.

NORTHERN SEOUL

Bongchu Jjimdak 봉추찜닭 Myeongnyun 4-ga 80-1 ☎02 745 6981; Hyehwa subway; map p.72. *Jjimdak* is a southeast Korean dish in which chicken and veggies are marinated in a soy-like sauce, and served with glass noodles – the tantalizing aroma will likely hit you as soon as you open the restaurant door. W20,000 for a two-person portion. Daily 11.30am–11.30pm.

Ggochiwa Chingudeul 꼬치와 친구들 Myeongnyun 2-ga ☎02 747 3020; Hyehwa subway; map p.72. With a name roughly meaning "skewered friends", this little shack sells divine chicken sticks for W1700 – just one reason why it's popular with students from the local university. Tues–Sun noon–midnight.

★**Jaha Sonmandoo** 자하 손만두 Buamdong 245-2 ☎02 379 2648; Gyeongbokgung subway; map p.72. Dumplings known as *mandu* are a cheap Korean staple, but unlike the regular processed fare, the handmade versions

served here (from W8000) are delicious, filled with chunks of quality beef, radish, shiitake mushrooms and the like. The setting is just as pleasant, a minimalist space with mountain views. Daily noon–10pm.

Samcheonggak 삼청각 Seongbukdong 330-115 ☎02 765 3700; Anguk subway; map p.72. This mountainside venue was once a *gisaeng* house of some repute (see box, p.74), and used by luminaries such as president Park Chung-hee as a secluded place of pleasure. It has since been converted into a traditionally styled restaurant serving a take on Korean royal cuisine, and still hosts occasional shows of traditional song and dance. Set meals W50,000–150,000. Daily 10am–11pm.

Saemaeul Sikdang 새마을 식당 Myeongnyun 4-ga 90 ☎02 3672 7004; Hyehwa subway; map p.72. So what if it's a chain restaurant – this pleasingly noisy venue still doles out the best-value barbecue meat in the wider

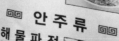

10

CULINARY CURIOSITIES

While even "regular" Korean food may be utterly alien to most visitors, there are a few edibles that deserve special attention; you'll find some of the following at restaurants, but street stalls and markets are the best places to go hunting.

Beonddegi (번데기) In colder months, stalls selling this local delicacy – silkworm larvae – set up on pavements and riverbanks across the whole country. The smell of these mites boiled up in a broth is so disgusting that it may well breach international law. The treat is also served as bar snacks in many *hofs*, bursting in the mouth to release a grimy juice – perfect drinking game material.

Dak-pal (닭발) So you've learnt the word for "chicken" in Korean (*dak*), spotted it on the menu and ordered a dish. Unfortunately, with this particular meal the suffix means "foot", and that's just what you get – dozens of sauced-up chicken feet on a plate, with not an ounce of meat in sight.

Gaegogi (개고기) This is dog meat, but let it be known that – contrary to the expectations of many a traveller – it rarely features on Korean menus: you're not going to get it on your plate unless you go to a dedicated restaurant. It's usually served in a soup: *yeongyangtang* and *bosintang* are its most common incarnations.

Sannakji (산낙지) Octopus tentacles served still-wriggling on the plate – every year, people die of suffocation when their still-wriggling prey makes a last bid for freedom, but as long as you don't throw down your tiny octoped whole (as many Korean guys do, in an effort to impress) you should be okay.

Sundae (순대) Don't let the romanization fool you – this is nothing whatsoever to do with ice cream. In Korea, it's actually a sausage made with intestinal lining, and stuffed with clear noodles. Head to the nearest market to try some.

Hyehwa area. Try the wafer-thin *yeoltan bulgogi* beef (열탄 불고기; W7000 per portion), washed down with some soybean broth (된장찌개; W5000). Daily 11.30am–midnight.

WESTERN SEOUL

Café Sukkara 카페 수까라 Seogyodong 327-9 ☎02 334 5919; Hongik University subway; map p.82. Not so much a café as a delightful light-food restaurant, in which vegan pumpkin pudding, chickpea salad, wholewheat spaghetti and the like are whipped up in the (very) open kitchen. Mains from W9000; wash them down with home-made ginger ale (W6000) or black shandy gaff (W7500). Tues–Sun 11am–3pm & 6–11pm.

Hannamdong Deungsin 한남동 등신 Eoulmadangno 145 ☎02 3144 0264; Hongik University subway; map p.82. At the time of writing, cheesy *deung-galbi* (barbecued pork ribs; 등갈비) was Korea's trendiest foodstuff, and a fad that's likely here to stay. This Hongdae joint is a great place to get a handle on it; W14,000 will buy you a portion, plus the gloves you'll need to eat it. Daily noon–2am.

Hwalhwasan Jogaegui 활화산 조개구이 Dong-gyodong 155-30 ☎02 323 8925; Hongik University subway; map p.82. A great place for a shellfish barbie (조개구이). A bellyful of clams, plus assorted side dishes, will set you back W27,000 for two, or W11,000 per person if part of a larger group. Daily 1pm–2am.

Jinnam Total Sashimi 진남 회집 Noryangjin Market ☎02 815 2732; Noryangjin subway; map p.82. The most reliable restaurant in fascinating Noryangjin market (see p.88), with a range of good seafood. Most dishes are for groups, but the *hoedeopbap* (sashimi on rice; 회덮밥) will please all for W10,000 a head. Daily 10am–10.30pm.

Jopok Deokbokki 조폭떡볶이 Seogyodong 407-1 ☎02 337 9933; Sangsu subway; map p.82. A dish of rice-cakes in spicy sauce, *deokbokki* (떡볶이) is available at street-stands all across the city, though this small sit-down restaurant is by far the most famous venue, since its staff are rumoured to be connected to the local Mafia (*jopok*). Fact or fib, the food's pretty good, especially if you have a few *twigim* (refried treats; 튀김) thrown on top – just point at what you'd like. Most dishes W3000. Daily 11am–6am.

Julio 후리오 Seogyodong 678 ☎02 3141 5324; Sangsu subway; map p.82. Stylish restaurant selling Mexican staples such as tacos and burritos from W8500 – try one of their Korean fusion specials, such as fried *kimchi carnitas* (W11,500). Daily noon–9.40pm.

★**Oyori** 오요리 Seogyodong 409-10 ☎02 332 5525; Sangsu subway; map p.82. One has to admire the thinking behind this restaurant, which not only gives employment to single mothers from other Asian countries, but uses the profit to send their children to kindergarten. The various nationalities working here take it in turns to enrich the menu, which contains Malaysian stir-fries,

Japanese noodles, Burmese curry and Russian desserts (around W15,000 for mains). Benevolence aside, the food is excellent, and the setting surprisingly stylish thanks to connections with a local art society. Daily 11.30am–11pm.

Park Yongseok Sushi 박용석 수시 Seogyodong 333-1, ☎02 3144 0131; Hongik University subway; map p.82. Popular little sushi restaurant, whose lunch sets (W10,000) are something of a bargain in this ever-more-pricey area. The fish slices are surprisingly large, and the rice components small – the opposite of most Korean *sushiya*. Daily noon–10pm.

Samgeori Pocha 삼거리포차 Seogyodong; Sangsu subway; map p.82. Nights out in Hongdae usually end late, meaning that this rustic raw fish restaurant can be heaving with drunken students at 6am: it's an integral part of the nightlife scene, and one of the most atmospheric places to be of a weekend. Having a bit of *soju* for Dutch courage makes it easier to handle the house speciality, *sannakji* (W15,000, feeds two) – chopped-up baby octopus that, while not exactly alive, is so fresh that it's still writhing on your plate when served. Daily 6pm–late.

ITAEWON

Copacabana 코파카바나 Itaewondong 119-9 ☎02 796 1660; Itaewon subway; map p.91. Anyone who's been to a Brazilian *churrascaria* will know exactly what to expect here – W29,000 buys as much grilled meat and salad as you can eat. Daily 11.30am–10pm.

Crow's Nest 크로즈 네스트 Itaewondong 112-2 ☎02 749 7888; Itaewon subway; map p.91. Now some Seoul pizzas are big, but the ones at this pizza pub are big big – their 20-inchers (W33,000) could feed you and your extended family. A fun group spot. Daily 11.30am–10pm.

Don Charly 돈 찰리 Itaewondong 650 ☎070 4219 4475; Noksapyeong subway; map p.91. Most Itaewon expats have heard of *Vatos Tacos*, the incredibly popular faux-Mex joint overlooking the main drag. For more authentic tacos, however, without having to queue for the pleasure of sitting down, try this relatively out-of-the-way place, beloved of Seoul's Hispanic community for its good, cheap fare; you'll fill up for W15,000. Tues–Sun noon–10pm.

Gecko's Garden 게코스 가든 Itaewondong 116-6 ☎02 790 0540; Itaewon subway; map p.91. Not to be confused with the nearby expat bar *Gecko's Terrace* (see p.126), this rambling restaurant is fenced off from Itaewon by a line of trees, and feels a world removed from smoky Seoul. The silver bistro tables impart a vaguely European air to the courtyard and the menu follows suit with pastas and risottos (from W17,000), while in the evening chefs will grill your choice of meat on an open barbecue. Daily noon–3.30pm & 5pm–1am.

Happy Home 해피홈 Itaewondong 64-15 ☎02 797 3185; Itaewon subway; map p.91. Itaewon isn't all English-teachers and soldiers – there's a sizeable Nigerian population here too, and a fair few restaurants catering to them. This is the best by far, a welcoming venue serving grilled plantains, black-eyed peas and beef-and-fish soups to eat with your *fufu* ("grinded" cassava). It's around W10,000 per dish, though ask first since prices are not on the menu. Daily noon–midnight.

Le Saigon 레사이곤 Itaewondong 74-33 ☎02 792 0336; Itaewon subway; map p.91. Vietnamese restaurant whose decor is pleasingly authentic, even if the food doesn't always hit the mark. If you want something beyond the inevitable *pho* noodles, try *banh mi* baguettes (W7000), or vermicelli salads with charbroiled pork (W8000). Daily 11.30am–9.30pm.

Le Saint-Ex 레손텍스 Itaewondong 119-28 ☎02 795 2465; Itaewon subway; map p.91. Check out the blackboard for the daily specials at this French bistro; expect grilled pork ribs, home-made sausage or something similar from the lunch sets (W25,000). Teasingly set out on the counter, the desserts are hard to resist, and there's a good wine list. Mon–Fri noon–3pm & 6pm–2am; Sat & Sun noon–2am.

★**Menya Sandaime** 멘야 산다이메 Itaewonno 206 ☎02 790 4129; Itaewon subway; map p.91. Ramen joint serving noodles that are almost as good as you'd find across the pond in Japan. Bowls go from W7000, though in summertime consider the delicious *tsukemen* (W8000), in which you dip noodles into a spicy soup; the *gyoza* dumplings (W3000) always go down well, too. Daily 10am–10pm.

Petra Palace 페트라 팰리스 Itaewondong 197 ☎02 749 9329; Itaewon subway; map p.91. Small, Jordanian-run place serving delicious falafel wraps (W5000), which are just the thing if you're pacing around Itaewon. Daily 10am–10pm.

Silence of the Lamb 사일런스 오브 더 램 Haenamuro 13-gil 9 ☎02 794 9002; Noksapyeong subway; map p.91. Wow, how's *that* for a morbid name? Lamb makes up almost the whole menu at this swanky Gyeongnidan restaurant – grilled, fried, burgers, in stews and much more. Figure on W15,000 per head, before drinks. Daily noon–3.30pm & 5pm–1am.

The Wolfhound 울프하운드 Itaewondong 128-6 ☎02 749 7971, ☻wolfhoundpub.com; Itaewon subway; map p.91. Irish-style drinking hole notable for an authentic selection of pub grub, including burgers, fish & chips and shepherd's pie. Best, however, are the fried breakfasts, which cost from W11,900 including a tea or coffee, and slide down quite nicely. Kitchen open daily noon–11pm.

Zelen 제렌 Itaewonno 27-gil 52 ☎02 749 0600; Itaewon subway; map p.91. Bulgarian cuisine is one of

10

10

the culinary world's best kept secrets, taking hearty meat and veg dishes from the Slavic lands to the west, and fusing them with kebabs and breads from the Turkic east. Meals here (around W22,000) are well prepared, though best may be the gigantic "couple" *shashlik* kebab. Daily 11am–3pm & 6–11pm.

SOUTHERN SEOUL

Bloom & Gouté 블룸 앤 구떼 Apgujeongno 10-gil 35-1 ☎02 545 6659; Apgujeong subway; map p.94. A great two-level brunch spot off the Garosugil shopping street. Eggs Benedict stands out (W15,000), or try quiche, salads, lasagne, or a range of organic teas. Daily 11am–11pm.

Bongohyang Matjip 본고향 맛집 Sinsadong 613-2 ☎02 544 9292; Apgujeong subway; map p.94. Don't let the unassuming appearance fool you – a number of highly prominent celebrities have dined at this simple meat restaurant. You can barbecue rounds from W25,000 per portion, though almost as many come for their *ddukbaegi bulbogi* (뚝배기 불고기; W9000), a sort of beef broth with glass noodles and rice. Mon–Sat 9am–9pm.

Ciné de Chef 씨네 드 쉐프 Nonhyeonno 848 ☎02 3446 0541; Apgujeong subway; map p.94. Immaculate Italian restaurant located in the bowels of the CGV cinema complex. The place is only really for couples, since dinner sets (from W70,000 per head, and usually including soup, a steak or pasta dish and dessert) include tickets to a private movie theatre, featuring just 30 comfy chairs laid out in couple formation; here you can watch the latest Hollywood blockbuster over a bottle of wine. Daily 3–11pm.

Lee's Gimbap 리스 김밥 Sinsadong 610 ☎02 548 5552; Apgujeong subway; map p.94. Korean staple foods are being trendified, one after another, so it was only a matter of time before the humble *gimbap* rice-tube received the treatment. Fillings here include Edam or Gouda cheese, shiitake mushrooms and paprika. Around W4000 a tube, take away only. Mon–Fri 9am–9pm, Sat 7.30am–8pm.

Marco Polo 마르코 폴로 52F Trade Tower, COEX complex ☎02 555 5656; Samseong subway; map p.94.

Seoul's top restaurant – in a literal sense, at least, sitting as it does on the 52nd floor of the World Trade Center, which rises from the centre of COEX. It's split into two halves: one serving Mediterranean cuisine and one Chinese, with prices slightly cheaper at the former. Either way, you'll be paying about W40,000 for lunch, and double that for dinner. Views are, of course, superb. Mon–Sat 11.30am–1am, Sun 11.30am–11.30pm.

Melting Shop 멜팅 샵 Apgujeongno 46-gil 55 ☎02 544 4256; Anguk subway; map p.94. Apgujeong probably has the full set of international comestibles now, after the addition of this dreamily pretty "retro ricotta bar". The ricotta itself sells for W12,000, pasta dishes for double that, and crab bisque for W13,000. A place to impress, especially if you can score the seats overlooking Dosan Park. Daily 11.30am–3pm & 5pm–midnight.

Pasha 파샤 Seochodong 1317-31 ☎02 593 8484; Gangnam subway; map p.94. Style and substance mix perfectly at this Turkish kebab house, whose attractive interior sets it apart from its dowdier counterparts in Itaewon. The meals (generally W15,000) are filling, with the familiar *döner* and *köfte* dishes supplemented by more unusual fish meals. *Pide* – a kind of Turkish pizza – is best washed down with some sour *ayran* yoghurt. Daily 11.30am–11.30pm.

Seventy Four 카페74 Cheongdamdong 83-20 ☎02 542 7412; Apgujeong subway; map p.94. This swanky venue serves up excellent brunches and light meals (from W20,000). Come early to grab a window seat, and watch bag-laden shoppers trooping up and down one of the most fashionable streets in the country. Daily 10am–1am.

★**Sushi Chohi** 수시 초히 Sinsadong ☎02 545 8422; Apgujeong subway; map p.94. Sushi fans will be in their

---

SELF-CATERING

Eating out is such good value for money that there's little need to make your own meals – even those staying at the cheapest guesthouses tend to eat out each day. However, if you do wish to self-cater, or simply throw together a picnic now and again, you'll find **convenience store** chains (many open 24hrs a day), such as 7-Eleven, CU and GS25, on almost every single corner. They carry simple foodstuffs like sandwiches (W1500 and up), instant noodles (from W800), crisps and chocolate bars; all have free hot water for making noodles, and chairs to sit on while you're eating. They also make good places to drink (see box, p.124). **Supermarkets and markets** are good for basics such as fruit, vegetables and salad ingredients, though non-native fruit can be almost absurdly expensive in Korea. **Western goods** can be tricky to find, with cheese at the top of many an expat's wish list. For these, it's best to head to one of the major hypermarkets such as *Lotte*, *E-Mart* and *Carrefour*. Each has a number of huge branches, but these tend to be out in the suburbs, and few are conveniently placed for foreign travellers; one Lotte store can be found in the basement of the *Lotte Hotel* (see map, p.64).

element at this pine-lined restaurant, overlooking Dosan Park. Absolutely no concessions are made regarding the fish or its preparation: the blades and chopping boards cost upwards of $1000 each, while each fish is selected from the best possible place, whether it be southwestern Korea or northern Japan. The head chef speaks English, and if you're seated at the main bar he will be happy to discourse on the merits of each creature as he performs his magic upon them. Sets from W50,000. Daily 11am–10pm.

Tutto Bene 투또베네 Cheongdamdong 118-9 ☎02 546 1489; Cheongdam subway; map p.94. The setting of this Italian restaurant is utterly gorgeous, its Orient Express-like wooden panelling offset by amber and honey-yellow lighting, and the scent of freshly cut flowers mingling with the creations of the chef. Pasta dishes are the most popular (from W25,000), but don't overlook the seafood menu – sourced from remote islands off Korea's west coast, the oysters are superb. Daily noon–midnight.

10

Cafés and tearooms

Seoul's **café** society has come a long way since the turn of the millennium – good coffee is now available on almost every corner, at almost any hour. You'll find a number of major chains around the city: *Hollys* and *Pascucci* have the best wi-fi access, while it's tough for foreigners to get online at *Starbucks*, and rarely possible for anyone at *The Coffee Bean and Tea Leaf*. Far more interesting, however, are the thousands of privately run ventures, which reach heights of quirky individuality around Hongdae and Samcheongdong; some effectively count as **dessert cafés**, focusing more on sweeties or baked goods than drinks.

For something more traditional, Insadonggil and its surrounding alleyways are studded with **tearooms**, typically decorated in a traditional style and therefore in keeping with the area. The teas are high-quality products made with natural ingredients (see box, p.120), and often come with traditional Korean sweets.

CAFÉS

Bau House 바우하우스 Seogyodong 394-44 ☎02 334 5152; Hapjeong subway; map p.82. Koreans are more famed abroad for eating dogs than owning them, but this café should show where the balance lies these days. Over a dozen cuddly pooches are on hand to greet customers, who are encouraged to bring their own dogs along. The coffee's good too (from W6000), but in such a bizarre atmosphere you may barely notice the taste. Daily 1.30–11.30pm.

Cat Café 고양이 다락방 Myeongdong 2-ga 51-14 ☎02 318 3123; Myeongdong subway; map p.64. Yes, that's right – a café filled with cats. It's hugely popular with visitors from China, who race up to this sixth-floor venue to take gazillions of pictures with the furry felines – great fun. W8000 entry gets you a free hot drink. Daily 1–10pm.

Café aA 카페aA Seogyodong 408-11 ☎02 3143 7312; Sangsu subway; map p.82. Several things set this place apart from the regular Korean café: the huge, church-like front door; a ceiling at least three times higher than the national average; the bespectacled, artsy clientele; and a range of chairs imported from Europe. The upstairs floor functions as a sort of furniture museum, featuring examples from luminaries such as Jean Prouvé and Salvador Dalí. Art aside, the coffee here is excellent (around W5000), as are the various cakes. Daily noon–2am.

★**Café Madang** 카페 마당 Sinsadong 630-26 ☎02 546 3643; Apgujeong subway; map p.94. The Hermès flagship store has a café discreetly tucked away on the basement level, and W11,000 will be enough to get you coffee. All cutlery, cups and glasses – plus the tables and chairs – are Hermès originals, and a fair proportion of the customers are local celebrities. There's no cheaper way to buy your way into high society, but dress smartly. Daily 10am–9pm.

Club Espresso 클럽 에스프레쏘 Buamdong 257-1 ☎02 764 8719; Gyeongbokgung subway; map p.72. If you're living in Seoul, this is where to buy your beans. The range of single-plantation Java is huge and truly global, from Zambian Munama Ndola to Brazilian Santo Antonio, and the pine interior is a pleasant place to compare and contrast a few samples. Daily 9am–9pm.

The Lounge 더 라운지 Teheranno 606 ☎02 2016 1205; Samseong subway; map p.94. Sitting atop the *Park Hyatt* (see p.107) alongside the infinity pool of the hotel's fitness centre, this is a superb place for a coffee or light snack. Better still is a range of smoothies designed by David Beckham's nutritionist, Patricia Teixeira: well worth the W16,000 splurge. Daily 9am–midnight.

Mille Crepe 밀크레이브프 Gahoedong 31-65 ☎02 745 9211; Anguk subway; map p.38. Jazz-playing café overlooking the prettiest road in Bukchon Hanok Village – try to score one of the four balcony seats if possible. Crêpes and cake W5000, coffee a bit more. Daily 10am–8pm.

Millimeter Milligram 밀리미터밀리그람 Itaewonno 240 ☎02 549 1520; Hangangjin subway; map p.91. Also known as MMMG, Millimeter Milligram is a local design team

10

producing arty stationery, postcards and other such items. This is the best place to buy their products – even the cool cup your coffee's served in will be available for sale. Daily 11am–9pm.

Rosen Cavalier 로젠 카발리에 Sinsadong 657-37 ☏02 512 1466; Apgujeong subway; map p.94. Decked out like a 1930s Viennese café, right down to the starched shirt of the waiter, and the delicious cakes on offer. *Rosen's* refined atmosphere is further enhanced by the tunes humming across from the classical music shop next door. Daily 10am–10pm.

Sanmotungi 산모퉁이 Buamdong 97-5 ☏02 391 4737; map p.72. Made famous by its use as a set in Korean drama *The Coffee Prince*, this remote coffee house is worth a visit for the fresh air and mountain views on offer from its upper level. Coffees W7000. Daily 11am–10pm.

Vecchia & Nuovo 베끼아 앤 누오보 Sinsadong 631-22 ☏02 514 0699; Apgujeong subway; map p.94. The nicest of several cafés in this uber-trendy area around Dosan Park. Pastries are surprisingly cheap (W3000 or so), though you won't get much change from W10,000 for a coffee. Daily 10am–10pm.

DESSERT CAFÉS

Bizeun 비즌 Insadonggil 16 ☏02 738 1245; Jonggak subway; map p.49. Waffles and ice cream are the regular snacks in Korean cafés, but here you'll be able to chow down on something more traditional: sweet rice-cakes, known as *ddeok* (떡), which come in a wonderful kaleidoscope of colours, with flavours running the gamut from pumpkin to black sesame. Daily 8.30am–10pm.

Books Cooks 북스쿡스 Bukchonno 8-gil 5 ☏02 743 4003; Anguk subway; map p.38. *Hanok*-like venue strung with cool lighting, this place is famed for its scones – made to order and served with jam for just W4000. There are tea sets all over the walls, and you can have a brew yourself for W7000 or so. Daily 10am–9pm.

★**Café Yung** 카페융 Palpandong 27-2 ☏02 736 7652; Anguk subway; map p.38. Set in a traditional *hanok*, this is a Samcheongdong dessert café *par excellence*, a quaint

place comparing favourably with the more pretentious competition on the main drag. Pride of place goes to the delectable *hoddeok* (호떡; W5000), a sweet pancake stuffed with seeds and brown sugar, and served with berries. The persimmon yoghurt (W6500) is also worth mentioning, and the coffee's good. Daily noon–10pm.

★**Fell & Cole** 펠앤콜 Seopyongdaero 8-gil 7 ☏010 8895 1434; Sangsu subway; map p.82. Divine ice cream in a tidy little hideyhole, secreted away in the alleys behind Sangsu station. Flavours change by the day, but expect things like carrot cake, fig mascarpone and caramel sweet potato. Daily noon–10pm.

O'Sulloc 오설록 Insadonggil 45-1 ☏02 732 6427; Anguk subway; map p.49. O'Sulloc is Korea's largest producer of green tea, but don't let that fool you into thinking that people come to their flagship tearoom to

---

KOREAN TEAS

Tea is no longer the national drink in this coffee-crazed country, which is a tremendous shame considering the wonderful concoctions available here. The following are particularly recommended:

Bori Cha (보리차) This barley tea is served with meals at many Korean restaurants, and is replenishable at no extra cost.

Daechu Cha (대추차) Apparently good for relieving muscle pain, this warming tea is made from the jujube, a type of oriental date.

Insam Cha (인삼차) Korea is the world's largest producer of ginseng, so it's no surprise to find that they make tea from the stuff. This hugely healthy drink is also available in powdered form at convenience stores, and many hotel lobbies.

Maesil Cha (매실차) Tea made from the Korean plum, and usually very sugary. Many Koreans make the stuff at home, and an alcoholic variety is available at most convenience stores.

Nok Cha (녹차) Korea's version of green tea, usually grown on the south coast or Jeju island, and available in many different varieties.

Omija Cha (오미자차) Shocking pink in colour, this tangy tea is made from the *omija* berry, whose name literally means "five tastes". Particularly good served cold as a refreshing summer drink.

Saenggang Cha (생강차) Made from ginger root, this throat-warming tea tastes just like a Chinese pharmacy smells, and is perfect for chasing away coughs or colds. Not to everyone's tastes, though for others it's the best of the bunch.

Yuja Cha (유자차) A citrus tea usually made with honey, and perfect if you've got a cold coming on. Unlike most other teas listed here, this one's pretty easy to make yourself – jars of condensed *yuja cha* are available in any convenience store, so all you'll need is hot water.

drink the stuff. Instead, this is a café and dessert bar *par excellence*, since the precious leaves have been blended into tiramisu, ice cream, lattes and chocolates (W5000–8000). Daily 9am–10pm.

Passion 5 파션5 Hannamdong 729-74 ☎02 2071 9505; Hangangjin subway; map p.91. Part bakery, part dessert café, part brunch spot, this stylish place is also the headquarters of the *Paris Baguette* chain. Their baked goods are delicious (from W2000), and the ice creams superb (W6000 for two scoops); head upstairs for eggs Benedict and hand-drip coffee (W7000). Daily 7.30am–10pm.

★**Second Best Place in Seoul** 서울에서 두번째 로잘하는집 Samcheongdong 122; Anguk subway; map p.38. A rarity on cosmopolitan and fast-changing Samcheongdonggil – not only has it been here for decades, but it also serves traditional fare. The menu is short and sweet, with an assortment of Korean teas and snacks. Best is the *patjuk* (W5500), something like a viscous red-bean fondue containing all manner of ingredients from cinnamon to chestnut chunks. Daily 10am–9pm.

TEAROOMS

★**Cha-teul** 차마시는뜰 Bukchonno 11-gil 26 ☎02 722 7006; Anguk subway; map p.38. Utterly gorgeous *hanok* tearoom with a splendid range of fine brews, including unusual local varieties such as mistletoe and pine mushroom, and some imported from China. It's right next to a decaying brick smokestack – an easy landmark to spot. Teas go from W5500. Daily 10am–10pm.

Dawon 다원 Gwanhundong 30-1 ☎02 730 6305; Anguk subway; map p.49. Located in the grounds of the Kyungin Museum of Fine Art (see p.52), in warm weather you can sit outside in the courtyard, while inside you'll find traditionally styled rooms where guests are encouraged to add their musings to the graffiti-filled walls. Teas from W6000 are on the menu, alongside information about their purported health benefits. Daily 10am–11pm.

Hue 휴 Gwanhundong 192-35 ☎02 722 8234; Anguk subway; map p.49. With an exterior seemingly fashioned from broken tiles, this looks a little like a Korean temple roof that has fallen down and been compressed into four floors of tearoom. Inside, you'll find interesting varieties such as medicinal herb and pomegranate (W5000 and up), as well as a number of fruit juices and shakes. There's a great view from the fifth-floor terrace. Daily 10am–midnight.

★**Mongmyeok Sanbang** 목멱산방 Minsokjaryo 11 ☎02 746 1736; Myeongdong subway; map p.64. This secluded Namsan restaurant (see p.114) also makes a wistful spot for tea, with most brews costing around W5000. Daily 11am–10.30pm.

★**Suyeon Sanbang** 수연산방 Seongbukdong 248 ☎02 764 1736; Hansung University subway; map p.72. Though a little out of the way and hard to find, this secluded *hanok* tearoom is highly recommended for those looking for a piece of old-world Seoul. Built in the 1930s, it exudes the charm of a bygone age, turning down the volume button of modern Seoul to leave only the sounds of bird chatter and running water. Teas around W10,000, desserts a little more. Daily 11.30am–10pm.

Su Yo Il 수요일 Gwanhundong 23 ☎02 8723 0191; Anguk subway; map p.49. Fancy tearoom with a few tables overlooking Insadonggil – a fine place for people-watching. Teas cost W7500, and many are served with floating flowers; in addition to the Korean options, they also offer Earl Grey, Darjeeling and other more familiar teas, as well as some fine desserts. Daily 10am–10.30pm.

10

Drinking and nightlife

Clubs pumping out techno, trance and hip-hop to wiggling masses; noisy live jazz and rock joints; neon-tinged cocktail bars in the bowels of five-star hotels; and a nascent craft beer scene – Seoul's nightlife scene has come of age. Not long ago drinking in Seoul was pretty much a male-only affair, taking place in restaurants or at a "hof", the once-ubiquitous faux-Western bars that are now being replaced by more authentic venues. The local drinking scene has been shaken up by an increase in demand for two particular alcoholic drinks. First came the *makgeolli* craze – for decades young Koreans pooh-poohed this rice beer, but the delicious drink has been given a new lease of life, and is now sold across the city, sometimes at bar-restaurants dedicated to the stuff. More recently, thanks to the arrival of some small-scale microbreweries, a whole generation of Koreans is now enjoying craft ale for the first time.

KNOW YOUR NEIGHBOURHOOD: WHERE TO GO OUT IN SEOUL

Koreans love going out, whether it's with family, colleagues, social acquaintances or friends, making Seoul a truly 24-hour city – day and night, year-round, its streets are a thrilling merry-go-round of noise, which ramps up as evening approaches, and stays at a maximum until the early hours. Each area of Seoul has its own particular flavour, with **Hongdae** by far the busiest. Its streets are saturated with bars, clubs and restaurants, and full every day of the week from early evening onwards. Towards midnight the crowds are swelled further with clubbers, who get the last subway of the day to Hongdae, party all night, then slink off home as dawn breaks. Almost as busy at the weekend is **Itaewon**, which has some of the best bars, clubs and restaurants in the capital. It has become very trendy of late, and is also Korea's most popular **gay district**, with some excellent bars catering to Seoul's ever-growing pink community (see p.126). Also full of cheap yet interesting bars is **Sinchon**, one subway stop from Hongdae, and studenty **Daehangno**, which is busy every evening (though most people drift towards Hongdae as midnight approaches), while **Samcheongdong** has a few relaxing places to wine and dine in. South of the river, **Gangnam** has a couple of good clubs, with trendy bars aplenty in nearby **Apgujeong**.

11

GYEONGBOKGUNG AND AROUND

Dugahun 두가헌 Sagandong 80 ☎02 3210 2100; Anguk subway; map p.38. A charmingly characteristic venue to fall into for a glass of wine, set as it is in a revamped *hanok* building. Their selection runs the gamut from under W70,000 to well over W1,000,000 a bottle, augmented by fine European cuisine from the kitchens. Some of the views disappoint, so choose your table carefully. **Mon–Sat noon–4pm & 6pm–midnight, Sun noon–4pm.**

★Jeon Daegamdaek 전대감댁 Angukdong 85 ☎02 735 0723; Anguk subway; map p.38. An integral part of the newly trendy Seochon district, this bar-restaurant sells a great range of *makgeolli* for W4000–8000 – try the slightly sour *Baedari* brand (배다리), once beloved of ex-president Park Chung-hee. It's great for meals, too; most

opt for the eponymous savoury *jeon* (전) pancakes. If there's room, head to the courtyard area at the back – an achingly beautiful place to drink, with occasional glimpses of the Seoul night sky. **Daily 11pm–midnight.**

★Sanchez 산체스 Angukdong 85 ☎02 735 0723; Anguk subway; map p.38. One of the best new *makgeolli* dens in Seoul, with a fantastic range (W6000 or so per bottle) sourced from all over the country – there's no English-language signage or advice, but you can't really go wrong. The food's great, too; try the super-tasty "America-style" *gamjajeon* (미국감자전; W15,000), a regular local potato pancake covered with bacon and egg. The only problem is a lack of table space – it's tiny and very popular, so you may well have to wait, or come back another day. **Daily 6pm–2am.**

INSADONG AND AROUND

Baekseju Maeul 백세주마을 Gwancheoldong 256 ☎02 0000; Jonggak subway; map p.49. This presentable bar-restaurant prides itself on its *baekseju* (see box, p.125), and serves local bar-food – entire meals, in other words – to go with it. It's also one of the few places in town where you'll find *ihwaju* (이화주; W29,000); something like evaporated *makgeolli*, it's pleasantly gloopy. **Daily 5pm–2am.**

Brew 3.14 브루 3.14 Donnamunno 11-gil 39 ☎010 6706 7769; Anguk subway; map p.49. What a pleasant addition to the Anguk neighbourhood this little place

is – somewhere to wash down a craft beer with a few slices of tasty pizza pie (from W8000). **Daily 5pm–midnight.**

Story of the Blue Star 푸른별주막 Gwanhundong 118-15 ☎02 734 3095; Anguk subway; map p.49. Though technically a restaurant serving earthy food from rural Gangwon province, this artily decorated *hanok*–style venue really comes alive in the evening, serving a variety of superb *makgeolli*: the rice wine is flavoured with ingredients such as green tea, pine needles and mugwort. You'll need to order at least one dish. **Daily 6–11pm.**

MYEONGDONG AND DONGDAEMUN

Neurin Maeul 느린 마을 Suhadong 67 ☎02 6030 0999; Jonggak subway; map p.64. The Neurin Maeul *makgeolli* brand has spotted a gap in the market, and run with it – they've dressed their tasty brew up to the nines as a boutique label, and are now selling it in myriad forms

(including seasonal flavours) in this highly presentable restaurant-bar. You'll have to buy some food, but it's very good too. **Daily 11.30am–11pm.**

Pierre's Bar 피에르스바 Euljiro 30 ☎02 317 7183, ⓦpierregagnaire.co.kr; Euljiro 1-ga subway; map p.64.

Adjoining the superb *Pierre Gagnaire* restaurant (see p.114) at the top of the *Lotte Hotel*, this stylish bar is a firm favourite with international businessmen. Despite the modern yet opulent surroundings, and the sky-high food prices next door, drinks aren't *that* dear – beer and spirits start at W13,000. Daily 6–11pm.

NORTHERN SEOUL

Dan Vie Myeongnyun 3-ga 154-2 ☎ 02 741 2550; Hyehwa subway; map p.72. Tucked into a basement just off Daehangno, this bar is a curious mix of decorative styles – some areas are cordoned off with dangling beads or shower curtains, others have space-station-style swivel chairs – and movies are projected onto the far wall. Daily 5pm–2am.

WESTERN SEOUL

Bar Da 바다 Seogyodong 365-5 ☎ 02 334 5572; Sangsu subway; map p.82. Getting to this bar is an adventure in itself – finding the entrance, crawling up the steep steps, then back outdoors to navigate what probably used to be a fire escape for the final leg to the top. Once you're there, it's wonderful: a broodingly dim, candle-studded hideaway for a nice drink. Daily 7pm–3am.

Club Naked 클럽 네이키드 Seogyodong 364-3 ☎ 010 8072 3461; Hongik University subway; map p.82. Hip-hop club that's not quite as packed or starchy as some of its neighbours, but still pretty darn busy at weekends. Drinks are cheap, too, and Thursday is Ladies' Night; entry usually W10,000 after 10pm on weekdays, and W20,000 at weekends. Daily 8pm–6am.

Gogos 고고스 Seogyodong 407-8 ☎ 02 337 8083; Sangsu subway; map p.82. Let's cut to the chase here – this is one of Hongdae's prime meat markets, with a good mix of Koreans and foreigners, cheap drinks, a fun vibe, and a W5000 entry fee. Tues–Thurs & Sun 8pm–2am, Fri & Sat 6pm–6am.

M2 클럽 엠투 Seogyodong 367-11 ☎ 02 3143 7573; Sangsu subway; map p.82. Focusing on electronica, this is the area's largest nightclub, which manages to rope in the occasional top international DJ. It's packed to the gills at weekends, when you may spend more than an hour waiting in line to get in. Entry W10,000–20,000. Tues–Thurs & Sun 9.30pm–5am, Fri & Sat 9.30pm–7am.

Samgeori Pocha 삼거리포차 Seogyodong; Sangsu subway; map p.82. Technically a restaurant (see p.117), though an integral part of Hongdae's nightlife – after a dance or a drink, Koreans love to eat (and drink a little more), so you may well find yourself dragged along to this rustic-looking place, where raw fish and steaming broths are on the menu, and the tables are littered with empty *soju* bottles. Daily 6pm–late.

★**Vinyl** 바이닐 Seogyodong 411-1 ☎ 02 322 4161; Sangsu subway; map p.82. Get takeaway cocktails from the window of this small bar, where Pina Coladas and Sex on the Beach are served in what appear, at first glance, to be colostomy bags. Such ingenuity brings the price down – just W5000 for a cocktail. It's a great place to drink too, if you can find a seat free. Sun–Thurs 4pm–midnight, Fri & Sat 4pm–2am.

ITAEWON

B1 비원 Itaewondong 119-7 ☎ 02 749 6164; Itaewon subway; map p.91. Underground club with a decent sound system, and usually DJs that know how to make the most of it – a mix of house, techno, electronic and more. With lounge areas and snazzy decoration, it's far classier than most dance venues in the area – at the beginning of

---

A KOREAN NIGHT OUT

A "proper" Korean night out has long followed the same format, one that entwines food, drink and entertainment. The venue for stage one (*il-cha*) is the **restaurant**, where a meal is chased down with copious shots of *soju*. This is followed by stage two (*i-cha*), a visit to a **bar**, where beers (W3000–10,000) or cocktails (from W7000) are followed with snacks (usually large dishes intended for groups). Those still able to walk then continue to stage three (*sam-cha*), the **entertainment** component of the night, which usually involves a trip to a *noraebang* room for a sing-along (see p.131), and yet more drinks. Stages four, five and beyond certainly exist, but few participants have ever remembered them clearly.

For a more relaxed night out, Seoul has many options for alfresco alcohol consumption. The capital's ubiquitous twenty-four-hour **convenience stores** – which in warmer months tend to be surrounded by plastic chairs and tables for customer use – make for one of Seoul's cheapest nights out, and can be just as good for meeting locals as the city's bars. Indeed, the choice of local liquor is far better at convenience stores than almost any bar in town. *Geonbae!*

KOREAN DRINKS

Though Koreans largely favour beer and imported drinks, the country has more than a few superb local hooches, many of which go down very well indeed with the few foreigners lucky enough to learn about them.

Baekseju (백세주) A nutty, whisky-coloured concoction, about the same strength as wine. Its name means "one-hundred-year alcohol", on account of its healthy ingredients including ginseng and medicinal herbs. Surely the tastiest path towards becoming a centenarian, *baekseju* is available at all convenience stores (W4500) and many barbecue houses (W7000 or so), though bar-restaurant chain *Baekseju Maeul* (see p.123) is the most entertaining place to try your first hit.

Bokbunjaju (복분자주) Made with black raspberries, this sweet, fruity drink is somewhat similar to sugary, low-grade port. Available at all convenience stores (W6500), though those off on a mountain hike in late summer may be lucky enough to try some freshly made fare: it's sold by farmers at makeshift stalls.

Dongdongju (동동주) Very similar to *makgeolli*, *dongdongju* is a little heavier taste-wise, and since it can only be served fresh you'll have to head to a specialist place to sample it. The restaurants most likely to have *dongdongju* are those also serving savoury pancakes known as *pajeon*; these establishments are usually rustic affairs decked out with Korean bric-a-brac, and serving *dongdongju* in large wooden bowls (W8000), to be doled out into smaller versions of the same. A word of warning: many foreigners have "hit the wall" on their first dabble, suddenly finding themselves floored by this deceptively quaffable drink.

Maehwasu (매화수) Similar to *baekseju* in colour, strength and price, this is made with the blossom of the *maesil*, a type of Korean plum, and some bottles come with said fruit steeping inside.

Makgeolli (막걸리) Usually around six percent alcohol by volume, this milky rice-beer was considered grandad fuel for years, but has recently seen an upsurge in its popularity. The stuff is now sold in upmarket bar-restaurants, and preliminary attempts at marketing it abroad have even been made. Although it's the most expensive of Korea's alcohols to make, it's actually the cheapest to buy (W1300 in a convenience store, W3000 in a restaurant), since its centuries-old heritage has afforded it a favourable tax status.

Soju (소주) *Soju* is Korea's national drink, with Seoulites alone getting through over a billion bottles a year – that's almost one hundred bottles of *soju* per adult. Locals refer to it as "Korean vodka", though it's only half the strength – a good thing too, as it's usually fired down in staccato shots, preferably over barbecued meat. It's traditionally made with sweet potato, but these days most companies use cheap chemical concoctions: the resultant taste puts many foreigners off, but some find themselves near-addicted within days of arrival. Expect to pay around W1300 from a convenience store, or W3000 at a restaurant.

the night, at least. W10,000–20,000 entrance fee at weekends. Daily 7pm–4am.

BricX 브릭스 Itaewondong 119-10 ☎02 3785 1555; Itaewon subway; map p.91. This candlelit underground lair is a popular place to take a date, with reasonably priced cocktails and excellent food – try the falafel. The seating areas are highly attractive, featuring curtains, oriental silk pillows and the like. Daily 6.30pm–3am.

Bungalow 번갈로 Itaewondong 112-3 ☎02 793 2344; Itaewon subway; map p.91. There are drinking options aplenty in this loungey, multilevel bar – sup sangria on the swing-seats, drink martinis in the sand pit, have a romantic glass of wine on a candle-lit table or kick back with a beer on the outdoor terrace. The cocktails, however, are best avoided. Daily 4.30pm–3am.

★**Craftworks Taphouse** 크라브워크스 Noksap-yeongdaero 238 ☎02 749 2537; Noksapyeong subway;

map p.91. One of the main drivers behind the recent surge in local demand for craft beer (see box, p.92). Their signature brews are all named after Korean mountains, including Geumgang Dark Ale, Halla Golden Ale, Seorak Oatmeal Stout and the Jirisan Moon Bear IPA; their popularity is such that they're starting to pop up in cities all over the country. Daily 11am–1am.

Damotori 다모토리 Yongsandong 2-ga 44-18 ☎070 8950 8362; Noksapyeong subway; map p.91. One of the best *makgeolli* bars in Seoul – the *mak*-menu is laid out geographically, showing you exactly which part of Korea your chosen hooch hails from. The best way to pick a batch (W5000–11,000) is by using their ridiculously good-value sampler sets – W2000 for five cups of *makgeolli*, selected to range from light to heavy. These cups, and the bottle you end up choosing, are served in handmade pottery – quite splendid. Food's good, too. Daily 6–11pm.

11

11

Gecko's Terrace 게코스 테러스 Itaewondong 178 ☎ 02 749 9425; Itaewon subway; map p.91. Unlike most Itaewon bars, this is busy every day of the week. With a lively mix of Koreans and foreigners, it's popular with people who don't feel like dancing, and those filling up on cheap beer before a night on the tiles – local draught beer is just W3000, and a pint of Guinness is a reasonable W8000. Sun–Thurs 11am–1am, Fri & Sat 11am–3am.

Hollywood Grill 할리우드 그릴 Itaewondong 123-33 ☎ 02 749 1659; Itaewon subway; map p.91. American-style bar-restaurant showing Premier League football, Major League baseball and any other sport coverage in demand from Seoul's expat community. At quieter times, it's a pleasant place for a game of pool or darts, while during major sporting events you'll be lucky to find standing room. If you're hungry, try one of their pizzas – some of the best in Seoul. Daily noon–2am.

★**Magpie** 맥파이 Itaewondong 691 ☎ 02 749 2537; Noksapyeong subway; map p.91. Started by a beer-curious expat, this little brewery has seen so much demand that they may eventually spread across several adjacent buildings; there are already branches in Hongdae, and on Jeju Island. The beers are great, with the varieties on sale rotated regularly; their pizzas are splendid, too. Daily 5pm–1am.

Prost 프로스트 Itaewondong 116-1 ☎ 02 796 6854; Itaewon subway; map p.91. This multi-floor drinking venue behind the *Hamilton Hotel* has been full to bursting almost every night since it first opened. Sassy staff, a global range of beers (including some of their own), and a bunch of people to rub shoulders with – whether you like it or not. Daily 11.30am–2am.

The Wolfhound 울프하운드 Itaewondong 128-6 ☎ 02 749 7971, ⓦ wolfhoundpub.com; Itaewon subway; map p.91. If you're feeling homesick, this Irish-style pub isn't a bad choice – they sell a bunch of good beer, and it's also a fine place to eat (see p.117). Daily noon–2am.

SOUTHERN SEOUL

Lound 라운드 Cheongdamdong 83-13 ☎ 02 517 7412; Apgujeong subway; map p.94. Under the same ownership as *Seventy Four* down the road (see p.118), this bar's pricey cocktails (W22,000) are regularly voted the best in Seoul by the bloggers and magazine writers who get to cast such judgement. The ground level is for drinking and dining; heading upstairs will get you into a club-like space with cool iPhone drink menus, which enable you to place orders electronically. Daily 7pm–3am.

★**Octagon** 오크타곤 Nonhyeondong 175-2, ☎ 02 516 8847, ⓦ cluboctagon.co.kr; Hakdong subway; map p.94. Seoul's most popular club at the time of writing, this EDM venue has state-of-the-art light and sound systems (and even a gourmet chef), and regularly hauls in superstar DJs from across the globe – Nic Fanciulli and Coyu have both played here. Entry is W30,000 on weekend evenings, and you'll have to be dressed up. Thurs–Sat 10pm–7am.

Syndrome 신드롬 Sinsadong 587-1, ☎ 02 544 7227, ⓦ clubsyndrome.com; Apgujeong subway; map p.94. A club with a swimming pool – no wonder this "new electronica" stomping ground was an immediate hit on opening in late 2013. Cover usually W10,000 before midnight, W30,000 after. Thurs–Sun 10pm–7am.

★**Woo Bar** 우바 Walkerhillo 177 ☎ 02 2022 0333; Gwangnaru subway; map pp.6–7. Located in the entrance lobby of the futuristic *W Hotel* (see p.108), this is almost a rite of passage for young Seoulites with a bit of cash to flash. Simply breathing ultra-trendiness, it's not for everyone, but if egg-shaped chairs, UV-lit sofas and space-helmet-like DJ booths sound appealing, this is the place to head. Drinks are expensive, but the staff are way too cool to make a fuss about those who spend all night sipping a single beer. Daily 10am–2am.

Gay & lesbian nightlife

Seoul's burgeoning queer nightlife scene has come on in leaps and bounds since 2000, when star actor **Hong Seok-cheon** came out of the closet – the first Korean celebrity to do so. Initially shunned by family and friends, he found himself out of work and living in a bedsit, before opening up an Italian restaurant named *Our Place* on **Itaewon's** famed "Hooker Hill". To Hong's surprise, *Our Place* proved a hit with repressed locals as well as gay foreigners, and similar places opened up in some of the newly vacant brothels neaby; Hong himself now runs almost a dozen venues in the area. One side-street, now known as "Homo Hill", remains the centre of the country's gay community, and home to numerous bars.

Although Itaewon tends to suffice for foreign visitors, Seoul *does* have other gay neighbourhoods. The zone around Jongno 3-ga station has long been home to underground gay bars, with the scene becoming more open in recent years. Unfortunately, few venues are foreigner-friendly, though the *pojangmacha* tent-restaurants outside exit 4 of the subway station are good places to get chatting to local gay guys. Finally, the university district of **Sinchon** is popular with the local **lesbian** community, many of whom congregate of an evening in "Triangle Park", a patch of concrete near exit 1 of Sinchon subway station (take the first right).

GAY AND LESBIAN BARS AND CAFÉS

Barcode 바코드 Myodong 41-1 ☎02 3672 0940; Jongno 3-ga subway; map p.49. The Jongno district has umpteen gay bars, but most of these are essentially off-limits to foreigners. This is a neat exception to the rule, a fun place with English-speaking staff, and a bearish, 30-something clientele. Daily 7.30pm–3am.

Coffee Bean & Tea Leaf 커프븐 앤 티리브 Nagwondong 272; Jongno 3-ga subway; map p.49. Located at the bottom of the *Fraser Suites* (see p.105), this Insadong branch of the popular coffee chain is something of a gay mecca. Young gay men congregate throughout the day, but most clamorously on weekend evenings – much to the bemusement of the elderly locals in this traditional neighbourhood. Daily 10am–9pm.

Pink Hole 핀크홀 Seogyodong 395-5; Hapjeong subway; map p.82. There are plenty of lesbian establishments in the wider Hongdae area, but this is one of the few options for those who feel like a dance – a pity, then, that they seem to put the same pop playlist on every night. Usually W10,000 entrance fee, with two free drinks. Daily 9pm–2am.

Labris 라브리 Seogyodong 362-2 ☎02 333 5276; Sangsu subway; map p.82. A long-established mainstay of the Seoul lesbian scene, this female-only bar and social space is one of the most welcoming places for foreigners; a mimimum charge of W15,000 is levied at weekends. Mon–Fri 7pm–2am, Sat & Sun 7pm–5am.

Queen 퀸 Itaewondong 136-42 ☎010 9039 2583; Itaewon subway; map p.91. The two most popular gay bars on "Homo Hill" are *Queen* and *Always Homme*, but visitors often get fleeced at the latter; head instead to this attractive venue, with inviting staff and highly comfortable chairs. On warm weekend evenings, even these can't stop the crowd – usually quite a mixed bag in terms of race and persuasion – spilling out onto the street for a dance. Tues–Sun 6pm–4am.

★**Why Not?** 와이낫? Itaewondong 137-4 ☎02 795 8193; Itaewon subway; map p.91. Now, this is a trip. Here you're likely to see dozens of young locals performing expertly choreographed K-pop dances – some of these guys are seriously talented. Other nights have drag shows, or more "regular" house music. Cover W10,000, includes a free drink. Daily 8pm–3am.

11

KARAOKE AT A SINGING ROOM

Entertainment

Seoul has a jaw-dropping amount going on almost every day of the year, anything from traditional dance performances to classical music or live jazz. Theatrical performances are big earners for the city, and some have been so popular with international visitors that they've been exported to other lands. Nowhere in Seoul is too far from a gigantic cinema, though there are also a couple of smaller-scale arthouse operations. More local – or at least East Asian – in nature is the opportunity to belt out a few hits at a *noraebang*, a karaoke-style singing room. While gambling is technically illegal in Korea, there are a couple of fun ways to lose your money – in a casino or at the races.

INFORMATION

Listings Two good sources of entertainment listings are the official city tourist site (@ visitseoul.net) and *10* magazine (@ 10mag.com), while the English-language dailies (see p.25) have comprehensive weekend supplements. For music and gig listings, check out @ koreagigguide.com.

CINEMA

Koreans love going to the movies – though the emphasis is firmly on Hollywood and Kollywood blockbusters – with most of the country having seen the major movies within a week of their release. *CGV* and *Megabox* are the two major cinema chains (sadly, neither has an English-language website); they show foreign films in their original language with Korean subtitles, though in most cinemas, local films are Korean-only. There are also a few options for those looking for something a little more arthouse, with some establishments catering to foreigners.

Ciné de Chef 씨네 드 쉐프 Nonhyeonno 848 ☎02 3446 0541; Apgujeong subway; map p.94. A combination of restaurant (see p.118) and theatre, located in the bowels of the Apgujeong *CGV* cinema complex; from W70,000 per head. Daily 3–11pm.

★**Cinematheque** 시네마테크 Nagwondong 284-6 ☎02 741 9782; Jongno 3-ga subway; map p.49. Also going under the name of "Seoul Art Cinema", this sits on top of the Nagwon Arcade, a building that local authorities have been planning to tear down for years. Now given a stay of execution, the cinema here has a rolling calendar of themed events, some of which are based around foreign films; pop by and pick up a pamphlet. Tickets around W8000.

★**CGV** Yongsan Station complex ☎1544 1122; Yongsan subway; map p.91. The Yongsan branch of Korea's biggest cinema chain shows some Korean films with English subtitles, as well as all the latest blockbusters from abroad. Some films are shown in "4D", with wind machines, vibrating chairs and choreographed scents making you feel part of the show. There's also a "Gold Class" theatre, designed to resemble the first-class section on a plane, and seating (should that be lying?) just forty. Lastly, some theatres here now have cushy "couple" seats at the back, for snuggling up with that special someone. Tickets W8000; 4D W21,000; Gold Class W30,000.

Korea Film Archive 한국영상자료원 World Cup Bungno 400 ☎02 0000, @ www.koreafilm.org; Digital Media City subway; map pp.6–7. This institution regularly screens films from home and abroad, and has a large selection of Korean classics that can be rented for viewing on the premises. Access is tricky; see their website for details. Tickets usually free.

Megabox 메가박스 Samseongdong 159-1 ☎1544 0070; Samseong subway; map p.94. The chain's huge COEX branch, now very attractive after renovation in 2014, shows some of its Kollywood hits with added English subtitles. There are other branches all over the city. Tickets usually W8000.

Mirospace 미로스페이스 Sinmunno 2-ga 1-153 ☎02 3210 3358; Seodaemun subway; map p.56. Interesting hundred-seat venue showing arty films, usually from abroad. For once, there's no popcorn on offer, and after the movie customers can glide into the sleek adjoining bar. Tickets W8000.

Sangsangmadang 상상마당 Eoulmadangno 65 ☎02 330 6243; Sangsu subway; map p.82. The basement of this arts complex has some arty English-language screenings, of which around half are from abroad. Interestingly, they try to show films whose themes match what's on show in the second-floor gallery. Tickets W8000.

THEATRE AND PERFORMANCE ARTS

Stage buffs will have plenty to choose from in Seoul. Most popular with foreign travellers are traditional performances and musicals; the latter tend to be based in dedicated theatres.

Battle B-Boy 배틀 비보이 Hongdae B-Boy Theater, Wausanno 121 ☎02 323 5233, @ sjbboys.com; Hongdae subway; map p.82. One way to get into the B-Boy breakdancing still enthralling the nation, this long-running stage concept gets refreshed every couple of years, but always has some pretty incredible dance routines. Tickets W55,000. Performances Wed–Fri 8pm, Sat 6pm & Sun 4pm.

Chongdong Theatre 정동극장 Jeongdonggil 43 ☎02 751 1500, @ chongdong.com; City Hall subway; map p.56. "Miso", an 80min traditional show of song and dance, has been extremely popular with foreign visitors

for many a year (tickets W40,000), while "Giparang" is newer, and tells a love story from the Silla dynasty (tickets W30,000). Performances are in Korean, though English subtitles appear next to the stage. Miso Tues–Sun 4pm & 8pm; Giparang Tues–Sun 7.30pm.

Dongsoong Art Center 동숭 아트센터 Dongsungdong 1-5 ☎02 766 3390, @ dsartcenter .co.kr; Hyehwa subway; map p.72. This well-established Daehangno arts complex puts on some of Seoul's best experimental drama, though as performances are in Korean only you'll need some language skills or an open mind.

12

PANSORI

Usually marketed to foreigners as "Korean opera", **pansori** performances are a modern-day derivative of the country's shamanic past. Songs and incantations chanted to fend off evil spirits or ensure a good harvest slowly mutated over the years into ritualized presentations. As might be expected, the themes also evolved, with tales of love and despair replacing requests to spirits unseen.

A good *pansori* may go on for hours, but each segment will be performed by a cast of just two – a female singer (the *sorikkun*) and a male percussionist (*gosu*). The *sorikkun* holds aloft a paper fan, which she folds, unfolds and waves about to emphasize lyrics or a change of scene. While the *gosu* drums out his minimalist finger taps on the *janggo*, he gives his singer words (or, more commonly, grunts) of encouragement known as *chuimsae*, to which the audience are expected to add their own. The most common are "*chalhanda!*" and "*olshi-gu!*", which are roughly equivalent to "you're doing good!", and "hm!", a grunt acknowledging appreciation, usually delivered with a refined nod. Just follow the Korean lead, and enjoy the show.

Jump 점프 Cinecore Theater, Jeongdong 22 ☎02 722 3995, ⓦhijump.co.kr; Jongno 3-ga subway; map p.56. Ever wondered what a family entirely made up of martial arts experts would be like? Experience all the inevitable jumps and kicks in this entertaining musical. Tickets W40,000. Performances Mon 8pm; Tues–Sat 4pm & 8pm, Sun 3pm & 6pm.

Korea House 한국의집 Toegyero 10 ☎02 2266 9101, ⓦkoreahouse.or.kr; Chungmuro subway; map p.64. Highly polished traditional performances from some of Korea's top artistes, combined with some of Seoul's best food (see p.113): this is one of the city's most popular nights out. The wonderful shows include fan dances, *pansori* opera and the long-ribboned hats of the "farmers' dance". Tickets W50,000. Performances daily at 6.30pm & 8.30pm.

Namsan Gugakdang 남간 국악당 Toegyero 34-gil 28 ☎02 2261 0500; Chungmuro subway; map p.64. Those looking for a traditional Korean performance should make this their first port of call. Part of the Namsangol complex (see p.66), its shows revolve around *gugak*, an ancient style of Korean music, but the savvy curators bring a pleasant variety to the offerings with regular themed

events of song, music, dance or a combination of the three. Ticket prices vary but are usually in the region of W30,000.

Nanta 난타 Myeongdong 2-ga 50-14 ☎02 739 8288, ⓦnanta.co.kr; City Hall subway; map p.64. This madcap kitchen-based musical has gone down a storm since opening in 1997 (making it Korea's longest-running show), with songs, circus tricks and all sorts of utensil drumming mixed in with a nice line in audience participation. Tickets W40,000. Performances daily at 2pm, 5pm & 8pm.

Sejong Centre 세종 문화 회관 Sejongdaero 175 ☎02 399 1114, ⓦsejongpac.or.kr; Gwanghwamun subway; map p.56. Gigantic venue offering a truly diverse array of music: everything from traditional Korean *gugak* to concerts from world-famous pianists. There's something going on every night of the week; check the website for details.

Seoul Arts Centre 예술의 정당 Seochodong 700 ☎02 580 1300, ⓦsac.or.kr; Nambu Bus Terminal subway; map p.94. The home of Korea's national ballet and opera companies, as well as the symphony orchestra, this rambling complex always has something interesting going on. See website for details of upcoming events.

MUSIC

Seoul isn't exactly renowned for the quality of its music. From pre-teen girls to bad-boy bike nuts, most of the country listens to sugary K-pop, generic hip-hop and little else. There's a decent little indie scene centred around Hongdae, though several once-great places have shut their doors in recent years. In addition, there are a few venues where you can hear more highbrow offerings such as jazz or classical music, and an ever-increasing number of international mainstream acts are arriving in Korea.

GIG VENUES

Badabie 바다비 Donggyodong 182-5 ☎02 4454 2343; Sinchon subway; map p.82. A short walk from central Hongdae, this venue showcases the talents of bands from the local universities and beyond – an eclectic mix of rock, punk, folk and more. There's not a lot of distance between performers and spectators, making for a

more immersive experience. Entrance fee is up to W15,000; bring your own drinks. Wed–Sun 7pm–midnight.

Bbang 빵 Seogyodong 327-18 ☎010 8910 1089; Hongik University subway; map p.82. Another good place to get a handle on local talent, this relaxed venue has been going since the mid-1990s – albeit in a few different locations. There are usually several bands on most nights;

entry is around W15,000. Wed–Sun 6.30–11pm.

FF 클럽FF Seogyodong 407-8 ⓣ010 9025 3407; Sangsu subway; map p.82. Both Fs stand for "funky", though you're more likely to see some good ol' rock at this highly popular live music venue. A great many of the bands are foreign, bringing their pals and Korean hangers-on, then staying for the DJ sets afterwards. A great place to make new friends. Entry W10,000–15,000. Tues–Thurs & Sun 8–11pm, Fri & Sat 6pm–6am.

LARGE PERFORMANCE VENUES

Ax 악스 Gwangjangdong 319-33 ⓣ02 457 5114; Gwangnaru subway; map pp.6–7. With room for 2000 spectators, this is where many international bands play during their time in Seoul. Ticket prices vary.

Olympic Arena 올림픽 아레나 Bangidong; Sports Complex subway; map p.94. With a capacity of more than 10,000, this is the venue of choice when the big-hitters play Korea – Lady Gaga, Oasis, Taylor Swift and Bruno Mars have all performed here. Ticket prices vary.

JAZZ VENUES

All That Jazz 올댓재즈 Itaewondong 112-4 ⓣ02 795 5701, ⓦallthatjazz.kr; Itaewon subway; map p.91. An Itaewon institution, this place has been attracting jazz lovers for donkey's years. The atmosphere is fun, and audience interaction is commonplace – some spectators have ended up playing on stage with the band. Tickets usually W5000. Performances begin Mon–Thurs at 8.30pm, Fri & Sat at 6.30pm, 8.30pm & 11.30pm, & Sun at 6.30pm & 8.30pm.

Club Evans 클럽 에반스 Seogyodong 407-3 ⓣ02 337 8361; Sangsu subway; map p.82. Hongdae's most popular jazz venue by a mile, this is small enough to generate some decent acoustics, but large enough to create a good atmosphere. The acts are usually of more than acceptable quality, and the experience surprisingly refined for this nightclub-filled street. Tickets usually W5000–7000. Daily 7pm–midnight.

Once in a Blue Moon 원스인어블루문 Seolleungno 824 ⓣ02 549 5490; Apgujeong subway; map p.94. Perhaps the most renowned of Seoul's many jazz bars, and certainly the closest approximation to a Western venue. The music spans the full gamut of styles, played while customers dine on French or Mexican cuisine, accompanied by a choice from the lengthy wine and cocktail lists. Admission free. Performances start at 7.30pm.

12

SINGING ROOMS

Karaoke may be a Japanese concept, but is even more common in Korea: you'll find a *noraebang* (노래방; literally "song room") on almost every street in Seoul. These "singing rooms" are wildly popular with people of all ages, and usually cost around W15,000 an hour between a group. The system is different from what Westerners may be used to – you don't sing in front of a crowd, but in a small room with your friends, where you'll find sofas, a television, books full of songs to choose from and a couple of maracas or tambourines to play. Foreigners are often intimidated at first, but after a few drinks it can be tough to get the microphone out of people's hands.

Luxury Su 수 노래방 Eoulmadangno 67 ⓣ02 322 3111; Sangsu subway; map p.82. Next door to *Sangsangmadang* (see p.129), this *noraebang* has achieved particular fame thanks to its sumptuously decorated rooms, and even a few with floor-to-ceiling windows visible from the street – show-offs, this is your big chance. Up to W20,000 per hour, per room at peak time. Daily 24hr.

GAMBLING

Seven Luck Casino 세븐럭 카시노 Teheranno 87-gil 58 ⓣ02 3466 6100; Samseong subway; map p.94. Foreigner-only casino in the Coex complex (see p.98); bring along your passport as proof that you're not about to break the law. There's another branch of the same casino north of the river in the *Millennium Hilton*. Casual attire permitted. Daily 24hr.

Seoul Racecourse Park 세븐럭 카시노 Teheranno 87-gil 58 ⓣ1566 3333; Seoul Racecourse Park subway. Gamble on the gee-gees at this venue just south of Seoul, near Seoul Grand Park (see p.101). It can be quite fun, and you'll also be able to bet on races from sister tracks in Jeju and Busan, which are simulcasted on large screens. Entry W2000. Sat & Sun only.

Shopping

Shopaholics will find themselves quite at home in Seoul: the city has everything from trendy to traditional and markets to malls. High on the itinerary of many tourists are the colossal markets of Dongdaemun and Namdaemun (see p.136), but there's much more on offer – clothing running the gamut from traditional to designer via tailored suits, a range of artistic produce including excellent pottery and Joseon-era antiques, and all the electrical goods you could possibly desire. Many of the city's shops stay open late into the evening and most accept the standard international credit cards, including Visa, Mastercard and Union Pay – making shopping in Seoul all the more seductive.

DUTY-FREE SHOPPING

Seoul has a few places in which you can do your **duty-free shopping** before getting to the airport, including the *Shilla* (see p.106) and *Sheraton Grande* (see p.108) hotels, and the dedicated Donghwa Duty Free just outside exit 6 of Gwanghwamun subway station. Cosmetics, beauty and body products, alcohol and designer bags are the most popular purchases, though you'll need to bring along your passport and plane tickets. In addition, you can get ten percent **tax back** on anything you've bought in Korea worth W30,000 or more from any shop sporting a "Tax Free" logo – usually the aforementioned goods, plus electrical equipment and some clothing.

ARTS, CRAFTS AND ANTIQUES

A good place to head for anything arty is Insadonggil and its side-streets, where you'll find numerous galleries (see box, p.52), as well as craft shops selling paints, brushes, calligraphy ink and handmade paper. For antiques, Itaewon is best, with the road known as "Antiques Alley" stretching south from the subway station. There's quite a lot of authentic Joseon-era furniture out there, too; this was once an absolute bargain (indeed, it's still occasionally possible to find antiques lying on the streets), but demand from abroad has pushed supply down and prices up. Replica dynastic furniture is cheaper and more abundant. All antiques shops can organize overseas shipping.

Curious Curious 큐리어스 큐리어스 Itaewondong 455-36 ☎02 795 5869; Noksapyeong subway; map p.91. Gorgeous jewellery including bangles, necklaces and earrings, all handmade at this charming Itaewon boutique store. Prices are reasonable – think W40,000 for a pair of earrings. Daily Tues–Sun 1–9pm.

Hyojae 효재 Seongbukdong 314-9 ☎02 720 5393; Hansung University subway; map p.72. Tiny shop with a big reputation for producing high-quality traditional fabrics, clothing and pottery. Of most interest to foreign customers will be the silk wrapping cloths known as *bojagi*, which make great small souvenirs. The shop is a bit out of the way – it's right opposite Gilsangsa temple (see p.74). Daily 10am–6pm.

Jeojip 저집 Buamdong 142-1 ☎02 3417 0119; Gyeongbokgung subway; map p.72. Blink and you'll miss this store, tucked way up north in Buamdong. It sells all manner of delightful chopsticks which, given the price – W100,000 or so – are for display, rather than use. Daily 10am–6pm.

★**Kwang Ju Yo** 광주요 Gahoedong 203 ☎02 741 4801, ⓦkwangjuyo.com; Anguk subway; map p.38. Korea has been at the forefront of world pottery for centuries, and this store is one of the best places to buy it. Celadon bowls and porcelain vases are among the items on offer, while they also sell Andong *soju* (a particularly potent form of the national drink, at 41 percent ABV) in elaborate jars: perfect souvenirs. Daily 10am–9pm.

Millimeter Milligram 밀리미터밀리그람 Itaewonno 240 ☎02 549 1520, ⓦmmmg.net; Hangangjin subway; map p.91. Seoul-based design team making cutesy cups, cutlery, stationery and the like. They have a few branches around the city, but their flagship store is the best, set into a lovely café (see p.119). Daily 11am–9pm.

Mono Collection ⓦmonocollection.com. Online store selling Korean-styled fabrics including curtains, pillowcases

and tablecloths. They occasionally also have an outlet at Incheon airport.

Myung Sin Dang 명신당 Insadonggil 34 ☎02 736 2466; Anguk subway; map p.49. The most renowned of Insadong's many art supplies shops, focusing solely on the humble paintbrush – there are hundreds of styles on offer here, including some made with baby hair. Daily 10am–6pm.

★**Royal Antiques** 로얄 엔틱 Bogwangdong 137-2 ☎02 794 9976, ⓦroyal-antique.com; Itaewon subway; map p.91. Near "Antiques Alley", this is the best place to head if you're hunting for a genuine Joseon-era piece of furniture. The owners are friendly and speak English. Tues–Sun 10am–6pm.

Sangsangmadang 상상마당 Eoulmadangno 65 ☎02 330 6243; Sangsu subway; map p.82. Although Hongdae is better known today for its bars than its art, the university that the area is named after is still artistically focused. This arty complex features a gallery, café and cinema, while the ground floor sells small lifestyle goods designed by local students. Daily 9am–9pm.

★**Ssamiziegil** 쌈지길 Gwanhundong 38; Anguk subway; map p.49. A wonderfully designed building whose spiral walkway plays host to countless small shops selling traditional clothing, handmade paper, jewellery and the like. There's also a rooftop market at weekends, selling all manner of quirky arts and crafts. Daily 10.30am–9pm.

Tongin 통인 가게 Insadonggil 32 ☎02 733 4867, ⓦtonginstore.com; Anguk subway; map p.49. Colonial structure with whole floors full of antique cases, cupboards, medicine racks and other furniture, much of it in a distinctively oriental style; at least one of the proprietors speaks English, and the store can arrange shipping. Daily 10am–8pm.

★**Yido Pottery** 이도 포터리 Changdokgunggil 191 ☎02 722 0756, ⓦyido.kr; Anguk subway; map p.38.

13

Just up the road from Kwang Ju Yo (see p.133), this pottery store is perhaps even more interesting. Here you'll find tea sets, plates and other great offerings from some of the country's top talents, many of whom learned their craft at Hongdae. Daily 10am–7pm.

BOOKS

Most of Seoul's larger bookshops have dedicated English-language sections stocked with novels, history books and language study-guides for those studying Korean or teaching English. There are also a couple of smaller specialist foreign-language stockists in Itaewon.

Bandi & Luni 반디 앤 루니 Jongno Tower B2, Jongno 2-ga 6 ☎02 2198 3000; Jonggak subway; map p.49. Large underground bookshop on the second basement level of Jongno Tower, with a fairly sizeable dedicated English-language section. Daily 9.30am–10pm.

Foreign Book Store 외국 서점 Itaewon 2-dong 533 ☎02 793 8249; Noksapyeong subway; map p.91. A rambling affair, and pleasingly messy, selling a selection of mostly secondhand books. Stick around a while and you're bound to find a gem or two, remnants of decades' worth of Itaewon expats. Daily 10am–9pm.

Hank's Bookstore 서울 셀렉션 Sagandong 10-2 ☎02 734 9565, ⓦseoulselection.com; Anguk subway; map p.38. Small, friendly shop run by the team behind *Seoul* magazine (see p.25), this is particularly good for English-language books about Korean culture. Mon–Sat 9.30am–6.30pm.

Kyobo Books 교보 문고 Kyobo Building B1, Jongno 1 ☎1544 1900; Gwanghwamun subway; map p.56. Filling the basement level of the huge Kyobo building, this is the country's largest bookshop, and fantastic for foreign-language books. There's also a branch in Gangnam, just south of Sinnonhyeon station. Daily 9.30am–10pm.

★**What the Book** 오오오 Itaewon 1-dong ☎02 797 2342, ⓦwhatthebook.com; Noksapyeong subway; map p.91. Dedicated foreign-language bookshop that's extremely popular with expats; everyone seems to end up here at some point. They've an extensive secondhand selection, and the country's best range of guidebooks, including many a *Rough Guide*. Daily 9.30am–9pm.

Youngpoong 영풍 Cheonggyecheonno 41 ☎02 399 5600; Jonggak subway; map p.49. The runt of the litter around Jonggak station, at least in foreign-language terms, but the selection is still fairly good. Daily 9.30am–10pm.

CAMERAS AND ELECTRONIC EQUIPMENT

Korea may be one of the world's most innovative producers of electronic goods, but the prices of such goods and the range on offer here are little different to most Western countries. You can take a peek at futuristic mobile phone designs at the fascinating Samsung D'light showroom in Gangnam (see p.97) or head to the streets south of Chungmuro station for used camera equipment: some shop owners here speak some English, too.

Techno Mart 테크노 마트 Cheongparo 125; Gangbyeon subway; map pp.6–7. Out near the Dongseoul bus terminal in eastern Seoul, this is a gigantic place stocking all manner of electronic goods. Prices are generally about twenty percent less than elsewhere in the country, though this can rise to fifty percent for imported goods. Daily 10am–7pm.

Yongsan Electronics Market 용산 전자 상가 Cheongparo 125; Yongsan subway; map p.91. This multi-level giant rises up alongside the Yongsan train station. Many staff speak a little English, and it's a great place just to look around, even if you're not buying. It's a bit more expensive than Techno Mart for some goods. Daily 10am–7.30pm.

TOP 10 SHOPPING PICKS

Seoul has an almost bewildering range of shopping possibilities, but since the city specializes in certain products, it may be best to put these on top of your list of priorities. Here are the best places to shop in each category:

Antique furniture Royal Antiques (see p.133)
Contemporary hanbok Lee Young Hee (see opposite)
Paintbrushes Myung Sin Dang (see p.133)
Hangeul-character ties Lee Geon Maan (see opposite)
Ladies' shoes Suecomma Bonnie (see opposite)

Oriental fabrics Mono Collection (see p.133)
Pottery Kwang Ju Yo (see p.133) or Yido (see p.133)
Tailored shirts Hamilton Shirts (see opposite)
Tailored suits Hahn's Custom Tailoring (see opposite)
Vintage clothing Gwangjang Market (see opposite)

CLOTHING

The city's department stores (see p.136) sell a wide range of largely expensive clothing, from both local and international brands. Apgujeong has the country's grandest such stores, as well as a parade of brand-name flagship shops such as Gucci, Prada and Louis Vuitton; there is also a clutch of boutique stores around nearby Dosan Park. The Hongdae area is full of cheaper clothing boutiques, though many cater for women only; oddly, men will find richer pickings outside Ewha Women's University, just down the road. Finally, the narrow lanes around Samcheongdonggil are home to a number of small clothing shops that span the full range from budget to designer. Itaewon is popular with foreign businessmen, so most shopkeepers can speak a little English: here you can get all sorts of things, including leather shoes and jackets, tailored suits and fake watches. Outside Itaewon, foreigners should note that sizes tend to be on the small side, particularly around the hips for females. Most upper-body wear is sold as small, medium and large (with a couple of extras on each side), while for waistlines a confusing mishmash of systems is employed; the American system is most common. Footwear is a different matter, with sizes almost exclusively in millimetres.

8Seconds 8세콘드 Sinsadong 535-12 ☎ 070 7090 1144; Sinsa subway; map p.94. Korea's closest answer to H&M, with striking yet affordable clothing. The flagship store is just off trendy Garosugil. Daily 10.30am–10pm.

Babo Shirts ⓦ baboshirts.com. This foreign-run online store has made money selling Koreans their own alphabet: their occasionally ironic T-shirt slogans have proven popular with locals and expats alike. Figure on around W20,000 per shirt-shaped slice of sarcasm.

Ccomaque 꼬마 Bukchonno 5-gil 25 ☎ 02 722 1547, ⓦ ccomaque.com; Itaewon subway; map p.38. Skirts and dresses featuring cutesey, cartoonish designs based around purportedly Korean motifs, including animals such as deer, turtles and cranes, and natural elements such as clouds and pine trees. Daily 10am–8pm.

Euijiro Tunnel 을지로 지하상가; map p.64. A trip back in time, this tunnel's shops have been serving the same people since the 1970s, and as such are a great place to head for a rare piece of retro Korea (see box, p.66). The tunnel stretches for several kilometres between City Hall and Dongdaemun History & Culture Park station, and has entrances every 50m or so. Many shops open from daybreak till midnight.

Gwangjang Market 광장시장; Jongno 5-ga subway; map p.64. Though best known for its culinary offerings (see p.113), this sprawling market has an excellent secondhand section, selling all manner of zany shirts, coats and jackets imported from abroad. It's a little hard to find: hunt down the staircase on the western side of the market, and head for the second floor. Mon–Sat 9am–6pm.

★ **Hahn's Custom Tailoring** 한스 양복 Itaewondong 34-16 ☎ 02 793 0830, ✉ hanstailor@hotmail.com; Itaewon subway; map p.91. Get a perfectly tailored suit for around US$500. Affable owner Hahn speaks excellent English, and will be pleased to discuss the particular style you're after; his tailors also make good shirts. Daily 10am–9pm.

Hamilton Shirts 해밀튼 셔츠 Hannam 2-dong 736-9 ☎ 02 798 5693, ⓦ hs76.com; Itaewon subway; map p.91. Tailored shirts at prices less than you'd pay for factory-made fare on your local high street: most shirts go for around W45,000. The quality is amazingly high for the price. Daily 10am–9.30pm.

★ **Lee Geon Maan** 이건만 Insadonggil 29 ☎ 02 733 8265, ⓦ leegeonmaan.com; Anguk subway; map p.49. Well-located store selling ties for men and handbags for women. Their unique selling point is an innovative use of *hangeul*, the Korean text conspicuous by its absence on Korean clothing. Daily 10.30am–8pm.

★ **Lee Young Hee** 오오오 Sinsadong 665-5 ☎ 02 544 0630, ⓦ leeyounghee.co.kr; Apgujeong subway; map p.94. Korea's traditional clothing, *hanbok* (한복), is alright to wear for a photo-shoot, but since it looks a little ridiculous on foreigners, few of them would actually go out and buy the stuff. This store sells striking contemporary versions of the style, and counts Hillary Clinton as a customer at their New York branch. Daily 11am–6.30pm.

Nohke 노케 Cheongdamdong 96-14 ☎ 02 517 4875, ⓦ nohke.com; Apgujeong subway; map p.94. Small local boutique selling futuristic feminine designs; the coats here are particularly striking. Although still young, designer Misun Jung has made clothing for several major Korean singers and models. Daily 11am–7.30pm.

Space Mue 스페이스 뮤 Cheongdamdong 93-6 ☎ 02 3446 8074; Apgujeong subway; map p.94. This Apgujeong multishop (a Konglish term for a store selling various brands) sells clothing from upmarket international brands, but even if you can't afford to spend US$100 on a T-shirt it's worth popping into for the gorgeous interior alone, its hexagonal motif making it look something like a futuristic beehive. Daily 11am–8pm.

Style Nanda 스타일 난다 Wausanno 29-gil 23 ☎ 02 333 9215; Hongik University subway; map p.82. From humble beginnings as an online retailer of secondhand clothes, this has become one of Korea's most famous youth labels – this three-storey flagship store has singlehandedly raised rent prices in the area. Daily 11am–11pm.

Suecomma Bonnie 슈콤마보니 Cheongdamdong 20-2 ☎ 02 3443 0217, ⓦ suecommabonnie.com; Apgujeong subway; map p.94. Superb ladies' footwear made by local diva Bonnie Lee. If her designs were good enough for *Sex and the City*, they're good enough for you. Daily 10am–7pm.

13

DEPARTMENT STORES AND MALLS

Department stores can be found all over the city, and most of them are pretty similar, with a wide range of cosmetics on their ground floor, level after level of clothing above, and usually a food court on top. Beware, though; as soon as you even look at an item of clothing, a grinning attendant in uniform will race up to you, invading your personal space until you try something on or leave. The bustling streets of Myeongdong host stores from the biggest nationwide chains – Migliore, Shinsaegae, Lotte and Galleria – and there are also luxury examples in Apgujeong. Given the prevalence of department stores, it's perhaps not much of a surprise that, bar the two examples listed below, mall culture has yet to truly permeate the Korean shopping scene.

Coex 코엑스 Samseongdong 159 ☎ 02 6000 0114; Samseong subway; map p.94. A huge underground shopping mall featuring a neat aquarium (see p.98), and all manner of local and international chain shops. Daily 10am–10pm.

Galleria 갤러리아 Apgujeongno 343 ☎ 02 3449 4114; Apgujeong subway; map p.94. The country's most exclusive department store, this is arranged in two buildings facing each other across a major road. The artistically designed west wing features a range of local designers, while the even more expensive east wing is home to international mega-labels. Daily 10.30am–8.30pm.

Hyundai 현대 Apgujeongdong 429 ☎ 02 547 2233; Apgujeong subway; map p.94. Nowhere near as exclusive as Galleria down the road, this is a better hunting ground for clothing from local designers – particularly recommended are Solidhomme for men, Son Jung Wan for women, and Andy & Debb for both. Daily 10.30am–8.30pm.

Lotte 롯데 Namdaemunno 81 ☎ 02 771 2500; Euljiro 1-ga subway; map p.64. Huge, slightly faceless department store popular with expats thanks to its well-stocked supermarket, located in the basement. Daily 10.30am–8pm.

Shinsegae 신세계 Sogongno 63 ☎ 1588 1234; Myeongdong subway; map p.64. Designed in the 1930s as a branch of the Japanese Mitsukoshi chain, this was Korea's first department store. Goods from luxury clothing and jewellery brands can be found inside, while the exterior of the old wing is quite charming at night, and extremely striking around Christmas. Daily 11am–8.30pm.

Times Square 타임스퀘어 Yeongdeungpodong 4-ga 442 ☎ 02 2638 2000; Yeongdeungpo subway; map pp.6–7. More of a Western-style mall than Coex (see above), this is a large, attractive space filled with all the chains you'd expect – the signage is dreadful, however, and it's an annoying walk from the subway station. Daily 10.30am–10pm.

MARKETS

Seoul has a quite phenomenal number of outdoor markets – there will be one within walking distance wherever you are, with the *kimchi* and fish products on offer making it possible to follow your nose. As well as a range of food, each market will also have a clothing section, with fake designer goods a particular speciality. The largest and most central markets are Dongdaemun (see p.69) and Namdaemun (see p.61), though the fish market at Noryangjin (see p.88) deserves a special mention, as does Gwangjang market (see p.69), an offshoot of the mammoth Dongdaemun complex. Though far smaller, there's also an interesting weekly flea market at Nolita Park in Hongdae (see p.84). Markets are the only places in Seoul where haggling is practised.

GRANDMOTHER TECHNO

While modern K-pop has swept across continental Asia, there are a couple of local strains of music that you may well come across on your way around Seoul: "**bongjak**" songs, fast-paced electronic ditties set to odd synthesized rhythms, and best described as a kind of grandmother techno; and "**trot**", slower (but still fast-paced) ballads, crooned out in a semi-compulsory warbly voice. *Bongjak* has been around since the 1970s, and remains hugely popular with Korea's older set, as anyone who's seen a clutch of grannies getting down to the beats will testify. *Trot* has its roots in the 1930s, but ironically this style is not the sole preserve of the elderly, and is unlikely to go out of fashion for some time – you'll find university students belting hits out in *noraebang* (Korean karaoke dens) and kids listening to them on tape, while young artists such as Jang Yoon-jeong have scored big by crossing the genre with the ballads that younger Koreans tend to prefer. Ubiquitous cabaret shows mean that *trot* is rarely off the television, and you can buy CDs (or, more commonly, tapes) at music shops across Seoul – the area around exit 12 of Jongno 3-ga is the best place to head.

MUSIC

13

The Korean music scene may be flooded with K-pop and local hip-hop, but there are a few shops dotted around Seoul that dare to venture underground. Mainstream fare can be found at one of the large bookstores (see p.134).

Nagwon Arcade 낙원 상가 Nagwondong 284-6; Jongno 3-ga subway; map p.49. If you want to play music rather than listen to it, head straight to this large arcade in Insadong, where more than a hundred small shops sell musical instruments. With customers and shop owners alike testing the products, this pleasantly crusty building can be quite atmospheric – and you can get a super-budget meal in the basement. Daily 9am–8pm.

Purple Record 퍼플 레코드 Seogyodong 343-5 ☎ 02 336 3023; Sangsu subway; map p.82. The best selection of foreign independent music in Korea, and a happy hunting ground for the works of local artists; a thoroughly pleasant place to hang out and sift through records. Daily 10am–11pm.

TAEKWONDO

Sports and health

Most Korean spectator sports will be familiar to Westerners, since martial arts are primarily active rather than passive affairs, and the local spectator sport – *ssireum*, a form of wrestling – can only really be seen during the Dano festival (see p.26). Sporty types can get their kicks with taekwondo, baseball, football, golf and rugby among the range of activities on offer. In warmer months it's possible to have a dip in one of several outdoor swimming pools or rent a bike; the Han-side banks of Yeouido are the best places for both (see box, p.87). Additionally, you'll find pool tables in many of Itaewon's foreigner bars, usually free to use. More common are pool halls that cater to four-ball, a pocketless version of the game so popular in Korea that live matches are regularly broadcast on television.

BASEBALL

Pro baseball Seoul has three main professional teams. The two biggest are the LG Twins and the Doosan Bears, long-time rivals who both play in Jamsil Baseball Stadium (Sports Complex subway); the Nexen Heroes are a newer team playing west of Yeouido in Mokdong (Omokgyo subway). Games take place most days from April to October, and tickets can cost as little as W5000, though they are often sold out during the playoffs.

Batting cages Avid players can get some practice at a number of batting nets dotted around the city, particularly in the student areas; these cost just W1000 for a minute's worth of balls. One is marked on the Insadong map (see p.49).

BOWLING

Pierrot Strike 삐에로 스트라이크 Cheongdamdong 86-4 ☎ 02 6007 8889; Apgujeong Rodeo subway; map p.94. Although bowling has not permeated Korean society as much as other American sports, there are a few alleys around the city – this is the most notable one, with a snazzily futuristic interior. Prices here are about average for the activity in Seoul – W5000 per person, per game.

14

FOOTBALL

K-League Those wanting to watch some professional K-League action can catch FC Seoul at the World Cup Stadium (ⓦ fcseoul.com; tickets from W10,000), with games taking place at weekends from March to October. Seongnam and Suwon, two of the most dominant Korean teams of recent times, also play near Seoul; the atmosphere at all grounds is fun but they can be on the empty side, unless you're lucky enough to be around for a major international game (ⓦ fifa.com).

Seoul Sunday League If you prefer to play rather than watch, you can try your luck with the highly competitive Seoul Sunday Football League (ⓦ ssflkorea.org); this has been in operation for a number of years, and most of the competing teams are based in or around Seoul, though as the standard is quite high you'll have to be a decent player to get a regular game.

GOLF

Korean golf courses are among the most expensive in the world – so much so that many local golfers visit Japan to *save* money. In addition, the courses around Seoul usually require membership – it's almost impossible to organize this independently, so any action is best arranged by your accommodation or a tourist office (see p.35).

Driving ranges You can keep your swing in shape at one of the many small driving ranges dotted around Seoul – look for the buildings topped with green nets. These are cheap at around W10,000 for an hour, and clubs can be borrowed for free.

Pro tournaments It's possible to watch the professionals in action near Seoul: an event on the men's OneAsia Tour, the Korea Open (ⓦ koreaopen.com) is held each September on the Woo Jeong Hills course, near the satellite city of Cheonan. This event has been growing in size and importance, and recent years have seen top golfers such as Vijay Singh, Sergio Garcia and Rickie Fowler lifting the trophy.

ICE-SKATING

Ice rinks In winter you can skate outdoors at various places in the city: Seoul Plaza (see p.61) and Gwanghwamun Plaza (see p.57) often turn into gigantic ice rinks for the season (usually Dec–Feb; daily 10am–10pm; W1000), though skaters are turfed off every 15 minutes or so for surfacing. There's also a year-round rink in Lotte World (see p.98), which charges W15,000 for entry and skate rental (daily 10am–9.30pm); far cheaper is the Olympic-size rink at Korea National University (daily 2–6pm; W5000), which is within walking distance of Korea University subway station.

RUGBY

Seoul Survivors RFC Although it's a minority sport in Korea, rugby players can keep in shape by training with Seoul Survivors RFC (ⓦ facebook.com/seoulsurvivors), an expat squad who practise most weeks. They take part in a few competitions in Korea, and make occasional international tours, including an annual pilgrimage to a 10s tournament in the Philippines. You'll likely need to be living in Seoul if you want to take part in the matches themselves, but they welcome casual visitors to their practice sessions.

SKIING

Winter sport fanatics will be in their element in Korea, which is hosting the Winter Olympics in 2018. The Games will take place near the east-coast town of Pyeongchang, but there are also a number of good resorts in the wider Seoul area. Prices are generally quite uniform, with packages available for ski trips of a day, multi-day, afternoon, night, day-and-night, and more. In general, you'll be able to get a good day's skiing for W50,000; ski/board rental will cost around W25,000, and all courses also offer instruction for beginners and children. The season usually runs from November to March, with artificial snow augmenting the real stuff in the shoulder periods.

Bears Town (🌐bearstown.com). An excellent major ski resort located to the northeast of Seoul, with ten slopes and good facilities for everyone from beginners to experts. In season, it's accessible via a free shuttle bus from Gangbyeon station (line 2).

Starhill (🌐starhillresort.com). You can be skiing in no time at this resort in the Cheonmasan mountain range, which lies just 32km from central Seoul. Buses from Cheongnyangni (line 1) and Jamsil (line 2) stations.

SWIMMING

Indoor pools Unless you're staying at a higher-end hotel or serviced apartment, you may find it tricky to get a swim in Seoul; the outdoor pool at the *Grand Hyatt* hotel (see p.107) is the easiest to sneak into. Municipal pools do exist in most parts of the city, but are often far out of the centre; ask at a tourist office (see p.35) to track down the one closest to you.

Outdoor pools In summer (usually June-August), a number of outdoor pools open up around the Hangang (see box, p.87); most convenient for visitors are those on the western side of Yeouido park (daily 9am–6pm; W5000). The *Hamilton Hotel* (see p.107) also opens its rooftop pool to non-residents during the summer months (daily 9am–6pm; W22,000).

TAEKWONDO

There are a number of places where foreign visitors can watch, or have a go at, this Korean martial art. The best place is Namsangol Hanok Village (see p.66), which puts on free performances every day bar Tuesday, and in summer often runs hands-on programmes for people to try themselves. Tourist information offices (see p.35) can advise on these as well as organizing longer programmes: figure on around W50,000 per day. In addition, there are occasional performances and tournaments at Kukkiwon (Mon–Fri 9am–5pm; free), a hall near Gangnam station and the home of Korea's national sport.

TENNIS

The Korean Open (🌐kiakoreaopen.com), a WTA event, is held at Seoul Olympic Park every September. This is a fairly major event on the women's calendar, and past winners have included Venus Williams, Maria Sharapova and Caroline Wozniacki. The few public courts around the city are members-only affairs, though it may be possible to get a game at some high-school courts (after classes have finished, of course).

SPAS AND MASSAGE

Spa culture has well and truly hit Seoul, with an ever-increasing number of world-class facilities sprouting up around the city. Most of the top hotels have a resident spa, while others are affiliated to major cosmetics brands.

Amore Spa 아모레 스파 Avenuel Building, Namdaemunno 2-ga 130 ☎02 2118 6221; Euljiro 1-ga subway; map p.64. No Korean cosmetics brand enjoys

as much global fame as Amore Pacific, who use Eastern elements such as ginseng, green tea and bamboo sap in their products. They're best enjoyed at the company's

---

TAEKWONDO

The martial art of **taekwondo** (태권도) is Korea's best-known cultural export to the wider world. It has its roots in the Three Kingdoms period (57 BC–668 AD), when several different forms of unarmed combat existed across the peninsula. Local martial arts faded away during the philosophical Confucianist heyday of the Joseon kingdom (1392–1910), and came close to extinction during the subsequent period of Japanese occupation (1910–45), when attempts were made at a systematic annihilation of Korean culture. Taekwondo only truly came into existence in 1955, at the close of the Korean War: short on money and equipment, the local military used martial arts as a cheap way of keeping soldiers fit, and lassoed together what remained of the dynastic styles – it is still used as an integral part of military training to this day. Taekwondo has since become a staple martial art around the world, with official organizations in more than one hundred countries. It was introduced as a demonstration sport at the **Seoul Olympics** of 1988, and became a medal event in 2000.

MEDICAL TOURISM

As strange as it may sound, **medical tourism** has been one of Seoul's biggest growth industries in recent years. The majority of customers hail from other Asian countries, and visit Korea to take advantage of Apgujeong's seemingly infinite number of plastic surgery clinics. It's not only aesthestic treatments that are on the rise; the price of **hospital care** in Korea is much lower than in most other developed countries, and in many cases the waiting time is minimal. The most popular clinic with foreigners is the Jaseng centre (ⓦjaseng.net) in Apgujeong, which specializes in spine and joint problems and uses a combination of Eastern and Western treatments. Though far from cheap, their services attract hundreds of foreigners each month, many of whom fly into Seoul especially for this purpose. For more on-the-ground recommendations, contact the **Medical Tourism Information Centre** (ⓣ02 752 2104), at the KTO Tourist Information Center, near Cheonggyecheon (see p.35), or at their desk at Incheon Airport.

14

renowned spa, located on the tenth floor of the huge Lotte complex; facials start at around W120,000, and it's at least double that for full-body treatments.

Dragon Hill Spa 드래곤힐 스파 Hangangno 3-ga 40 ⓣ02 792 0001, ⓦdragonhillspa.co.kr; Yongsan subway; map p.91. Abutting Yongsan station, this is more of an oversized *jjimjilbang* (see p.107) than a spa, but you'll find spa-like facilities – including Thai massage, and skin- and bodycare programmes – in the grounds of this vast complex.

Guerlain Spa 겔랑 스파 Donghoro 249 ⓣ02 2233 3131, ⓦguerlainspa.com; Dongguk University subway;

map p.64. Have your tootsies pampered while enjoying a mountain view in this elegant spa, tucked away inside the *Shilla* hotel (see p.106). Treatments range from simple hour-long facials (from W165,000) to full-day packages (from W900,000).

Healing Hands 힐링 핸드 Itaewondong 124-7 ⓣ010 3158 5572, ⓦhealinghands.co.kr; Cheongdamdong subway; map p.91. Overlooking Itaewon's main drag, this is a decent enough massage parlour, though occasional weird stories – and sounds – come out of its booths. A one-hour full-body massage will set you back around W70,000, or W40,000 for a foot massage alone.

FARMERS' DANCE AT THE KOREAN FOLK VILLAGE

Around Seoul

There's no reason for your trip to begin and end with the city centre, since there's a wonderful array of sights within easy day-tripping range of the capital. Most popular is a visit to the Demilitarized Zone (DMZ) separating North and South Korea, a 4km-wide buffer zone often described as one of the most dangerous places on Earth. It's even possible to step across the border here, in the infamous Joint Security Area. The DMZ forms the northern boundary of Gyeonggi (경기), a province that encircles Seoul. This is one of the world's most densely populated areas – including the capital, over 25 million people live here.

Most cities here are commuter-filled nonentities, but a couple are worthy of a visit. **Incheon**, to the west of Seoul, was the first city in the country to be opened up to international trade, and remains Korea's most important link with the outside world thanks to its hub airport and ferry terminals. It sits on the shores of the West Sea, which contains myriad tranquil **islands**. Heading south of Seoul you come to **Suwon**, home to a renowned fortress, and useful as a springboard to several nearby sights. Further south again is the small city of **Gongju**, now a sleepy place but once capital of the famed Baekje dynasty.

The Demilitarized Zone

As you head slowly north out of Seoul through the traffic, the seemingly endless urban jungle gradually diminishes in size before disappearing altogether. You're now well on the way to a place where the mists of the Cold War still linger, and one that

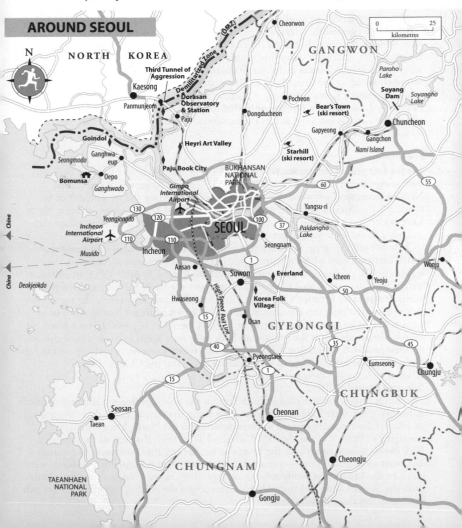

BEST OF AROUND SEOUL

The DMZ Walk through a tunnel beneath the world's most heavily fortified border, or take a couple of steps into official North Korean territory in the eerie Joint Security Area. See opposite

Incheon Gaze out over the Lego-like jumble of container ships surrounding this city, before filling your stomach at Korea's largest Chinatown. See p.149

West Sea islands It's hard to believe that the clean air, homely villages and thriving fishing industry of these peaceful islands can be easily visited on a day-trip from Seoul. See p.152

Suwon Scramble up a UNESCO-listed fortress wall, and watch the colourful ceremonies and dancing at a nearby folk village. See p.154

Yangsu-ri Seoul's best sunsets can be found east of the city centre, on this charming, mountain-surrounded island. See p.157

15

could well have been ground zero for the Third World War – the **DEMILITARIZED ZONE**. More commonly referred to as "the DMZ", this no man's land is a 4km-wide buffer zone that came into being at the end of the Korean War in 1953. It sketches an unbroken spiky line across the peninsula from coast to coast, separating the two Koreas and their diametrically opposed ideologies. Although it sounds forbidding, it's actually possible to enter this zone, and take a few tentative steps into North Korean territory – thousands of civilians do so every month, though only as part of a **tightly controlled tour**. Elsewhere are a few platforms from which the curious can stare across the border, and a **tunnel** built by the North, which you can enter.

Brief history

For the first year of the **Korean War** (1950–53), the tide of control yo-yoed back and forth across the peninsula. Then in June 1951, General Ridgeway of the United Nations Command got word that the Korean People's Army (KPA) would "not be averse to" armistice talks. These took place in the city of Kaesong, now a major North Korean city, but were soon shifted south to **Panmunjeom**, a tiny farming village that suddenly found itself the subject of international attention.

Cease-fire talks went on for two long years and often degenerated into venomous verbal battles littered with expletives. One of the most contentious issues was the repatriation of prisoners of war, and a breakthrough came in April 1953, when terms were agreed; exchanges took place on a bridge over the River Sachon, now referred to as the **Bridge of No Return**. "Operation Little Switch" came first, seeing the transfer of sick and injured prisoners (notably, six thousand returned to the North, while only a tenth of that number walked the other way); "Operation Big Switch" took place shortly afterwards, when the soldiers on both sides were asked to make a final choice on their preferred destination. Though no **peace treaty** was ever signed, representatives of the KPA, the United Nations Command (UNC) and the Chinese People's Liberation Army put their names to an **armistice** on July 27, 1953; South Korean delegates refused to do so.

An uneasy truce has prevailed since the end of the war – the longest military deadlock in history – but there have been regular spats along the way. In the early 1960s a small number of disaffected American soldiers **defected** to the North, after somehow managing to make it across the DMZ alive, while in 1968 the crew of the captured USS *Pueblo* walked south over the Bridge of No Return after protracted negotiations. The most serious confrontation took place in 1976, when two American soldiers were killed in the **Axe Murder Incident** (see box opposite), and in 1984, a young tour leader from the Soviet Union fled from North Korea across the border, triggering a short gun battle that left three soldiers dead.

THE AXE MURDER INCIDENT AND OPERATION PAUL BUNYAN

Relations between the two Koreas took a sharp nose dive in 1976, when two American soldiers were killed by axe-wielding North Korean soldiers because of a **poplar tree** which stood next to the Bridge of No Return: there was a UNC outpost beside the bridge, but its direct line of sight to the next Allied checkpoint was blocked by the leaves of the tree, so on August 18 a five-man American detail was dispatched to perform some trimming. Nobody is quite sure how this military gardening descended into violence, since both sides claim to have acted in self-defence; the American story is accepted in the West, though the key moments are missing from their video of the incident. Whoever made the first attack, KPA troops were soon attacking UNC personnel, in some cases using the axes the team had been using to prune the tree. The attack lasted less than a minute, but claimed the life of First Lieutenant Mark Barrett, as well as Captain Bonifas, who was apparently killed instantly with a single karate chop to the neck (one of the few facts that both sides agree on).

Three days later, the US launched **Operation Paul Bunyan**, with a convoy of two dozen UNC vehicles streaming towards the poplar tree, carrying more than eight hundred men, some trained in taekwondo, and all armed to the teeth. These were backed up by attack helicopters, fighter planes and B-52 bombers, while an aircraft carrier had also been stationed just off the Korean shore. This carefully managed operation drew no response from the KPA, and the tree was successfully cut down.

15

The Joint Security Area

"The visit to the Joint Security Area at Panmunjeom will entail entry into a hostile area, and possible injury or death as a direct result of enemy action"   Disclaimer from form issued to visitors by United Nations Command

There's nowhere in the world quite like the **Joint Security Area** ("the JSA"), a settlement squatting in the middle of Earth's most heavily fortified frontier, and the only place in DMZ territory where visitors are permitted. Visits here will create a curious dichotomy of feelings: on the one hand, you'll be in what was once memorably described by Bill Clinton as "the scariest place on Earth", but on the other hand as well as soldiers, barbed wire and brutalist buildings you'll see trees, hear birdsong and smell fresh air. The only way to get into the JSA is on a guided tour (see p.146), which takes you to the village of **Panmunjeom** (판문점) in jointly held territory – though this has dwindled to almost nothing since it hosted the armistice talks in 1951 (see opposite).

Once inside the JSA, you'll see seven buildings at the centre of the complex, three of which are **meeting rooms**. If you are lucky, you'll be allowed to enter one of these to

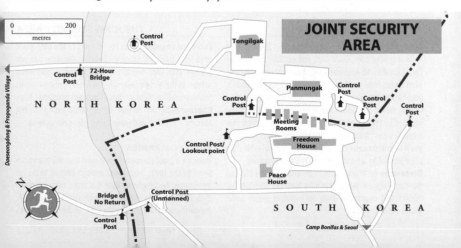

DAESEONGDONG AND "PROPAGANDA VILLAGE"

The DMZ is home to two small settlements, one on each side of the Line of Control. With the southern village rich and tidy and its northern counterpart empty and sinister, both can be viewed as a microcosm of the countries they belong to.

The southern village – **Daeseongdong** (대성동) – is a small farming community, but one off-limits to all but those living or working here. These are among the richest farmers in Korea: they pay no rent or tax, and DMZ produce fetches big bucks at markets around the country. Technically, residents have to spend 240 days of the year at home, but most commute here from their condos in Seoul to "punch in", and get hired hands to do the dirty work; if they're staying, they must be back in town by nightfall, and have their doors and windows locked and bolted by midnight. Women are allowed to marry into this tight society, but men are not; those who choose to raise their children here also benefit from a school that at the last count had twelve teachers, and only eight students.

North of the line of control is **Kijongdong** (기정동), an odd collection of empty buildings referred to by American soldiers as "**Propaganda Village**". The purpose of its creation appears to have been to show citizens in the South the communist paradise that they're missing – a few dozen "villagers" arrive every morning by bus, spend the day taking part in wholesome activities and letting their children play games, then leave again in the evening. With the aid of binoculars, you'll be able to see that none of the buildings actually has any windows; lights turned on in the evening also seem to suggest that they're devoid of floors. Above the village flies a huge North Korean flag, so large that it required a fifty-man detail to hoist, until the recent installation of a motor. It sits atop a 160m-high flagpole, the world's tallest, and the eventual victor in a bizarre contest between the two Koreas, each hell-bent on having the loftier flag.

earn some serious travel kudos – the chance to step into North Korea. The official Line of Control runs through the centre of these cabins, the corners of which are guarded by South Korean soldiers, who are sometimes joined by their Northern counterparts, the enemies almost eyeball to eyeball. Note the microphones on the table inside the room – anything you say can be picked up by North Korean personnel. The rooms are closed to visitors when meetings are scheduled.

From a **lookout point** outside the cabins you can soak up views of the North, including the huge flag and shell-like buildings of **Propaganda Village** (see box above). You may also be able to make out the jamming towers it uses to keep out unwanted imperialist signals – check the reception on your phone. Closer to the lookout point, within JSA territory, the **Bridge of No Return** was the venue for POW exchange at the end of the Korean War (see p.144), and also for James Bond in *Die Another Day* – though for obvious reasons it was filmed elsewhere.

ARRIVAL AND DEPARTURE

Guided tours The only way to visit the Joint Security Area is on a guided tour. Tours start just outside the DMZ at Camp Bonifas, an American army base just over an hour from Seoul. Here you'll meet your guides (usually young, amiable recruits from the infantry), and be given a briefing session telling you about a number of restrictions, most imposed by the United Nations Command. Be warned that schedules can change in an instant, and remember that you'll be entering an extremely dangerous area – this is no place for fooling around or wandering off by yourself.

Dress code An official dress code applies in the JSA (no flip-flops, ripped jeans, "clothing deemed faddish" or "shorts that expose the buttocks"), but in reality most things are OK.

THE JOINT SECURITY AREA

Entrance requirements For all tours to the DMZ you'll need your passport. Citizens of certain countries are not allowed into DMZ territory, including those from most nations in the Middle East, some in Africa, and communist territories such as Vietnam, Hong Kong and mainland China.

Photography In certain areas photography is not allowed – you'll be told when to put your camera away.

TOUR COMPANIES

There are a great number of companies that sell tours from Seoul to the DMZ; most speak enough English to accept reservations by telephone. Note that some tours are much cheaper than others – these probably won't visit the JSA, the most interesting place in the DMZ, so check to see if it's

FROM TOP THE DMZ (P.143); GANGHWADO (P.152) >

15

15

on the schedule: expect to pay around W77,000 to include the JSA. Most tours also include lunch. We've listed a couple of recommended operators below, but you'll find pamphlets from other companies in your hotel lobby.
Panmunjom Travel Center ☎ 02 771 5593, ⓦ korea dmztour.com. Offers the regular tour, plus a session with a North Korean defector willing to answer questions about

life on the other side. Runs from the *Lotte Hotel*, near Euljiro 1-ga subway (line 2). W77,000
★**USO** ☎ 02 6383 2570, ⓦ koridoor.co.kr. Run in conjunction with the American military, these are the best tours to go for, and include a 20min presentation by a US soldier in Camp Bonifas. Book at least four days in advance. Runs from Camp Kim near Namyeong subway (line 1). $80

The Third Tunnel of Aggression

제3땅굴 • Only accessible as part of a tour (see p.146)

A short drive south of Panmunjeom, the **Third Tunnel of Aggression** is one of four tunnels dug under the DMZ by North Korean soldiers in apparent preparation for an invasion of the South. North Korea has denied responsibility, claiming them to be coal mines (though they are strangely devoid of coal), but to be on the safe side the border area is now monitored from coast to coast by soldiers equipped with drills and sensors. The tunnel was discovered in 1974 by a South Korean army patrol unit; tip-offs from North Korean defectors and some strategic drilling soon led to the discovery of another two tunnels, and a fourth was found in 1990. The third tunnel is the closest to Seoul, which would have been just a day's march away if the North's invasion plan had succeeded.

Many visitors emerge from the depths underwhelmed – it is, after all, only a tunnel, even if you get to walk under **DMZ territory** up to the Line of Control that marks the actual border. On busy days it can become uncomfortably crowded – not a place for the claustrophobic.

Dorasan observatory and station

도라전망대 • Observatory Tues–Sun 10am–5pm • Free • Light-rail from Seoul station to Dorasan station, at the end of the Gyeongui line, or "DMZ Train" from Seoul station (departs Seoul at 8.30am & 1.15pm, returns at 12.10pm & 5.30pm; Tues–Fri W8700; Sat & Sun W8900)

South of the Third Tunnel is **Dorasan observatory**, from where visitors can stare at the North through binoculars. The observatory is included on many DMZ tours (see p.146), but unlike the JSA you can also visit independently.

The gleaming, modern **Dorasan station** was built in early 2007 at the end of the Gyeonghui light-rail line. The line continues to China, via Pyongyang: as one sign says, "it's not the last station from the South, but the first station toward the North". In May 2007, the first train in decades rumbled up the track to Kaesong in North Korea (another went in the opposite direction on the east-coast line), while regular freight services started in December. Such connections were soon cut, but there remains hope that this track will one day handle high-speed services from Seoul to Pyongyang; in the meantime, a map on the wall shows which parts of the world Seoul will be connected to should the line ever see regular service, and there's a much-photographed sign pointing to Pyongyang.

Paju and around

파주

The Seoul satellite city of **PAJU** contains some of the most interesting sights in the border area and, for once, they do not revolve solely around North Korea. The **Paju Book City** is a publisher-heavy area more notable for its architecture than anything literary, while the **Heyri Art Valley** is a twee little artistic commune.

Paju Book City

파주 출판도시 문화재단 • ⓦ pajubookcity.org • Bus #200 (every 30min; 1hr) from Hapjeong subway (lines 2 & 6)

Quirky **Paju Book City** is ostensibly a publishing district. Many publishers were encouraged to move here from central Seoul (though a whole glut of smaller printing houses remain in the fascinating alleyways around Euljiro) and most of the major companies based here have **bookstores** on their ground levels. However, the main attraction for visitors is the area's excellent **modern architecture** – quite a rarity in this land of the sterile high-rise. There's no focus as such, but strolling around the quiet streets dotted with great little book cafés is enjoyable.

Heyri Art Valley

헤이리 문화예술마을 • ⓦ heyri.net • Bus #200 (every 30min; 45min) from Hapjeong subway (lines 2 & 6)
Seven kilometres to the north of Paju Book City, similar architectural delights are on offer at **Heyri Art Valley**. This artists' village is home to dozens of small **galleries**, and its countryside air makes it an increasingly popular day-trip for young, arty Seoulites. They come here to shop for paintings or quirky souvenirs, or to sip a latte in one of the complex's several cafés. However, such mass-market appeal means that the atmosphere here in general is more twee than edgy.

Incheon

인천

15

Almost every international visitor to Seoul passes through **INCHEON**, Korea's third most populous city. It's home to the country's main airport and receives all Korea's ferries from China, though most new arrivals head straight on to Seoul as soon as they arrive. However, in view of its colourful recent history, it's worth at least a day-trip from the capital. This was where Korea's "Hermit Kingdom" finally crawled out of self-imposed isolation in the late nineteenth century and opened itself up to international trade, spurred on by the Japanese following similar events in their own country (the "Meiji Restoration"). Incheon was also the landing site for **Douglas MacArthur** and his troops in a manoeuvre that turned the tide of the Korean War (see box, p.150).

Incheon's most interesting district is **Jung-gu**, home to Korea's only official Chinatown and **Jayu Park**, where a statue of MacArthur gazes out over the sea. Downhill from here, you can visit a couple of **former Japanese banks** in a quiet but cosmopolitan part of town, where many Japanese lived during the colonial era. Lastly, Incheon is also a jumping-off point for ferries to a number of islands in the West Sea (see p.152).

Jung-gu

중구 • Incheon subway (line 1)
Jung-gu district lies on the western fringe of Incheon, though it forms the centre of the city's tourist appeal. On exiting the gate at Incheon station, you'll immediately be confronted by the city's gentrified **Chinatown**. Demarcated by the requisite oriental gate, it's a pleasant and surprisingly quiet area to walk around with a belly full of Chinese food.

Jayu Park

자유 공원 • 24hr • Free
Within easy walking distance of the subway station, **Jayu Park** is most notable for its statue of **General Douglas MacArthur**, staring proudly out over the seas that he conquered during the Korean War (see box, p.150). Also in

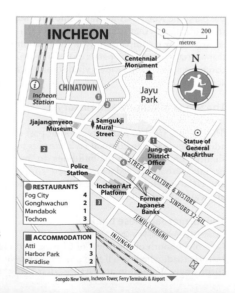

INCHEON

0   200
metres

N

Centennial Monument

ⓘ CHINATOWN
Incheon Station

Jayu Park

Jjajangmyeon Museum

Samgukji Mural Street

Statue of General MacArthur

Jung-gu District Office

Police Station

STREET OF CULTURE & HISTORY

Incheon Art Platform

Former Japanese Banks

SINPORO 32-GIL

JEMULLYANGNO

INJUNGNO

● RESTAURANTS	
Fog City	4
Gonghwachun	2
Mandabok	1
Tochon	3

■ ACCOMMODATION	
Atti	1
Harbor Park	3
Paradise	2

Songdo New Town, Incheon Tower, Ferry Terminals & Airport ▼

GENERAL MACARTHUR AND THE INCHEON LANDINGS

"We drew up a list of every natural and geographic handicap... Incheon had 'em all."

Commander Arlie G. Capps

On the morning of September 15, 1950, the most daring move of the **Korean War** was made, an event that was to alter the course of the conflict entirely, and is now seen as one of the greatest military manoeuvres in history. At this point the Allied forces had been pushed by the North Korean People's Army into a small corner of the peninsula around Busan, but **General Douglas MacArthur** was convinced that a single decisive movement behind enemy lines could be enough to turn the tide.

MacArthur wanted to attempt an amphibious landing on the Incheon coast, but his plan was greeted with scepticism by many of his colleagues – both the South Korean and American armies were severely under-equipped, Incheon was heavily fortified, and its natural island-peppered defences and fast tides made it an even more dangerous choice.

However, the plan went ahead and the Allied forces performed **successful landings** at three Incheon beaches, during which time North Korean forces were shelled heavily to quell any counterattacks. The city was taken with relative ease, the People's Army having not anticipated an attack on this scale in this area, reasoning that if one were to happen, it would take place at a more sensible location further down the coast. MacArthur had correctly deduced that a poor movement of supplies was his enemy's Achilles heel – landing behind enemy lines gave Allied forces a chance to cut the supply line to KPA forces further south, and Seoul was duly retaken on September 25.

Despite the Incheon victory and its consequences, MacArthur is not viewed by Koreans – or, indeed, the world in general – in an entirely positive light, feelings exacerbated by the continued American military presence in the country. While many in Korea venerate the General as a hero, repeated demonstrations have called for the **tearing down** of his statue in Jayu Park, denouncing him as a "war criminal who massacred civilians during the Korean War", and whose statue "greatly injures the dignity of the Korean people". Documents obtained after his eventual dismissal from the Army suggest that he would even have been willing to bring nuclear weapons into play – on December 24, 1950, he requested the shipment of 38 atomic bombs to Korea, intending to string them "across the neck of Manchuria". Douglas MacArthur remains a controversial character, even in death.

the park, the Korean–American **Centennial Monument** is made up of eight black triangular shards that stretch up towards each other but never quite touch – feel free to make your own comparisons with the relationship between the two countries. Views from certain parts of the park expose Incheon's port, a colourful maze of cranes and container ships that provide a vivid reminder of the city's trade links with its neighbours across the seas.

The Street of Culture and History
역사문화의 거리

The city has tried to evoke its colonial past on the **Street of Culture and History** by adding new wooden colonial-style facades to the street's buildings. The effect is slightly bizarre, though the buildings do, indeed, look decidedly pretty. Most of the businesses that received a facelift were simple shops such as confectioners, laundries and electrical stores; many are still going, though they are now augmented by bars, arty cafés and the like.

The former Japanese banks
Sinporo 23-gil • Both daily 9am–6pm • W1500 combined ticket

One block south of the Street of Culture and History is a genuinely cultural and historic road, where you'll find a few distinctive **Japanese colonial buildings** which are surprisingly Western in appearance (that being the Japanese architectural fashion of the time). Three of the buildings were originally banks, of which two have now been turned into small **museums**. The former **58th Bank of Japan** contains interesting photo and video exhibits of life in colonial times, while the former **1st Bank** down the road has a less interesting display of documents, flags and the like. Check out, too, the small outdoor display area between the two banks, where you'll find some fascinating pictures taken here in the 1890s, on what was then a quiet, dusty road almost entirely devoid of traffic, peopled with white-robed gents in horsehair hats – images of a Korea long gone.

ARRIVAL AND INFORMATION   INCHEON

By plane Incheon international airport is on an island west of the city and connected to the mainland by bridge: there are dedicated airport bus connections to Seoul and all over the country. Several limousine bus routes connect the airport with central Incheon, or take city bus #306 to Incheon subway station.

By ferry Incheon has three ferry terminals, served by ferries from China (see p.23) and some Korean islands in the West Sea (see p.152). From all three terminals, it's an

easy taxi-ride to Jung-gu.

By subway Despite the city's size, there's no train station: Incheon is served by subway line 1 from Seoul (1hr), though check that your train is bound for Incheon, as the line splits when leaving the capital.

Tourist information The helpful booth outside Incheon subway station (daily 9am–6pm; ☎ 032 773 2225) usually has an English-speaker; further offices can be found in the ferry terminals.

15

ACCOMMODATION

Atti 아띠 호텔 Songhak 1-dong 9-6 ☎ 032 772 5233, ⓦ attihotel.com. This little gem is tucked away in a quiet area behind the Jung-gu district office, near *Tochon* restaurant (see below). Recently renovated, it is perhaps a little too trendy – with glass partitions that make the bathrooms too visible. However, the surrounding area is highly pleasant, away from the big-city bustle. **W60,000**
Harbor Park 하버파크 호텔 Jemullyangno 217 ☎ 032 770 9500, ⓦ harborparkhotel.com. Value-for-money option in Jung-gu, with excellent service and great

sea views. Unfortunately, the standard rooms can be extremely small, so try to check a few if possible; suites, on the other hand, are generously sized. **W125,000**
Paradise 향만성 Jemullyangno 257 ☎ 032 762 5181, ⓦ incheon.paradisehotel.co.kr. Though service can be a little ropey at times, and the crane-filled views may not appeal to some, this is the best hotel in the area. Despite being just a stone's throw from Incheon subway station, the hotel entrance is uphill and hard to reach, so you may prefer to take a taxi. **W250,000**

EATING

Rarely for a Korean city, and perhaps uniquely for a Korean port, Incheon isn't renowned for its food, though the presence of a large and thriving Chinatown is a boon to visitors. Don't expect the food to be terribly authentic, since Koreans have their own take on Chinese cuisine. Top choices here, and available at every single restaurant, are sweet-and-sour pork (탕수육; *tangsuyuk*), fried rice topped with a fried egg and black-bean paste (볶음밥; *beokkeumbap*), spicy seafood broth (짬뽕; *jjambbong*), and the undisputed number one, *jjajangmyeon* (자장면), noodles topped with black-bean paste.

Fog City 포그시티 Jungangdong 1-ga 19-1 ☎ 032 766 9024. Steakhouse-cum-café which stands out in the wider Chinatown area. The coffee's poor, but the pizzas are fine (W16,000), as is the clam chowder (W6000). Pride of place, however, goes to their excellent homemade sourdough bread, or a weird-but-tasty variety made with *makgeolli*. Tues–Sun 11am–10pm.
Gonghwachun 공화춘 Chinatown-no 43 ☎ 032 765 0571. This is where Korea's *jjajangmyeon* fad started – it has been served here since the 1890s. W5000 will buy you a bowl, or you could try the sautéed shredded beef with green pepper (W20,000), and finish off your meal with fried, honey-dipped rice balls. Daily 11am–11pm.

Mandabok 만다복 Bukseongdong 2-ga 9-11 ☎ 032 773 3838. There are various Chinese dishes on offer at this vaunted, authentic Chinatown institution, whose interior is resplendent with cheesy golden wallpaper. The shark fin, scallop and abalone dishes are pricey and made for small groups, though single diners and those on a budget can enjoy the rice staples, such as the shredded chilli pork (W7000). Daily 10am–10pm.
★Tochon 토촌 Songhakdong 1-ga 10 ☎ 032 464 5511. A wonderfully rustic warren, whose ground floor is surrounded on three sides by interconnected fish tanks. Try the *ddeok-galbi* Korean burgers for W20,000, filling *jeongsik* (set meals) from W20,000, or a *meonggae bibimbap*. Daily 10am–10pm.

West Sea Islands

Incheon's perforated western coast topples into a body of water known as the **West Sea** to Koreans, and the Yellow Sea to the rest of the world. Land rises again across the waves in the form of dozens of **islands**, almost all of which have remained pleasantly green and unspoilt; some also have excellent **beaches**. Life here is predominantly fishing-based and dawdles by at a snail's pace – a world away from Seoul and its environs, despite a few being close enough to be visited on a day-trip. The easiest to reach are **Ganghwado**, a slightly over-busy dot of land studded with ancient dolmens, and its far quieter neighbour **Seongmodo**, both of which are best accessed directly from Seoul. However, you'll have to head to Incheon for ferries to the beautiful island of **Deokjeokdo**, which is sufficiently far away from the capital to provide a perfect escape.

Ganghwado

강화도 • Bus #3000 (every 15–20min; 1hr 40min) from Sinchon subway in Seoul (line 2); walk directly up from exit 1

Unlike most West Sea islands, **GANGHWADO** is close enough to the mainland to be connected by road – buses run regularly from Seoul to **Ganghwa-eup** (강화읍), the island's ugly main settlement; from here local buses head to destinations across the island, though the place is so small that journeys rarely take more than thirty minutes. While this accessibility means that Ganghwado lacks the beauty of some of its more distant cousins, there's plenty to see. One look at a map should make clear the strategic importance of the island, which not only sits at the mouth of Seoul's main river, the Han, but whose northern flank is within a frisbee throw of the **North Korean border**.

Before the latest conflict, this unfortunate isle also saw **battles** with Mongol, Manchu, French, American and Japanese forces, among others (see p.166). However, Ganghwado's foremost sights date from even further back – a clutch of **dolmens** scattered around the northern part of the island dates from the first century BC and is now on UNESCO's World Heritage list.

Goindol

고인돌 • 24hr • Free • From Ganghwa-eup, take one of the buses bound for Changhu-ri, which depart every hour or so, and tell the driver where you want to get off

Misty remnants from bygone millennia, Ganghwa's **dolmens** are overground burial chambers consisting of flat capstones supported by three or more vertical megaliths. The Korean peninsula contains more than 30,000 of these ancient tombs – almost half of the world's total – and Ganghwado has one of the highest concentrations in the country. Most can only be reached by car or bike, though one, **Goindol**, is situated near a main road and accessible by bus. This granite tomb sits unobtrusively in a field, as it has for centuries: a stone skeleton long divested of its original earth covering, with a large 5m by 7m capstone.

Oepo

외포 • Buses (hourly; 25min) from Ganghwa-eup; some come straight through from Sinchon

Small and delightfully old-fashioned, the settlement of **OEPO** (pronounced "Way-paw") on the island's west coast is a little like stepping into Korea in the 1970s, before the country's "economic miracle" mopped up old traditions by the bucketload. There are no particular sights, so you can just wander around soaking up the atmosphere, stopping at the appealing little fish market near the dock, with restaurants all around it.

Seongmodo

석모도 • Ferries (every 30min; 10min) run from Oepo's tiny terminal on Ganghwado; the last one back is at 8.30pm. Buses to Bomunsa (15min) meet the ferries

The wonderfully peaceful island of **SEONGMODO** lies just a short ferry trip across the water from Ganghwado; ornithophobes should note that large flocks of seagulls tend to circumnavigate the vessel for the entire journey, waiting to catch thrown crisps.

The island's main sight is the charming temple of **Bomunsa** (보문사), a five-minute walk uphill from the bus stop, with a small tearoom at its entrance. A mountain path behind the temple leads to a clutch of small grottoes that function as **Buddhist shrines** and boast wonderful sea views. There are restaurants (plus simple accommodation) around both the temple and ferry terminal, as well as **bicycle rental** immediately off the ferry ramp for those with the muscle to pump up and down the island's hilly roads.

Deokjeokdo

덕적도 • Two fast ferries (1hr) run from Incheon's Yeonan pier, departing at 9.30am & 2.30pm; slower ferries (1 daily; 2hr 30min) leave at 8am from the same terminal

Possibly the prettiest and most tranquil of the West Sea isles, **DEOKJEOKDO** feels a world away from Seoul, though it's quite possible to visit from the capital on a day-trip. There's little in the way of sightseeing, save an easy climb up to the island's main peak, and not much to do, but that's just the point – the island has a couple of stunning beaches and some gorgeous mountain trails, and makes a refreshing break from the hustle and bustle of the mainland. Around the ferry berth are a few shops, restaurants and guesthouses, while a bus meets the ferries and makes its way round to **Seopori Beach** (서포리 해수욕장) on the other, quieter, side of the island – also home to a few guesthouses.

Suwon and around

수원

Heading south from Seoul by train, the capital's dense urban sprawl barely thins before you arrive in **SUWON**, a city with an impressive history of its own, best embodied by the gigantic **fortress** at its centre. Suwon, in fact, came close to usurping Seoul as Korea's seat of power following the murder of prince Sado (see box, p.73), but though it failed to overtake the capital, the city grew in importance in a way that remains visible to this day. Its fortress walls, built in the late eighteenth century, once enclosed the whole of Suwon, but from the structure's upper reaches you'll see just how far the city has spread.

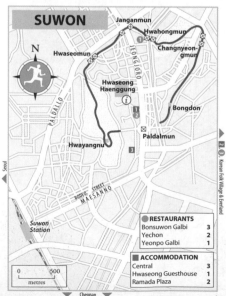

never-ending hotchpotch of buildings now forming one of Korea's largest urban centres. Making up for the dearth of sights in Suwon itself is an interesting and varied range of possibilities in a corridor stretching east of the city. Twenty kilometres away, the **Korean Folk Village** is a vaguely authentic portrayal of traditional Korean life; though too sugary for some, it redeems itself with some high-quality dance, music and gymnastic performances. Twenty-five kilometres further east is **Everland**, a huge amusement park.

Hwaseong fortress

화성 • Daily 9am–6pm • W1000, or free out of hours; ticket also includes Hwaseong Haenggung (see opposite); archery W2000 for 10 arrows • Buses #2-2, #11 and any beginning with #13, #16 or #50 from Suwon train station; #36 from bus terminal

Central Suwon has just one notable sight – **Hwaseong fortress**, whose gigantic walls wend their way around

MISTER TOILET

Although Suwon's sightseeing potential is limited, it does boast what may be the world's greatest concentration of **public toilets** – they all have names, and some are even marked on tourist maps. This concept was the brainchild of Sim Jae-deok, aka "**Mister Toilet**", who has even had his house custom-built to resemble a giant loo. Sim claims to have been born in a public restroom, but transcended these humble beginnings to become mayor of Suwon, and a member of the National Assembly. He then went on to create, and declare himself head of, the World Toilet Organization (the *other* WTO). Undoubtedly spurred on by his team's debatable finding that the average human being spends three years of their life on the toilet, Sim set out to improve his home city's facilities for the World Cup in 2002, commissioning dozens of individually designed public toilets. They're still around today, with features including skylights, mountain views or piped classical music, though such refinement is sadly sullied by the baskets of used toilet paper discarded throne-side.

the city centre. Completed in 1796, the complex was built on the orders of **King Jeongjo**, one of the Joseon dynasty's most famous rulers, in order to house the remains of his father, **Prince Sado**. Sado never became king, and met an early end in Seoul's Changgyeonggung Palace at the hands of his own father, King Yeongjo (see box, p.73); it may have been the gravity of the situation that spurred Jeongjo's attempts to move the capital away from Seoul.

Towering almost 10m high for the bulk of its course, the **fortress wall** rises and falls in a 5.7km-long stretch, most of which is walkable, the various peaks and troughs marked by sentry posts and ornate entrance gates. From the higher vantage points you'll be able to soak up **superb views** of the city, though you'll often have your reverie disturbed by screaming aircraft from the nearby military base. Most visitors start their wall walk at **Paldalmun** (팔달문), a gate at the lower end of the fortress, exuding a well-preserved magnificence now diluted by its position in the middle of a traffic-filled roundabout. From here there's a short but steep uphill path to Seonammun, the western gate.

Hwaseong Haenggung

화성행궁 • Daily 9am–6pm • Martial arts displays Tues–Sun at 11am; traditional dance and music performances April–Nov Sat & Sun at 2pm • Entry included in fortress ticket (see opposite)

In the centre of the area bounded by the fortress walls is **Hwaseong Haenggung**, once a government office, then a palace, and now a fine place to amble around; its pink walls are punctuated by the green lattice frames of windows and doors, which overlook dirt courtyards from where you can admire the fortress wall that looms above. The building hosts a daily **martial arts display** and occasional performances of traditional **dance and music**.

Korean Folk Village

한국 민속촌 • Generally daily 9.30am–6pm; farmers dance at 11am & 2pm; tightrope-walk at 11.30am & 2.30pm; horseriding at 11.30am & 3pm; wedding ceremony at 12pm & 4pm • W15,000 • ⓦ koreanfolk.co.kr • Free shuttle buses (30min) from Suwon station at 10.30am, 12.30pm & 2.30pm (returning at 2pm, 3.30pm & 4.30pm), or take regular city bus #10-5 or #37 (50min). From Seoul take bus #5001-1 or #1560 from Gangnam station (50min), or #5500 from Jonggak station (1hr 20min)

This re-creation of a traditional **Korean Folk Village** has become one of the most popular day-trips for foreign visitors to Seoul, its thatch-roofed houses and dirt paths evoking the sights, sounds and some of the more pleasant smells of a bygone time, when farming was the mainstay of the country. Its proximity to the capital makes this village by far the most-visited of the many such facilities dotted around the country, which tends to diminish the authenticity of the experience. Nevertheless, the riverbank setting and its old-fashioned buildings are impressive, though the emphasis is squarely on performance, with **tightrope-walking** and horseriding shows taking place regularly

15

throughout the day. **Traditional wedding ceremonies** provide a glimpse into Confucian society, with painstaking attention to detail including gifts of live chickens wrapped up in cloth like Egyptian mummies. Don't miss the **farmers' dance**, in which costumed performers prance around in highly distinctive ribbon-topped hats amid a cacophony of drums and crashes – quintessential Korea.

Everland

에버랜드 • Daily, usually 9.30am–9pm • W46,000, W38,000 after 3pm, W20,000 after 5pm; discount and combination tickets often available on website • ⓦ everland.com • Bus from Suwon train station departs on the half-hour (around 1hr). From Seoul, bus #5700 from the Dong-Seoul bus terminal via Jamsil subway station (1hr 10min), or #5002 from Gangnam subway station, via Yangjae (45min); more expensive daily shuttles (50min; W12,000) run from Hongdae at 9am, from City Hall at 9.30am & from Jongno 3-ga at 9.40am (returning at 6pm & 9pm); or take the Everline, a spur running from the Bundang line (around 2hr in total)

Everland is a colossal theme park that ranks as one of the most popular domestic tourist attractions in the country – male or female, young or old, it's hard to find a *hangukin* (Korean person) who hasn't taken this modern-day rite of passage. Most are here for the fairground rides, and the park has all that a roller-coaster connoisseur could wish for. Other attractions include a **zoo** (which features a safari zone that can be toured by bus, jeep or even at night), a speedway track, a golf course, and the surprisingly good **Hoam Museum**, which contains a few excellent examples of Buddhist art, and some interesting French sculpture in an outdoor garden.

Caribbean Bay

캐리비언 베이 • Daily, usually 9.30am–6pm; outdoor section June–Aug only • W35,000, W30,000 after 2.30pm; discount and combination tickets often available on website

The most popular part of the theme park is **Caribbean Bay**, with a year-round indoor zone containing several pools, a sauna and a short river that you can float down on a tube, as well as massage machines and relaxation capsules. The **outdoor section** with its man-made beach is what really draws the summer crowds. Other facilities include an artificial surfing facility, and a water bobsleigh, which drops you the height of a ten-floor building in just ten seconds.

ARRIVAL AND INFORMATION

By train and subway Within walking distance of the fortress, Suwon's main train station handles both national rail and Seoul subway trains (line 1), though this splits south of Seoul. The train from Seoul is quicker (30min) and far more comfortable than the subway (1hr), though it's more expensive.

SUWON AND AROUND

Transport cards Seoul transport cards (see box, p.24) can be used for buses or subway trains in Suwon.

Tourist information The main information office is currently being moved – it will eventually be in or around the train station. A smaller branch office is visible from Hwaseong Haenggung.

ACCOMMODATION

Although accommodation in Suwon is markedly cheaper than similar places in Seoul, most travellers visit on day-trips from the capital. There are plenty of motels in the area bounded by the fortress wall, though it's one of the seediest parts of the city. True budget-seekers can make use of an excellent *jjimjilbang* just off Rodeo Street (W7000).

Central 센터럴 호텔 Gyodong 1-2 ☎ 031 246 0011, ⓦ suwoncentral.com. In an excellent location for the fortress, and not too run-down for a Korean tourist hotel. The rooms are reasonably good value and have cable TV; a small breakfast is also thrown in for free, but the bar-filled street outside can get noisy at night. **W77,000**

Hwaseong Guesthouse 화성 게스트하우스 Jeongjoro 801-gil 11 ☎ 031 245 6226, ⓦ hsguesthouse .com. Central Suwon's first hostel is decent enough, if a little sterile – though the dorms have no a/c (it's fine in

winter thanks to underfloor heating). The big plus here is the location, smack bang in the centre of the fortress area. Dorm beds **W18,000**, doubles **W30,000**

★ **Ramada Plaza** 라마다프라자 Jungbudaero 150 ☎ 031 230 0001, ⓦ ramadaplazasuwon.com. Suwon's best hotel, though in an uninteresting corner of the city, attracts well-heeled visitors – primarily Europeans on business – and offers all the comfort you'd expect. Some of the suites are stunning, and even standard rooms have been designed with care. **W220,000**

EATING

Suwon is famous for a local variety of *galbi*, whereby the regular meat dish is given a salty seasoning. You will more than likely find something appealing on Rodeo Street, where the city's youth flocks to in the evening to take advantage of the copious cheap restaurants.

Bonsuwon Galbi 본수원 갈비 Uman 2-dong 103-1 ☎ 031 211 8434. Around the back of *Hotel Central* is what may well be the best *galbi* restaurant in the city. The succulent meat doesn't come cheap (at least W25,000 per portion), but is worth it for the chance to try Suwon's local take on Korea's most pyromaniacal eating experience. Daily 11.30am–8.30pm.

Yechon 예촌 Namchangdong 132-1 ☎ 031 254 9190. It's retro to the max at this little hidey-hole near Paldalmun, a folk-styled establishment serving savoury pancakes known as *jeon* (전) in many different styles (from W10,000), as well as superb *makgeolli* from Jeonju, in the southwest of the country. Tues–Sun 3.30pm–midnight.

★**Yeonpo Galbi** 연포 갈비 Buksudong 25-4 ☎ 031 255 1337. In a quiet area just inside the fortress wall lies the best restaurant in the area. The *galbi* meat is expensive (from W33,000), but cheaper noodle dishes are available: before 3pm you can get a huge *jeongsik* (set meal) for W20,000, which includes several small fish and vegetable dishes. Daily 9am–9pm.

15

Yangsu-ri

양수리

A tranquil village surrounded by mountains and water, **YANGSU-RI** sits at the confluence of the Namhangang and Bukhangang, two rivers that merge to create the Hangang, which pours through Seoul. The village has long had a reputation as a popular spot for extra-marital affairs – a fact made evident by its large number of seedy motels – though in recent years its natural charm has also started to draw in an ever-increasing number of families, students and curious foreign visitors.

The focus of the village is a small **island**, with farmland taking up much of its interior. A pleasant walking or cycling track skirts the perimeter – the stretch to the south of the island is particularly enjoyable, with the very southern tip being a spectacular spot to watch the sunset.

ARRIVAL AND GETTING AROUND   YANGSU-RI

By subway Yangsu is a stop on the Jungang line, which starts in Yongsan – the journey takes around an hour. It's a 15min walk to the island from Yangsu station, though there's also a bus. You can also access the island from Gukcheon, the station immediately west of Yangsu – from here, simply find the bridge, and walk across.

By bike Though it may be more than 35km from central Seoul, Yangsu-ri is a popular bike trip from the capital (see p.87 for rental information), and is certainly within day-trip distance. You can also rent bikes at Yangsu-ri itself: there's a booth immediately outside Yangsu station, and another near Gukcheon station. Cycling the island's perimeter is very pleasant, and the track even continues way down to the southeast of the peninsula.

EATING

★**Gelateria Panna** 빤나 Yangsu-ri 649-5 ☎ 031 775 4904. Seoul's best ice cream can be found here in Yangsu-ri – the couple that run this tiny place lived in Milan for a decade, where they learned how to make some kick-ass gelato (W3500 for a cup). The flavours change daily – the ginger and vanilla are particularly tasty – and they also make a mean espresso. It's in the village, just south of the main road. Daily except Wed 11am–8pm.

Gongreungdong Myeolchiguksu 경릉동 멸치국수 Yangsu-ri 565-11 ☎ 031 772 1560. The cold, spicy noodles (비빔국수; W4500) at this simple sit-on-the-floor joint are just the thing after a summer walk; there are warmer noodle broths available too, and portions are huge. It's on the main road heading across the island, near the bridge on the western side. Thurs–Tues 11am–8pm.

Gongju

공주

Presided over by the large fortress of Gongsanseong, small, sleepy **GONGJU** is one of Korea's most charming cities, and the best place to see relics from the Baekje dynasty that it ruled as capital in the fifth and sixth centuries. Once known as Ungjin, Gongju became the second capital of the realm in 475, but only held the seat of power for 63 years before it was passed to Buyeo, a day's march to the southwest. Today, the city is largely devoid of bustle, clutter and chain stores, and boasts a number of wonderful sights, including a hilltop **fortress** and a **museum** containing a fine collection of Baekje jewellery. It is also home to some excellent restaurants, and hosts the **Baekje Cultural Festival** (𝕨baekje.org) each September/early October, with colourful parades and traditional performances in and around the city.

Gongsanseong

공산성 • Ungjinno 280 • Daily: summer 9am–6pm; winter 9am–5pm • Changing of the Guard April–June, Sept & Oct daily at 2pm • W1500

For centuries, Gongju's focal point has been the hilltop **fortress of Gongsanseong**, whose 2.6km-long perimeter wall was built from local mud in Baekje times, before receiving a stone upgrade in the seventeenth century. It's possible to walk the entire circumference of the wall, a flag-pocked, up-and-down course that occasionally affords splendid views of Gongju and its surrounding area. The grounds inside are worth a look too, inhabited by striped squirrels and riddled with paths leading to a number of carefully painted **pavilions**. Of these, **Ssangsujeong** has the most interesting history – where this now stands, a Joseon-dynasty king named Injo (r.1623–49) once hid under a couple of trees during a peasant-led rebellion against his rule; when this was quashed, the trees were made government officials, though sadly they're no longer around to lend their leafy views to civil proceedings. Airy, green **Imnyugak**, painted with meticulous care, is the most beautiful pavilion; press on further west down a small path for great views of eastern Gongju. Down by the river there's a small temple, a refuge to monks who fought the Japanese in 1592, and on summer weekends visitors can dress up as a Baekje warrior and shoot off a few arrows.

Tomb of King Muryeong

무령왕릉 • Ungjindong 57 • Daily 9am–6pm • W1500

West over the creek from Gongsanseong, the **Tomb of King Muryeong** is one of many regal burial groups dotted around the country from the Three Kingdoms period (see p.162), but the only Baekje mound whose occupant is known for sure. Muryeong, who ruled for the first quarter of the sixth century, was credited with strengthening his kingdom by improving relations with China and Japan; some accounts suggest that the design of Japanese jewellery was influenced by gifts that he sent across the sea. His gentle green burial mound was discovered by accident in 1971 during a civic construction project – after fifteen centuries, Muryeong's tomb was the only one that hadn't been looted, and it yielded thousands of pieces of jewellery that provided a fascinating insight into the craft of the Baekje people. All the tombs have now been sealed off for preservation, but a small exhibition hall contains replicas of Muryeong's tomb and the artefacts found within.

Gongju Hanok Village

공주 한옥 마을 • Pungnamdong 15–11 • Daily 24hr • Free

A short walk from the regal tombs, **Gongju Hanok Village** is a fairly decent re-creation of a Baekje-era village – though one complete with café, restaurants and a convenience store. Unlike its counterpart in Seoul (see p.44), this is a tourist construct rather than a functional part of the city; nevertheless, it makes for good camera fodder, and you may find yourself tempted to stay for a meal, or even overnight (see opposite).

Gongju National Museum

공주 국립 박물관 • Ungjindong 360 • Tues–Sun 9am–6pm • Free

In a quiet wooded area by the turn of the river, **Gongju National Museum** is home to many of the treasures retrieved from Muryeong's tomb. Much of the museum is devoted to jewellery, and an impressive collection of Baekje bling reveals the dynasty's penchant for gold, silver and bronze. Artefacts such as elaborate golden earrings show an impressive attention to detail, but manage to be dignified and restrained in their use of shape and texture. The highlight is the king's flame-like **golden headwear**, once worn like rabbit ears on the royal scalp, and now one of the most important symbols not just of Gongju, but of the Baekje dynasty itself. Elsewhere in the museum exhibits of wood and clay show the dynasty's history of trade with Japan and China.

ARRIVAL AND INFORMATION   GONGJU

By bus Direct buses from the express bus terminal in Seoul arrive at Gongju's bus terminal, just north of the Geumgang River; you can walk from here to all the main sights, though taxi rides are cheap.

Information The main tourist information centre (☎ 041 856 7700; daily: summer 9am–6pm; winter 9am–5pm) is beneath Gongsanseong, and usually has helpful, English-speaking staff.

ACCOMMODATION AND EATING

Gongju has a poor selection of accommodation, with motels centred in two areas: north of the river, to the west of the bus terminal, is a bunch of new establishments (including a couple of cheesy replica "castles"), while a group of older cheapies lies south of the river across the road from Gongsanseong. The latter is a quainter and more atmospheric area, and slightly closer to the sights, but the newer rooms are far more comfortable.

★**Hanok Gongju** 한옥 공주 Ungjindong 337 ☎ 041 840 8900. A pretty little faux hamlet of traditional wooden *hanok* housing, sitting in calm isolation between the tombs and museum. Though recently constructed, the buildings feel authentic enough, and are heated from beneath by burning wood; they're spartan, for sure, but the location is relaxing, and the experience unique. W50,000

Hotel Kumgang 호텔 금강 Singwandong 595-8 ☎ 041 852 1071. The only official hotel in town, though in reality it's a less-seedy-than-average motel with a few twins and triples. However, it has friendly staff, spacious bathrooms, internet-ready computer terminals in most rooms and a moderately priced bar-restaurant on the second floor, and should suffice for all but the fussiest travellers. W50,000

EATING

Geumganggwan 금강관 Ungjindong 337 ☎ 041 840 8900. The best and most rustic of the restaurants around the Hanok Gongju complex (see above), featuring suitably traditional platters of Korean food – there's no à la carte menu, but sets start at W18,000. Daily 10am–8pm.

★**Gomanaru** 고마나루 Geumseongdong 184-4 ☎ 041 857 9999. This unassuming restaurant is, quite

simply, one of Korea's most enjoyable places to eat. Here W15,000 per head (minimum two) will buy a huge *ssam-bap* (쌈밥), which features a tableful of side dishes, and more than a dozen kinds of leaves to eat them with; there are a few choices for the centrepiece of the meal, though the barbecued duck is highly recommended. An extra W5000 will see the whole meal covered with edible flowers – absolute heaven. Daily 9am–10pm.

15

CHANGDEOKGUNG PALACE

Contexts

History

Modern Seoul has functioned continuously as a capital city since 1394, when the nascent Joseon dynasty selected it as the most auspicious place from which to rule their new kingdom, though Neolithic remains prove the area had already been a major centre of population for several thousand years prior to this. Seoul most likely first served as a place of power at around the same time that Augustus was inaugurating the Roman Empire: the Baekje dynasty proclaimed their first capital in 18 BC, on a site likely to have been within the present-day city limits. They soon moved the throne southwest to Ungjin (now known as Gongju), and Seoul was passed this way and that between the Three Kingdoms until the Joseon dynasty came to power in 1392, and favoured Seoul's position at the centre of the peninsula. Over a period of more than five centuries a full 27 kings came and went, alliances were made and broken with the Chinese and Japanese dynasties of the time and in the seventeenth century Korea retreated into its shell, becoming a "Hermit Kingdom", effectively shut off to the rest of the world. In 1910, at a time of global turmoil, Joseon rule was snuffed out by the Japanese, bringing to an end Korea's monarchy. World War II ended Japanese annexation, after which Korea was split in two in the face of the looming Cold War. There then followed the brutal Korean War, and in 1953 the communist North and the capitalist South went their separate ways; Seoul remained a capital city, but only of the south of the peninsula, while Pyongyang became the northern centre of control. With its position almost exactly on the line of control, Seoul inevitably suffered widespread destruction, making it all the more remarkable when, within just one generation, the city rose from the ashes to become an industrial powerhouse.

The beginnings

Rivers tend to provide a road map of civilization, and with its fertile valley, the wide **Hangang** likely proved a tempting base for hunter-gatherers during Paleolithic times. However, the first tangible evidence of habitation in Seoul itself is a clutch of **Neolithic** remains found in what is now the east of the city; dating from 7000 to 3000 BC, these artefacts detail the area's transition from the Stone to the Bronze Age. In addition to the use of metal tools, from 7000 BC **pottery** was being produced with distinctive comb-toothed patterns (*jeulmun*) similar to those found in Mongolia and Manchuria.

2333 BC	7th century BC	c.109 BC
Founding of Gojoseon, Korea's first known kingdom, by semi-mythical bear-child Dangun	First mentions of Gojoseon in Chinese records	Demise of Gojoseon at hands of Chinese Han dynasty

> **KOREA'S MAJOR HISTORICAL ERAS**
> **Gojoseon** c.2333 BC to c.109 BC
> **Three Kingdoms** c.57 BC to 668 AD
>   Silla c.57 BC to 668 AD
>   Goguryeo c.37 BC to 668 AD
>   Baekje c.18 BC to 660 AD
> **Unified Silla** 668–935
> **Goryeo** 918–1392
> **Joseon** 1392–1910
> **Japanese colonial period** 1910–1945
> **Republic of Korea (South)** 1945 to present day
> **Democratic People's Republic of Korea (North)** 1945 to present day

Fired earth also came to play a part in death rituals, a fact made evident by small, shell-like "jars" into which the broken bodies were placed together with personal belongings; these were then lowered into a pit and covered with earth. An even more distinctive style of burial was to develop in the first millennium BC, with some tombs covered with **dolmens**. Korea is home to over thirty thousand such burial mounds; these are spread across the country, but are most prevalent in **Ganghwado**, an island west of Seoul whose collection is recognized by UNESCO as a World Heritage Site.

Today the peninsula's first kingdom is usually referred to as **Gojoseon** ("Old Joseon") in an effort to distinguish it from the later Joseon period (1392–1910). Its origins are obscure, to say the least, but most experts agree that it got going in 2333 BC under the leadership of **Dangun**, who has since become the subject of one of Korea's most cherished myths – apparently, he was the son of a tiger turned human. Gojoseon initially functioned as a loose federation of fiefdoms covering not only parts of the Korean peninsula but large swathes of Manchuria too. By 500 BC it had become a single, highly organized dominion, even drawing praise from Confucius and other Chinese sages. Accounts of the fall of Gojoseon are also rather vague, but Seoul seems to have been at the forefront: the kingdom was apparently conquered by the nascent Chinese Han dynasty in 109 BC, who were in turn forced out over the following few decades by natives of the Hangang area at the start of what's now known as the "Three Kingdoms" period. Joseon's historical name lives on: North Korea continues to refer to itself as such (and South Korea as Namjoseon, or "South Joseon"), while many South Korean tourist brochures use "The Land of Morning Calm" – a literal translation of the term – as a national motto.

The Three Kingdoms period

By 109 BC, after the fall of Gojoseon, the peninsula had split into half a dozen fiefdoms, the most powerful of which – **Silla**, **Goguryeo** and **Baekje** – became known as the Three Kingdoms. Around this time, close ties with China brought **Buddhism** to Korea, while **Confucianism** (another Chinese import) provided the social building blocks, with a number of educational academies supplying the *yangban*, scholars at the

57 BC	**c.37 BC**	**18 BC**
Founding of Silla dynasty, first of Korea's "Three Kingdoms", by horse-egg king Hyeokgeose	Founding of Goguryeo dynasty by Jumong, another king hatched from an egg	Founding of Baekje dynasty by King Onjo

head of the aristocracy. Great advances were made in the arts, particularly with regard to jewellery and pottery, and thousands of wonderful relics have been discovered in the grassy hill-tombs of dead kings and other formerly sacred sites.

Fertile and with good transportation routes, the Hangang valleys were in demand, and Seoul was to fall under the banner of all three kingdoms at different times. First in were the **Baekje**, a kingdom created in 18 BC as the result of great movements of people on the western side of the Korean peninsula. The dynasty was inaugurated by King Onjo, a man jealous of his brother's inheritance of the rival Goguryeo kingdom, itself started by their father Dongmyeong. **Wiryeseong**, which almost certainly lay within Seoul's present-day borders, became the first Baekje capital.

Goguryeo got their own back several generations down the line when the great king Gwanggaeto seized control of the Hangang area in 329 AD. Baekje retreated southwest, establishing new capitals at what are now Gongju and Buyeo, and cultivating an artistic reputation. Baekje became friendly with the **Japanese kingdom of Wa**, and evidence of this close relationship can still be seen today – the lacquered boxes, folding screens, immaculate earthenware and intricate jewellery of Japan are said to derive from the influence of Baekje artisans. This relationship allowed Baekje to grow in power, and they were to retake Seoul, only to see it snatched back by Goguryeo's King Jangsu in 475, after which the city was renamed **Hanseong**.

Baekje were not done with Seoul, and formed an alliance with **Silla**, the peninsula's third kingdom. Together, they pushed Goguryeo north and out of Seoul in 551, though Silla was to become the senior party in the relationship, since the Japanese Wa did not provide Baekje such protection as the **Chinese Tang** dynasty gave Silla. After taking control of Seoul, Silla enlisted Tang help in 660 to eliminate the Baekje kingdom, whose last pockets of resistance literally toppled from a cliff in Buyeo's riverside fortress. This left only Goguryeo as peninsular rivals, and with a vice-like position between Silla to the south and the Tang to the north, it was only a matter of time (eight years, to be precise) before they too were vanquished, setting the scene for a first-ever **unified rule** on the peninsula.

Unified Silla

Following the quickfire defeats of its two competitor kingdoms in the 660s, the **Silla dynasty** instigated the Korean peninsula's first-ever unification. They kept the southeastern city of Gyeongju as their seat of power, renaming Seoul "**Hanyang**" but relegating it to a provincial power base. Silla set about cultivating a peninsular **sense of identity**, and the pooling of ideas and talent in the eighth century created a high-water mark of artistic development, particularly in metalwork and earthenware. However, rulers stuck to a rigidly Confucian "bone rank" system, which placed strict limits on what an individual could achieve in life, based almost entirely on their genetic background. Though it largely succeeded in keeping the proletariat quiet, this highly centralized system was to lead to Silla's demise: the late eighth century and most of the ninth were characterized by **corruption and in-fighting** at the highest levels of Silla society, and a near-permanent state of civil war. With the Silla king reduced to little more than a figurehead, the former kingdoms of Baekje and Goguryeo were resurrected (now known as "**Hubaekje**" and "**Taebong**" respectively). Silla shrank back to within its

372 AD	**660**	**668**
Buddhism introduced to Korea; it slowly starts to replace Shamanism	Silla defeats Baekje	Silla defeats Goguryeo, leading to unified Silla rule on the peninsula

---

SEOUL'S HISTORICAL NAMES

Wiryeseong under Baekje rule, partly as capital   c.18 BC to 475 AD
Hanseong under Goguryeo rule   475 to 668
Hanyang under Unified Silla rule   668 to 918
Namgyeong under Goryeo rule   918 to 1392
Seoul as capital of the Joseon dynasty   1392 to 1910
Gyeongseong (Keijo) during Japanese occupation   1910 to 1945
Seoul again as capital of the Republic of Korea   1945 to present

---

Three Kingdoms-era borders, and after a power struggle Taebong took control of the peninsula; in 935, King Gyeongsun ceded control of his empire in a peaceful transfer of power to Taebong leader **Wang Geon**, who went on to become Taejo, the first king of the Goryeo dynasty.

The Goryeo dynasty

Having grown from a mini-kingdom known as Taebong, one of the many battling for power following the collapse of Silla control, it was the Goryeo dynasty that eventually gave its name to the English term "Korea". It began life in 918 under the rule of **Taejo**, a powerful leader who needed less than two decades to bring the whole peninsula under his control. One of his daughters married Gyeongsun, the last king of Silla, and Taejo himself wed a Silla queen, two telling examples of the new king's desire to cultivate a sense of national unity – he even gave positions of authority to known enemies. Relations with China and Japan were good, and the kingdom became ever more prosperous.

Following the fall of Silla, Taejo moved the national capital to his hometown, Kaesong, a city in present-day North Korea, while Seoul became **Namgyeong**, the "Southern Capital". Taejo and successive leaders also changed some of the bureaucratic systems that had contributed to Silla's downfall: power was centralized in the king but devolved to the furthest reaches of his domain, and even those without aristocratic backgrounds could, in theory, reach lofty governmental positions via a system of state-run examinations. Despite the Confucian social system, **Buddhism** continued to function as the state religion, and repeated refinements in the pottery industry saw Korean produce attain a level of quality only bettered in China. In fact, despite great efforts, some **pottery techniques** perfected in Goryeo times remain a mystery today, perhaps never to be replicated.

In 1248, Goryeo was attacked by Mongol hordes, and became a vassal state of the Great Khans. Annexation came at a great human cost, one echoed in a gradual worsening of Goryeo's economy and social structure. This lasted almost a century, before **King Gongmin** took advantage of a weakening Chinese–Mongol Yuan dynasty (founded by Kublai Khan) to regain independence. He made an attempt at reform, purging the top ranks of those he felt to be pro-Mongol, but this instilled fear of yet more change into the *yangban* elite, and he was eventually murdered. After a series of short-lived kings, powerful Joseon General **Yi Seong-gye** decided to take the mantle himself, and in 1392 declared himself King Taejo, the first leader of the Joseon dynasty.

918	**935**	**1145**
Inauguration of Goryeo dynasty by King Taejo	Official transfer of power from Silla to Goryeo	Completion of *Samguk Sagi*, a historical annal of the Three Kingdoms period

The Joseon dynasty

The **Joseon era** started off much the same as the Goryeo dynasty had almost five centuries before, with a militaristic king named **Taejo** on the throne, a name that translates as "The Grand Ancestor". Joseon was to last even longer, with a full 27 kings ruling from 1392 until the Japanese annexation in 1910. Taejo moved the capital from Kaesong to **Seoul** (the first time the city had used its present name), and immediately set about entrenching his power with a series of mammoth projects. The first few years of his reign saw the wonderful palace of Gyeongbokgung, the ancestral shrines of Jongmyo and a gate-studded city wall go up. His vision was quite astonishing – the chosen capital and its palace and shrine remain to this day, together with sections of the wall. More grand palaces would rise in due course, while another four would at various times house the royal throne. From the start of the dynasty, Buddhism declined in influence as **Confucianism** permeated society ever more in its stead. Joseon's social system became more hierarchical in nature, with the king and other royalty at the top, and the hereditary **yangban** class of scholars and aristocrats just beneath, followed by various levels of employment, with the servants and slaves at the bottom of the pile. All of these social strata were governed by heredity, but the *yangban* became increasingly powerful as the dynasty progressed, gradually starting to undermine the power of the king. They were viewed as a world apart by the commoners, and they placed great emphasis on study and the arts. However, only the *yangban* had access to education and literacy, as Chinese characters were used. In the 1440s **King Sejong** (reigned 1418–50) devised **hangeul**, a new and simple local script that all classes could read and write (see box, p.180); the *yangban* were not fond of this, and it was banned at the beginning of the sixteenth century, lying largely dormant until it was resurrected by waves of nationalist sentiment that greeted the end of Japanese annexation in 1945.

The "Hermit Kingdom"

In 1592, under the command of feared warlord **Hideyoshi**, Japan set out to conquer the Ming dynasty, with China a stepping stone towards possible domination of the whole Asian continent. The Korean peninsula had the misfortune to be both in the way and loyal to the Ming. After King Seonjo refused to allow Japanese troops safe passage, Hideyoshi mustered all his military's power and unloaded the lot at Korea, with another major wave of attacks coming in 1597. Korea was then also affected by the internal strife of its closest ally, China. Following the dynastic transfer from Ming to Qing in the 1640s Joseon became a vassal state, forced to spend substantial sums paying tribute to the emperors in Beijing. After all this, it was no surprise that Korea turned inwards: it became known as the "**Hermit Kingdom**", one of which outsiders knew little, and saw even less. One exception was a Dutch ship that crashed off Jeju Island in 1653 en route to Japan; the survivors were brought to Seoul, but their appeal for release was turned down by King Hyojong. They were essentially kept prisoner in Korea for thirteen years but finally managed to escape, and the accounts of one survivor, **Hendrick Hamel**, provided the Western world with one of its first windows into isolationist Korea.

The Dutch prisoners had entered a land in which corruption and factionalism were rife, one that achieved little social or economic stability until the rule of **King Yeongjo** (1724–76), who authorized a purge of crooked officials, but also murdered his son (see box, p.73). Yeongjo's grandson **Jeongjo**, who came to the throne in 1776, became one

1231	1248	c.1350
First of the Mongol invasions	Korea becomes a vassal state of the Mongol khans	Mongols driven away from Korean peninsula as their Chinese Yuan dynasty crumbles

of the most revered of Korea's kings, instigating top-to-bottom reform to wrench power from the *yangban* elite, and allowing for the creation of a small middle class. The lot of the poor also gradually improved.

The end of isolation

Following Japan's **opening up** to foreign trade in the 1860s (the Meiji Restoration), Korea found itself under pressure to do likewise, not just from the Japanese but from the United States and the more powerful European countries – warships were sent from around the globe to ensure agreement. Much of the activity occurred on and around the island of Ganghwado, just west of Seoul. The French occupied the isle but failed to advance on the mainland in 1866, their battle fought partly as retaliation for the murder of several French missionaries. Five years later, and in the same location, the Americans also attempted – and failed – to prise the country open to trade. The third bout of gunboat diplomacy – this time by the Japanese in 1876 – resulted in the Treaty of Ganghwa, which dragged Korea into the global marketplace on unfair terms. From this point until well after the Korean War, Korea would be a ship largely steered by foreign powers.

Through means both political and economic, the Japanese gradually strengthened their position in Korea. Local resentment boiled over into occasional riots and protests, and peaked in 1895 after the Japanese-orchestrated **murder of Empress Myeongseong** – "Queen Min" to the Japanese – in Gyeongbokgung palace. After this event, **King Gojong** (r.1863–1910) fled to the Russian embassy for protection; in 1897, when things had quietened down sufficiently, he moved into the nearby palace of Deoksugung where he set up the short-lived **Empire of Korea**, a toothless administration under almost full Japanese control.

In 1902 Japan forged an alliance with the British Empire, recognizing British interests in China in return for British acknowledgement of Japanese interests in Korea. Sensing shifts in power, Russia began expanding into Korea, though they ran into the Japanese on the way. To avoid confrontation, Japan suggested that the two countries carve Korea up along the **38th parallel**, a line roughly bisecting the peninsula. Russia refused to accept, and the two fought the Russo-Japanese War across Manchuria and the Yellow Sea in 1904–05; after its surprise victory, Japan was in a position to occupy the peninsula outright. They were given tacit permission to do so in 1905 by US Secretary of State and future president William Taft, who agreed in a secret meeting to accept Japanese domination of Korea if Japan would accept the American occupation of the Philippines. Korea became a Japanese protectorate that year, and Japan gradually ratcheted up its power on the peninsula before a final **outright annexation** in 1910. Joseon's kings had next to no say in the running of the country during its last quarter-century of dynastic succession. Sunjong, the peninsula's final monarch, retreated into early retirement in Changdeokgung, and the book softly closed on Korea's near two thousand years of unbroken regal rule.

The Japanese occupation

After the signing of the Annexation Treaty in 1910, Japan wasted no time in filling all the top posts in politics, banking, law and industry with its own personnel; despite the

1392	1443	1592–1598
General Yi Seong-gye executes last Goryeo kings and declares himself King Taejo of new Joseon dynasty	Creation of *hangeul*, Korea's official script, a project of King Sejong	Japanese invasions of Korea

fact that they never represented more than four percent of the peninsular population, they came to control almost every sphere of the country. Korea was but part of the Empire of Japan's dream of **continental hegemony**, and being the nearest stepping stone from the motherland, it was also the most heavily trampled on. While the Japanese went on to occupy most of Southeast Asia and large swathes of China, only in Korea did they have the time and leverage necessary to attempt a total annihilation of **national identity**. Some of the most powerful insults to national pride were hammered home early. The royal palace of **Gyeongbokgung** had all the Confucian principles observed in its construction shattered by the placing of a modern Japanese structure in its first holy courtyard, while Changgyeonggung suddenly found itself home to a decidedly un-royal theme park and zoo. Korean currency, clothing and even the language itself were placed under ever stricter control, locals were required to take Japanese names, and thousands of local "**comfort women**" were forced into sexual slavery. Korean productivity grew, but much of this was also for Japan's benefit – within ten years, more than half of the country's rice was heading across the sea.

The local populace, unsurprisingly, objected to this enforced servitude. In 1919, the **March 1st Movement** saw millions of Koreans take to the streets in a series of non-violent nationwide protests. A declaration of independence was read out in Seoul's Tapgol Park, followed by processions through the streets and the singing of the Korean national anthem. The Japanese police attempted to suppress the revolt through force; around seven thousand died in the months of resistance demonstrations that followed. A government-in-exile was established across the sea in Shanghai, but in Korea itself the main result of the resistance movement was a marked change of Japanese policy towards Korea, with Saito Makoto (the admiral in charge of quelling the chaos) agreeing to lift the bans on Korean radio, printed material and the creation of organizations, a policing that aimed to promote harmony rather than pushing the militarist line. The pendulum swung back towards oppression on the approach to World War II – in the late 1930s, Japan began forcing Koreans to worship at Shinto shrines, speak Japanese and even adopt a Japanese name (a practice known as *soshi-kaimei*), all helped by local **collaborators** (*chinilpa*).

The end of annexation
Throughout the occupation period, the **Korean government-in-exile** had been forced ever further west from China's eastern seaboard, eventually landing near the Tibetan plateau in the Sichuanese city of Chongqing. Modern Korean museums and history books extol the achievements of what was, in reality, a largely toothless group. In doing this they gloss over the fundamental reason for Korea's independence: the American A-bombs that fell on **Hiroshima and Nagasaki**, thereby ending both World War II and the Empire of Japan itself. With Tokyo busy elsewhere, Seoul was little affected by the war: the main change in city life was the conscription of tens of thousands of Korean men, many of whom never returned.

An even greater number of Koreans had moved to Japan prior to the war. Some, of course, were collaborators fearful of reprisals should they head home, but the majority were simply squeezed out of their impoverished homeland by **Japanese land confiscations**. Many of these Korean families remain in Japan today, and are referred to there as "Zainichi Koreans".

1767	1866	1895
Murder of Crown Prince Sado by his father, King Yeongjo	The French occupy the island of Ganghwado, but fail to move into Seoul	Murder of Queen Min by Japanese

The Korean War

Known to many as the "**Forgotten War**", sandwiched as it was between World War II and the war in Vietnam, the Korean conflict was one of the twentieth century's greatest tragedies, laying waste to the city of Seoul, which stood more or less in the middle of the two warring parties. The impoverished Korean peninsula had already been pushed to the back of the global mind during World War II; the land was under Japanese control, but the Allied forces had developed no plans for its future should the war be won. In fact, at the close of the war US Secretary of State Edward Stettinius had to be told in a meeting where Korea actually was. It was only when the **Soviet Union** sent troops into Korea in 1945 that consideration was given to Korea's postwar life. During an emergency meeting on August 10, 1945, American officials and high-rankers (including eventual Secretary of State Dean Rusk) sat with a National Geographic map and a pencil, and scratched a line across the 38th parallel, just north of Seoul – a simple solution, but one that was to have grave repercussions for Korea.

The build-up to war

With World War II rapidly developing into the **Cold War**, Soviet forces occupied the northern half of the peninsula, Americans the south. Both countries imposed their own social, political and economic norms on the Koreans under their control, thereby creating two de facto states diametrically opposed in ideology that refused to recognize each other. The **Republic of Korea** (now more commonly referred to as "South Korea") declared independence in Seoul on August 15, 1948, exactly three years after liberation from the Japanese, and the **Democratic People's Republic of Korea** followed suit just over three weeks later. The US installed a leader favourable to them, selecting **Syngman Rhee** (ironically born in what is now North Korea), who had degrees from American universities. Stalin chose the much younger **Kim Il-sung**, who like Rhee had been in exile for much of the Japanese occupation. The foreign forces withdrew, and the two Koreas were left to their own devices, each hellbent on unifying the peninsula by absorbing the opposing half; inevitably, locals were forced into this polarization of opinions, one that split friends and even families apart. Kim wanted to wade into war immediately, and Stalin turned down two requests for approval of such an action. The third time, for reasons that remain open to conjecture, he apparently gave the nod.

War breaks out

Nobody knows for sure exactly how the **Korean War** started. Or, rather, everyone does: the other side attacked first. The South Korean line is that on June 25, 1950, troops from the northern **Korean People's Army** (KPA) burst across the 38th parallel, then little more than a roll of tape. The DPRK itself claims that it was the south that started the war, and indeed both sides had started smaller conflicts along the line on several occasions; declassified Soviet information seems to show that the main battle was kicked off by the north. With the southern forces substantially ill-equipped in comparison, Seoul fell just three days later, but they were soon aided by a sixteen-nation coalition fighting under the **United Nations** banner – the vast majority of troops were from the United States, but additional forces arrived from Britain, Canada, Australia, the Philippines, Turkey, the Netherlands, France, New Zealand, Thailand, Ethiopia, Greece, Colombia, Belgium, South Africa and Luxembourg; other countries provided non-combative support.

1897	1910	1919
King Gojong sets up the short-lived Empire of Korea	Japanese Empire annexes Korea	Mass protests against Japanese rule on March 1

Within three months, the KPA had hemmed the United Nations Command (UNC) into the far southeast of the country, behind a short line of control that became known as the **Pusan Perimeter**, a boundary surrounding the (now re-romanized) city of Busan. Though the KPA held most of the peninsula, American general Douglas MacArthur identified a weak logistical spine and poor supply lines as their Achilles heel, and ordered amphibious landings behind enemy lines at **Incheon**, just west of Seoul, in an attempt to cut off their enemy. The ambitious plan worked to perfection, and UNC forces pushed north way beyond the 38th parallel, reaching sections of the Chinese border within six weeks. At this stage, with the battle seemingly won, the **Chinese** entered the fight and ordered almost a million troops into North Korea; with their help, the KPA were able to push back past the 38th parallel. The UNC made one more thrust north in early 1951, and after six months the two sides ended up pretty much where they started. The lines of the conflict settled around the 38th parallel, near what was to become the **Demilitarized Zone**. The fighting did not end for well over two years, until the signing of an **armistice agreement** on July 27, 1953. North Korea, China and the United Nations Command signed the document, but South Korea refused to do likewise, meaning that the war is still technically being fought today.

In effect, both sides lost. Seoul had **fallen four times** – twice to each side – and Korea's population was decimated, with over two million civilians killed, wounded or missing over the course of the war; to this can be added a combined total of around two million troops killed or injured in action. Had the war been "contained" and brought to an end when the line of control stabilized in early 1951, these figures would have been far lower. The war split thousands of families as the front line yo-yoed up and down the land, and as people were forced to switch sides to avoid starvation or torture, or to stay in contact with other family members. Though the course of the war was easy enough to understand, propaganda clouded many of the more basic details, and the conflict was largely forgotten by the West. For all the coverage of Vietnam, few know that a far greater amount of **napalm** fell on North Korea, a much more "suitable" target for the material thanks to its greater number of large urban areas. Also kept quiet was how close they came to using **nuclear weapons**. Since the end of the war there have been innumerable accounts of atrocities committed on both sides, many detailing beatings, torture and the unlawful murder of prisoners of war, others documenting the slaughter of entire villages. Korea lay in ruins, yet two countries were slowly able to emerge from the ashes.

To the present day

Considering its state after the war, Seoul's transformation is nothing short of astonishing. A rapid phase of industrialization, one often referred to as the "**Economic Miracle**" in the West, saw South Korea become one of Asia's most ferocious financial tigers, and Seoul morph from battle-scarred wasteland into one of the world's largest and most dynamic cities. The country's GDP-per-head shot up from under US$100 in 1963 to almost US$30,000 in 2010. Thanks in large part to the bullishness of large conglomerates (known as *jaebeol*) such as Samsung, Hyundai and LG, it now sits proudly on the cusp of the world's ten most powerful economies. And, since flinging

1945	1948	1950
American bombing of Hiroshima and Nagasaki effectively ends Japanese annexation	Two separate Korean republics declared, one either side of 38th parallel	Start of Korean War, in which over three million were killed

off its autocratic straitjacket in the 1980s, it developed sufficiently to be selected as host of two of the world's most high-profile sporting events – the **Summer Olympics** in 1988, and football's **World Cup** in 2002 – plus the **G20 Summit** in 2010.

Problematic beginnings

Today's visitor to Seoul will scarcely be able to imagine the state that the city was in after the double whammy of Japanese occupation and the Korean War. Korea was, essentially, a third-world country, with shantytowns widespread even in central Seoul. Indeed, more than half the city's population was homeless and the construction of new housing was hampered by the fact that Japan had stripped the peninsula's trees for its own use. Neither were Korea's problems merely structural or economic in nature – every single person in the land carried memories of wartime atrocities in their minds, and countless families had been torn apart. In addition, accusations and recriminations were rife, and everyone knew that hostilities with the North could resume at any moment. American-educated **Syngman Rhee**, who had been selected as president before the war, ruled in an increasingly autocratic manner, making constitutional amendments to stay in power and purging parliament of those against his policies. In 1960 disgruntled students led the **April 19 Movement** against Rhee's rule, and after being toppled in a coup he was forced into exile, choosing Hawaii as his new home.

One dictator was swiftly replaced with another: Yun Bo-seon came to office as a puppet of military general **Park Chung-hee**, who then swiftly engineered a coup and took the presidency himself in 1962. To an even greater degree than Rhee before him, Park's name became synonymous with corruption, dictatorship and the flouting of human rights – thousands were jailed merely for daring to criticize his rule. To his credit, Park introduced the economic reforms that allowed his country to push forward – until the mid-1970s, the South Korean economy actually lagged behind that of North Korea – and the country made great advances in automotive, electronic, heavy and chemical industries. This was, however, achieved at a cost, since Korean tradition largely went out of the window in favour of bare economic progress. These policies were a major factor behind the **loss of Korea's traditional buildings**: today, Seoul has almost none left. Park's authoritarian rule continued to ruffle feathers around the country, and the danger from the North had far from subsided – Park was the subject, and Seoul the scene, of two failed **assassination** attempts by North Korean agents. It was, however, members of his own intelligence service who gunned him down in 1979, claiming that he was "an insurmountable obstacle to democratic reform". Those responsible were hanged the following year.

Park's eventual successor, **Chun Doo-hwan**, was also from the southeast of the country, and the resultant Seoul–Gyeongsang tangent of power saw those parts of the country developing rapidly, while others languished far behind. The arrest of liberal southwestern politician **Kim Dae-jung**, as well as the botched trials following the assassination of Park Chung-hee, were catalysts for mass uprisings across the land, though mainly concentrated in Jeju Island and the southwestern provinces. These culminated in the **Gwangju Massacre** of May 1980, where over two hundred civilians died after their protest was crushed by the military.

1953	**1962**	**1979**
Fighting over and armistice agreement signed	General Park Chung-hee assumes power in a coup and embarks South Korea on a course of rapid industrialization	Park Chung-hee shot dead by his own intelligence service

THE SINKING OF THE CHEONAN, AND THE YEONPYEONGDO ATTACKS

On March 26, 2010, the *Cheonan*, a South Korean naval vessel, sank in the waters off Baengnyeongdo, killing 46 of its crew of just over one hundred, and claiming the life of one rescue worker. With the incident taking place in waters so close to the North Korean border, there was immediate worldwide suspicion that Pyongyang was behind the attack; Seoul refused to be drawn into such a conclusion, choosing instead to wait for the results of a full investigation. South Korean **conspiracy theorists** initially blamed an American submarine which had "gone missing", though such rumours were hurriedly put to bed when the sub resurfaced a few days later on the other side of the world. One rumour that refused to go away was that the attack may have been an internal show of force from **Kim Jong-un**, who was at the time being groomed for leadership in North Korea. It was suggested that Kim may have used the incident to prove himself to the country's military leadership, who were known to be unhappy with a dynastic transfer of power from his father, Kim Jong-Il. Two months after the incident, an international team found that the *Cheonan* was sunk by a torpedo, most likely fired by a North Korean vessel.

Pyongyang continues to deny responsibility for the sinking of the *Cheonan*, but the attacks of November 23, 2010, were more directly attributable to North Korea. Almost two hundred shells and rockets were fired from North Korea's southern coast at the South Korean island of **Yeonpyeongdo** in response to Seoul's refusal to halt a military training exercise in nearby waters. The northern shelling appeared to be indiscriminate, killing two civilians and two soldiers from the South, which responded in kind with howitzers of its own. This was one of the most serious cross-border incidents since the Korean War, and many southerners formerly sympathetic to the North were suddenly favouring a powerful military response to any future attacks. At the time of writing, the situation remained tense.

The Olympic legacy

Rather incredibly, just one year after the massacre, Seoul was given the rights to host the **1988 Summer Olympics**. Some estimates say the Gwangju Massacre resulted in a similar death count to the Tiananmen Square massacre, though it's hard to imagine Beijing being granted a similar honour the year after those events. Originally the brainchild of Park Chung-hee, the Olympic plan was followed through by Chun Doo-hwan in an apparent attempt to seek international recognition of his authoritarian rule. Though he may have regarded the winning of the 1981 Olympic vote as a tacit global nod of acceptance, the strategy backfired somewhat when the country was thrust into the spotlight. Partly as a result of this increased attention, Korea's first-ever free elections were held in 1987, with **Roh Tae-woo** taking the helm. During the same period Korean conglomerates, known as the *jaebeol*, were spreading their financial arms around the world. Korea's aggressive, debt-funded expansion worsened the effect of the Asian Currency Crisis on the country in 1997, and for several years after it struck, the bare shells of over a hundred partially finished buildings stood around Seoul.

In 1998, once-condemned liberal activist **Kim Dae-jung** completed a remarkable turnaround by being appointed president himself. The first South Korean leader to favour a peaceable reunification of the peninsula, he wasted no time in kicking off his "**Sunshine Policy**" of reconciliation with the North; some minor industrial projects were outsourced across the border, and new Seoul-funded factories were built around the city of Kaesong, just north of the DMZ. In 2000, after an historic Pyongyang summit with North Korean leader Kim Jong-Il, he was awarded the **Nobel Peace Prize**.

1980	1988	2002
Massacre of student protestors in Gwangju; Seoul awarded Olympics the following year	Seoul hosts Olympic Games	South Korea co-hosts football's World Cup

Into the twenty-first century

South Korea's international reputation was further enhanced by its hugely successful co-hosting of the **2002 Football World Cup** with Japan. However, that same year a series of incidents gave rise to something of an anti-American (and, by extension, anti-Western) sentiment. Most significant was the accidental killing of two local schoolgirls by an American armoured vehicle, which led to large protests against the US military presence (one that has declined, bit by bit, ever since). Later that year, **Roh Moo-hyun** was elected president on a slightly anti-American ticket; soon after taking office in early 2003, however, he sent Korean troops to Iraq, which made him instantly unpopular, and he committed suicide in 2009, following a bribery scandal. Roh's presidency coincided with **Lee Myung-bak**'s tenure as mayor of Seoul. In 2003, Lee announced plans to gentrify the **Cheonggyecheon** creek, which was an expensive and therefore deeply unpopular project – today, however, it is much beloved by the public.

Lee was elected president of Korea in 2008, but as with Roh before him, there were almost immediate protests against his rule, this time thanks to a beef trade agreement made with the USA. Fears that mad cow disease would be imported to this beef-loving land resulted in mass protests around the city, and **rioting** around **Gwanghwamun Plaza**; one man died after setting fire to himself in protest. The plaza itself was renovated shortly afterwards, and other major projects followed, including the **Dongdaemun Design Plaza**, the new **City Hall** and some futuristic **floating islands** in the Hangang. Like Incheon Airport, these designs all display a curvy, chrome-and-glass style of architecture, intended to portray Seoul as a city of the future, surely one factor behind its selection as host of the **G20 Summit** in 2010. In 2014, however, Seoul was again rocked by protests after the sinking of the *Sewol* off Korea's southwestern coast, a tragic incident in which almost 300 died – the vast majority were of school age. The issue turned into a political hot potato, with opposition parties stoking widespread protests against president **Park Geun-hye**.

2010	2012	2014
North Korea sinks frigate from the South, and shells Yeonpyeongdo island	Psy's hit *Gangnam Style* brings the wealthy Seoul suburb to the attention of the world	Sinking of the Sewol ferry; hundreds of children perish

Religion

Korea has a long and fascinating religious history, one that continues to inform local life. Buddhism is the religion most closely identified with Korea, though Christianity now has a greater number of followers. The rise of the latter is particularly interesting when laid over Korea's largely Confucian mindset, which is often diametrically opposed to Christian ideals and beliefs – priests and pastors preach equality at Sunday service, but outside church relative age still governs many forms of social interaction, and women remain socially inferior to men.

Buddhism

Buddhism is a religion deriving from the teachings of the Buddha, also known as the Siddhartha Gautama or Sakyamuni, who lived in India sometime between the fourth and sixth centuries BC. Although there are two main schools of thought and several smaller ones, Buddhist philosophy revolves around the precept that karma, rebirth and suffering are intrinsic elements of existence, but that the cycle of birth and death can be escaped on what is known as the "Noble Eightfold Path" to nirvana.

An import from China (which had in turn imported it from the Indian subcontinent), Buddhism arrived in Korea at the beginning of the Three Kingdoms period. **Goguryeo** and **Baekje** both adopted it at around the same time, in the last decades of the fourth century – Goguryeo king Sosurim accepted Buddhism almost as soon as the first Chinese monks arrived in 372, while Baekje king Chimnyu adopted it after taking the throne in 384. The **Silla** kings were less impressed by the creed, but a major change in regal thought occurred in 527 after an interesting episode involving an official who had decided to switch to Buddhism. He was to be beheaded for his beliefs, and with his final few gasps swore to the king that his blood would not be red, but a milky white; his prediction was true, and the king soon chose Buddhism as his state religion.

Even in China, Buddhism was at this point in something of an embryonic phase, and Korean monks took the opportunity to develop the **Mahayana** style by ironing out what they saw to be inconsistencies in the doctrine. Disagreements followed, leading to the creation of several **sects**, of which the **Jogye** order is by far the largest, including about ninety percent of Korea's Buddhists; other notable sects include **Seon**, largely known in the West as Zen, the Japanese translation, and **Cheontae**, which is likewise better known under its Chinese name of Tiantai.

Ornate **temples** sprang up all over the peninsula during the **Unified Silla** period, but although Buddhism remained the state religion throughout the **Goryeo** era, the rise of Confucianism squeezed it during **Joseon** times. Monks were treated with scant respect and temples were largely removed from the main cities (one reason why there are relatively few in Seoul, the Joseon capital), but though the religion was repressed, it never came close to extinction. Further troubles came during the **Japanese occupation period**, during the latter years of which many Koreans were forced to worship at Shinto shrines. Mercifully, although many of the temples that weren't closed by the Japanese were burnt down in the Korean War that followed the Japanese occupation, reconstruction programmes have been so comprehensive that in most Korean cities you will seldom be more than a walk away from the nearest temple, each one still an active place of worship. Seoul has fared less well in this regard, but there are some temples in the city centre, and more on the slopes of the city's surrounding mountains.

Temples

Korea's many **temples** are some of the most visually appealing places in the country, though there are precious few good examples in Seoul. Most run along a similar design scheme: on entry to the temple complex you'll pass through the *iljumun* (일주문), or "first gate", then the *cheonwangmun* (천왕문). The latter almost always contains **four large guardians**, two menacing figures towering on each side of the dividing walkway; these control the four heavens and provide guidance to those with a righteous heart. The central building of a Korean temple is the **main hall**, or *daeungjeon* (대웅전). Initially, it was only Sakyamuni – the historical Buddha – who was enshrined here, but this was soon flanked on left and right by bodhisattvas (a term for those who have reached nirvana). Most of these halls have doors at the front, which are usually only for elder monks; novices, and visiting foreigners, use side-entrances. Among the many other halls that you may find on the complex are the *daejeokgwangjeon* (대적광전), the hall of the Vairocana Buddha; *gwaneumjeon* (관음전), a hall for the Bodhisattva of Compassion; *geungnakjeon* (극락전), the Nirvana Hall and home to the celestial Amitabha Buddha; *mireukjeon* (미륵전), the hall of the future Maitreya Buddha; and *nahanjeon* (나한전), the hall of disciples. Some also feature the *palsangjeon* (팔상전), a hall featuring **eight paintings** detailing the life of the Sakyamuni Buddha, though these are more often found on the outside of another hall.

Somewhere in the complex you'll find the *beomjonggak* (범종각), a "**bell pavilion**" containing instruments to awaken the four sentient beings – a drum for land animals, a wooden fish for the water-borne, a bronze gong for creatures of the air, and a large bell for monks who have slept in. The bell itself can sometimes weigh upwards of twenty tonnes, and the best will have an information board telling you how far away they can be heard if you were to strike them lightly with your fist. Needless to say, you shouldn't test these contentions.

Confucianism

Like Buddhism, **Confucian thought** made its way across the sea from China – the exact date remains a mystery, but it seems that it first spread to Korea at the beginning of the Three Kingdoms era. Although Confucianism can't be classified as a religion – there's no central figure of worship, or concept of an afterlife – it is used as a means of self-cultivation, and a guide to "proper" conduct, particularly the showing of respect for those higher up the social hierarchy. For centuries it co-existed with the state religion, informing not only political thought but also national ethics, and in many ways it still governs the Korean way of life today. Central to the concept are the **Five Moral Disciplines** of human-to-human conduct, namely ruler to subject, father to son, husband to wife, elder to younger and friend to friend.

During the Three Kingdoms period, the concepts of filial piety began to permeate Korean life, with adherence to the rules gradually taking the form of ceremonial rites. In the Silla kingdom there developed a "bone rank" system used to segregate social strata, one that was to increase in rigidity until the Joseon era. This was essentially a **caste** system, one that governed almost every sphere of local life – each "level" of society would have strict limits placed on what they could achieve, the size of their dwelling, whom they could marry and even what colours they were allowed to wear.

At the dawn of the Joseon dynasty in 1392, King Taejo had the **Jongmyo shrines** built in central Seoul, and for centuries afterwards, ruling kings would venerate their ancestors here in regular ceremonies. At this time, Confucianism truly took hold, with numerous academies (*hyanggyo*) built around the country at which students from the elite *yangban* classes would wade through wave after wave of punishing examinations on their way to senior governmental posts. Buddhism had been on the decline for some time, with Confucian scholars arguing that making appeals to gods unseen had a detrimental effect on the national psyche, and that building ornate temples absorbed funds too readily. Some, in fact, began to clamour for the burning of those temples, as well as the murder of monks. As with other beliefs, some followers violated the core principles for their own ends and, despite the birth of great neo-Confucian philosophers such as **Yi-Yi** and **Toegye**, enforced slavery and servitude meant that the lot of those at the lower caste levels changed little over the centuries.

Confucianism today

It's often said that Korea remains the **most Confucian** of all the world's societies. In addition to several remaining academies and shrines – there's one of the latter at Inwangsan, just west of Gyeongbokgung – colourful ancestral ceremonies take place each year at Jongmyo in Seoul. Its impact on everyday life is also evident: on getting to know a local, you'll generally be asked a series of questions both direct and indirect (particularly with regard to age, marriage, education and employment), the answers to which will be used to file you into mental pigeonholes. Though foreigners are treated somewhat differently, this is the main reason why locals see nothing wrong in barging strangers out of the way on the street or showing no mercy on the road – no introduction has been made, and without knowledge of the "proper" behaviour in such a situation no moves are made towards showing respect. Among those who do know each other, it's easy to find **Confucian traits**: women are still seen as inferior to men (their salaries continue to lag far behind, and they're usually expected to quit their job on having a child, never to return to the workplace); the boss or highest earner will usually pay after a group meal; family values remain high, and paper qualifications from reputable universities carry more weight than actual intelligence. Also notable is **bungsu**, a concept that involves the moving of ancestral grave sites. Perhaps the most high-profile examples of corpse-shifting have been before general elections. After Kim Dae-jung lost the elections in 1987 and 1992, he decided to move the graves of his ancestors to more auspicious locations, and he duly won the next election in 1998. However, Confucian ideas are slowly being eroded as Westernization continues to encroach, particularly as the number of Christians continues to grow.

Christianity

Making up well over a quarter of the country by population, **Christianity** is now Korea's leading religion by number of worshippers, having surpassed Buddhism at the start of the twenty-first century. Surprisingly, the religion has been on the peninsula since the end of the eighteenth century, having been brought across the waters by missionaries from various European empires. At the time, the Confucian *yangban* in charge were fearful of change, hardly surprising considering how far apart the fundamental beliefs of the two creeds are. Christianity's refusal to perform ancestral rites eventually led to its repression, and hundreds of Christians were **martyred** in the 1870s and 1880s. A number of French missionaries were also murdered in this period, before Korea was forcefully opened up for trade. The numbers have been growing ever since, the majority now belonging to the Presbyterian, Catholic or Methodist churches.

Churches tend to be monstrous concrete edifices (many visitors note that most sport rather Satanic-looking red neon crosses), and some are huge, with room for thousands of worshippers. In fact, the island of Yeouido, near Seoul, officially has the largest church in the world, with 170 pastors and over 100,000 registered deacons.

Film

For all of its efforts in finance, electronics and promoting its food and tradition, it's Korea's film industry that has had the most success in pushing the country as a global brand. While Korean horror flicks have developed an international cult following, and a number of esteemed directors have set international film festivals abuzz, special mention must also be made of the locally produced television dramas that have caught on like wildfire across Asia. Like many of the movies, these are highly melodramatic offerings that don't seek to play on the heartstrings so much as power-chord the merry hell out of them. All of these form part of the Hallyeo movement, a "New Wave" of Korean production that has been in motion since cinematic restrictions were lifted in the 1980s.

After the Korean War, the film industries in North and South Korea developed separately; leaders on both sides saw movies as a hugely useful **propaganda tool**, and made immediate efforts to revive local cinema. In the south, President Syngman Rhee conferred tax-exempt status on movie-makers, who made films looking back at the misery of wartime and the occupation, and forward to a rosy future for non-Communist Korea. By the end of the 1950s, annual movie output had reached triple figures, with the most popular being watched by millions. The accession of Park Chung-hee to president in 1961, however, brought an end to what passed for cinematic freedom – in addition to the **censorship** and hard-fisted restrictions over local productions, foreign films were vetted and placed under a strict quota system, elements of which remained in place until 2006. As Park's rule grew ever more dictatorial, he inaugurated a short-lived era of **"governmental policy" films**; these were hugely unpopular, and cinema attendance dropped sharply.

The Hallyeo "New Wave"

After Park's death, democratization and the gradual relaxation of restrictions gave rise to the **Hallyeo movement**. With the loosening of controls in the 1980s, a clutch of talented directors was finally able to give Korea exposure in the West. Foremost among them was **Im Kwon-taek**, a maverick who shrugged off his role as a creator of commercial quota-fillers to unleash some striking new films. The government continued to provide funding for the movie industry until the 1999 release of *Shiri*, the country's first fully independent film. Since then, Korean films have reached an ever-greater international audience, and a number of directors such as **Kim Ki-duk** and **Park Chan-wook** are now globally acclaimed. The films recommended below are those that give an insight into Korea in general and Seoul in particular.

Chihwaseon (2002) Sometimes going under the title *Painted Fire*, this beautifully shot tale of Jang Seung-eop – a nineteenth-century Seoulite painter best known by his pen name Owon – won the Best Director award at Cannes for Im Kwon-taek, a maverick who had been around for decades but was previously ignored on the international stage.

Joint Security Area (2000) Any Korean film about the DMZ is worth a look, as is anything by acclaimed director Park Chan-wook. Here, two North Korean soldiers are killed in the DMZ; like *Memento* (which came out the following year), the story plays backwards, revealing the lead-up piece by piece.

Ode to my Father (2014) A look at Korea from the 1950s to the present day, through the eyes of an ordinary man who gets caught up in the Korean and Vietnamese wars. The film was criticized by some for glorifying the country's dictatorial past – the fact that it was a huge hit demonstrates the local appetite for such selective nostalgia, and the politics which continue to divide South Korea.

NORTH KOREAN CINEMA

Cinema is big business in **North Korea** – cinephile Kim Jong-Il poured funds into the industry for decades before he became leader of the country, and in 1978 even organized the kidnapping of **Shin Sang-ok** – a prominent South Korean director – in an effort to improve the quality of local cinema. North Korea produces some of the world's most distinctive films, a few of which have started to trickle onto the international market; to buy, go to Ⓦ north-korea-books.com. The themes stick rigidly to brave North Korean resistance during the Korean War and the Japanese occupation, depicting Americans as unspeakably evil and South Koreans as their puppets.

A State of Mind (2004) On the surface, this is a documentary about two young girls training for the Arirang Mass Games in Pyongyang, but it amounts to a first-ever stab at a genuine portrayal of the average life of today's North Koreans. It was evidently a success: after the film was shown on DPRK state TV, locals complained that it was "dull", having merely filmed them going about their daily lives; little did they know how compelling this kind of realistic reportage is to the average foreign viewer.

★ **Comrade Kim Goes Flying** (2012) Produced and directed by Nick Bonner, this was the first foreign film to be made in North Korea, receiving the personal approval of Kim Jong-Il. In Korean and with an all-DPRK cast, this light-hearted "commie rom-com" tells the story of an ambitious young trapeze artist.

Crossing the Line (2006) James Joseph Dresnok is a movie-maker's delight, but this fascinating documentary is the world's only peek inside the mind of "Comrade Joe", one of four American soldiers known to have defected to North Korea after the Korean War. With a candour that shows a genuine love of his new country, Dresnok tells of his journey from a troubled adolescence to old age in Pyongyang, including his crossing of the treacherous DMZ, a failed attempt at escape, and his stint as a star on the North Korean silver screen.

The Interview (2014) This dumb comedy became a giant global news story even before its release. Its plot – two boobs are sent to assassinate Kim Jong-un – angered the establishment in North Korea, and Sony Pictures had their systems hacked as an apparently direct result. The storyline of the film itself is less interesting, but it's still worth a watch.

Shiri (1999) Also known as *Swiri*, this was a landmark film in Korean cinema, marking the dawn of a Hollywood style long suppressed by the government. The mix of explosions and loud music is not of as much interest to foreigners as it is to Koreans, but the plot – South Korean cops hunt down a North Korean sniper girl – is interesting enough. The girl was played by Yunjin Kim, who later found fame on the American TV series *Lost*.

Silmido (2003) Loosely based on events in the 1960s, which saw South Korean operatives receive secret training on the island of Silmido to assassinate North Korean leader Kim Il-sung. The film broke Korean box office records, and provides a fascinating depiction of the tensions of the time.

The Host (2006) The tranquil life of a riverside merchant is blown to smithereens when formaldehyde disposed into the river by the American military creates a ferocious underwater creature. This comic thriller smashed box office records in Korea; although the international reception was nowhere near as fervent, it's worth a look.

★ **The King and the Clown** (2005) A period drama with homosexual undercurrents, this was an unexpected smash hit at the box office. Set during the reign of King Yeonsan – whose short rule began in 1494 – it tells of a pair of street entertainers who find themselves in Seoul's royal court. One of them fosters an ever-closer relationship with the king.

The President's Last Bang (2005) Korea has long been crying out for satire, particularly something to inject a little fun into its turgid political reportage, and this hits the nail squarely on the head (as demonstrated by the lawsuit that followed). It's based on a true story, namely the assassination of president Park Chung-hee in 1979; the portrayal of Park as something of a Japanese-sympathetic playboy certainly ruffled a few feathers.

Welcome to Dongmakgol (2005) Too twee for some, but heart-warming to others, this beautifully shot film tells of a motley assortment of American, South Korean and North Korean combatants from the Korean War who somehow end up in the same village, among people unaware not only of the conflict raging around them but of warfare in general.

Books

Despite Korea's long and interesting history, the East Asian sections in most bookshops largely focus on China and Japan. The majority of books that are devoted to Korea cover North Korea or the Korean War; far less biased than most newspaper or television reports, these are the best form of reportage about the world's most curious state and how it was created.

FICTION

Cho Se-hui *The Dwarf*. Even miracles have a downside: Seoul's economy underwent a truly remarkable transformation in the 1970s, but at what cost to its people and culture? This weighty, tersely delivered novel uncovers the spiritual decline of Seoul's nouveaux riches, via twelve interconnected stories; *A Dwarf Launches a Little Bell* is particularly recommended, and has been reprinted hundreds of times in Korea.

★**Adam Johnson** *The Orphan Master's Son*. Winner of the 2013 Pulitzer Prize for fiction, this tells the story of an orphan who struggles through life in North Korea, and ends up employed as a kidnapper of Japanese citizens.

Park Wan-Suh *Who Ate Up All the Shinga?* A semi-autobiographical mother-daughter story from one of Korea's most highly acclaimed writers, set during the Korean War. Fans of Park should also check out *Sketch of the Fading Sun*, a collection of short stories.

★**Yi Munyeol** *Our Twisted Hero*. This tale of psychological warfare at a Korean elementary school has a deceptively twee plotline, managing to explore the use and misuse of power while providing metaphorical parallels to Korean politics of the 1970s.

Young Ha Kim *Your Republic is Calling You* and *I Have the Right to Destroy Myself*. Two books from a man whose international reputation is growing by the year, his popularity and his existentialist tendencies marking him out as a potential Korean Murakami. The first book revolves around a North Korean spy torn between his homeland and the South, while the second, set in Seoul, is the dark tale of a refined thinker with suicidal tendencies.

HISTORY AND SOCIETY

Michael Breen *The Koreans: Who They Are, What They Want, Where Their Future Lies*. Although the four main sections of this book – society, history, economy and politics – may seem dry, the accounts are relayed with warmth and a pleasing depth of knowledge.

Bruce Cumings *Korea's Place in the Sun: A Modern History*. The Korean peninsula went through myriad changes in the twentieth century, and this weighty tome analyzes the effects of such disquiet on its population, showing that the South's seemingly smooth trajectory towards democracy and capitalism masked a great suffering of the national psyche.

Euny Hong *The Birth of Korean Cool*. A good rundown of Korea's attempts to conquer Asia, then the world at large, with its pop culture – as well as the more obvious drama and music, it looks at how this impacted upon Korea's place on the global economic stage.

Keith Pratt *Everlasting Flower: A History of Korea*. This thoroughly readable book provides a chronicle of Korean goings-on from the very first kingdoms to the modern day, its text broken up with interesting illustrated features on the arts and customs prevalent at the time.

Daniel Tudor *Korea: The Impossible Country*. Written by Korea's former *Economist* correspondent, this looks at how the country transformed from a failed state to an economic powerhouse in the space of a generation or two – and what today's generation has in store.

NORTH KOREA AND THE KOREAN WAR

★**Bruce Cumings** *North Korea: Another Country*. The US-North Korean dispute is far more complex than Western media would have you imagine, and this book provides a revealing – if slightly hard to digest – glance at the flipside. Cumings' meticulous research is without parallel, and the accounts of American atrocities and cover-ups both in the "Forgotten War" and during the nuclear crisis offer plenty of food for thought.

Guy Delisle *Pyongyang*. A comic strip describing his time as a cartoonist in Pyongyang, Delisle's well-observed and frequently hilarious book is a North Korean rarity – one that tells it like it is, and doesn't seek to make political or ideological statements. His illustrations are eerily accurate.

★**Barbara Demick** *Nothing to Envy*. An admirably well-researched look at modern life in North Korea, based on the experiences of six residents of Chongjin, a major city in the northeast of the country. Gulags, the Kim cult, famine and poverty all get a mention, juxtaposed with the views of a seemingly unwavering believer in the regime.

Max Hastings *The Korean War*. A conflict is not quite a war until it has been given the treatment by acclaimed historian Max Hastings. Here, he has provided more than his usual mix of fascinating, balanced and well-researched material; the account of the stand of the Gloucesters on the Imjin is particularly absorbing.

Kang Chol-Hwan *The Aquariums of Pyongyang*. Having fled his homeland after spending time in a North Korean gulag, Kang's harrowing accounts of squalor, starvation and brutality represent one of the few windows into the world's most fenced-off social systems. He's not a natural author, however, and the confused sermonizing at the end rather dilutes the book's appeal.

Bradley K. Martin *Under the Loving Care of the Fatherly Leader*. Almost 900 pages long – 200 of which are references – this isn't a tome to carry around in your backpack, but for an in-depth look at the Kims and the perpetration of their personality cult, it's hard to beat.

★**Don Oberdorfer** *The Two Koreas: A Contemporary History*. Lengthy, but engaging and surprisingly easy to read, this book traces various events in postwar Korea, as well as examining how they were affected by the actions and policies of China, Russia, Japan and the US. You'd be hard pressed to find a book about North Korea more neutral in tone.

RECIPE BOOKS

Debra Samuels and **Taekyung Chung** *The Korean Table*. One hundred easy-to-follow recipes "from barbecue to *bibimbap*", accompanied by photos that will make you drool, this book will have your kitchen covered with chilli paste in no time at all.

Marja Vongerichten and **Jean Georges Vongerichten** *The Kimchi Chronicles: Korean Cooking for an American Kitchen*. A very useful cookbook, which takes account of the fact that its readers may not have access to a full Korean kitchen's-worth of utensils.

Korean

The sole official tongue of both North and South Korea, the Korean language is spoken by almost eighty million people, making it one of the world's twenty most-spoken tongues. It's a highly tricky language to pick up – much to the chagrin of linguists, it remains stubbornly "unclassified" on the global language tree, its very origins something of a mystery. Some lump it in with the Altaic group (itself rather vague), which would put it on the same branch as Turkish and Mongolian, though many view it as a language isolate. Korean is therefore in the same boat as Japanese, its closest linguistic brother; both share a subject-object-verb syntax and similar grammar, though well over half of the Korean words themselves actually originate from China. Korea also used Chinese text for centuries, even after creating its own characters (known as *hangeul*; 한글) in the 1440s, but now almost exclusively uses the local system for everyday functions.

Native speakers of European languages will encounter some pretty significant **grammatical differences** when attempting to get a handle on the Korean tongue. Korean **nouns** remain unaffected whether they refer to singular or plural objects, very little use is made of **articles**, and **verbs** do not change case according to whom or what they're referring to – *gayo* can mean "I go", "he/she/it goes" or "we/they go", the meaning made clear by the context. Verbs do, however, alter depending on which **level of politeness** the speaker wants to use, and the relationship between speaker and listener; the conversation will sound quite different depending on whether it's between a child and a mother, a boss and an employee, or even good friends of slightly different age. In general, it's pretty safe to stick to verbs with the polite **–yo** ending; the verb forms given here are in a formal style which should suffice for most travellers. Unfortunately, there are few good books from which to learn Korean; those from the *Teach Yourself* and *Colloquial* series fall short of the two companies' usually high standards, but are about as good as you'll find.

THE ORIGINS OF HANGEUL

Though it may seem surprising, *hangeul* was actually a royal creation, having been the brainchild of **King Sejong** in the 1440s. Up until then, his Joseon kingdom and the dynasties that went before had been using Chinese characters, but seeing that most of his citizens were illiterate and denied education, the king devised a system that would be easier for the common man to learn. He was forced to do much of his work in secret, as the change did not go down well with the Confucian *yangban* scholars, some of whom were almost king-like in their power at the time; as the only members of society to receive an education strong enough to make reading Chinese characters a possibility, they argued against the change in an effort to maintain their privileged access to historical texts and suchlike. *Hangeul* experienced periodic bursts of popularity, but was kept down first by the *yangban*, and then almost erased entirely by the Japanese during their occupation of the peninsula (1910–45). Today, it's the **official writing system** of both North and South Korea, as well as a small autonomous Korean pocket in the Chinese province of Jilin. Students in Korea study at least two thousand Chinese characters at school, and some of the simpler ones are still used in daily life.

Korean characters

Though it consists of a highly distinctive scrawl of circles and Tetris shapes, many foreigners find Korean text surprisingly **easy to learn**. Koreans tend to assume that foreigners don't have the inclination or mental capability to decipher *hangeul*, so your efforts will not go unappreciated. Koreans are immensely proud of *hangeul*, which they see as the world's most logical written system (see box opposite). While this is no great exaggeration, the efficiency also has a downside – user-friendly it may well be, but in reality *hangeul* is a very narrow system that cannot cope with sounds not found in the Korean language, a fact that partially explains the Korean people's occasionally curious pronunciation of foreign words.

Korean characters are grouped into **syllabic boxes** of more or less equal size, and generally arranged left to right – if you see a line of text made up of eighteen of these character-chunks, it will have eighteen syllables when spoken. The way in which the **characters** fall into the boxes is unique and takes a bit of figuring out – some have two characters in the top half and one at the bottom (the top two are read left to right, followed by the bottom one, so 한 makes *han*), while others have two or three characters arranged vertically (these are read downwards, so 국 makes *guk*). Thus put together, we have 한국 – *hanguk*, meaning "Korea".

Pronunciation

Pronouncing Korean words is tough – some sounds simply do not have English-language equivalents. You'll see from the *hangeul* box (see below) that there's only one character for "l" and "r", with its actual sound some way in between the two – try saying both phonemes at the same time. The letters "k", "d", "b" and "j" are often written "k", "t", "p" and "ch", and are pronounced approximately halfway towards those Roman equivalents; unfortunately, the second set also have their place in the official system, and are usually referred to as **aspirated consonants**, accompanied as they are by a puff of air. Consonants are fairly easy to master – note that some are doubled up, and spoken more

---

HANGEUL CHARACTERS

The basic building blocks of *hangeul* are listed below. Note that some consonants are pronounced differently depending on whether they're at the beginning or end of a syllable or word (syllable-ending sounds are in brackets below), and that "ng" is used as an initial null consonant for syllables that start with a vowel.

ㄱ	g (k)	ㅗ	o
ㄴ	n	ㅛ	yo
ㄷ	d (t)	ㅜ	u
ㄹ	r/l	ㅠ	yu
ㅁ	m	ㅡ	eu
ㅂ	b (p)	ㅣ	i
ㅅ	s (t)	ㅔ	e
ㅈ	j (t)	ㅐ	ae
ㅊ	ch (t)	ㅖ	ye
ㅋ	k	ㅒ	yae
ㅌ	t	ㅟ	wi
ㅍ	p	ㅞ	we
ㅎ	h	ㅙ	wae
ㅇ	ng	ㅘ	wa
ㅏ	a	ㅚ	oe
ㅑ	ya	ㅢ	ui
ㅓ	eo	ㅝ	wo
ㅕ	yeo		

TRANSLITERATARY TROUBLES

Rendering the Korean language in Roman text is, simply, a battle that can never be won – a classic problem of square pegs and round holes. Numerous systems have been employed down the years, perhaps best exemplified in the Korean family name now usually romanized as "Lee": this has also been written as Rhee, Li, Ri, Lih, Rhi, Ree, Yi, Rii and more besides. Under the current system it would be "I", but the actual pronunciation is simply "ee" – it's amazing how much trouble a simple vowel can cause (especially when almost a fifth of the country has this name).

A Korean's age, schooling, family and even lifestyle influence the way that they'll romanize a given word, but official standards have long been in place. The **Yale** and **McCune–Reischauer** systems became widely accepted in the 1940s, and the latter is still much in evidence today; under its rules, aspirated consonants are marked with apostrophes, and certain vowels with breves. One problem – other than looking ugly – was that these punctuation markings are often neglected, even in language study books; though it remains the official system in North Korea, the South formulated its own system of **Revised Romanization** in 2000. While this is far from perfect, it's the official standard, and has been used throughout this book; exceptions include names of the many hotels, restaurants, universities and individuals who cling to the old ways. One other issue is the Korean syllable *shi*; this is now romanized as *si*, a rather ridiculous change since it takes Koreans years of language classes before they can pronounce the syllable without palatalizing it – "six" and "sister" will be pronounced "shix" and "shister". We've written it as *shi* in the language listings to help you achieve the correct pronunciation, but obeyed the official system in the rest of the book – Sinchon is pronounced "Shinchon", and so on.

Koreans themselves find it hard to render **foreign words** in *hangeul* as there are many sounds that don't fit into the system – the difficulties with "l" and "r" sharing the same character being an obvious example – but even when parallels exist they are sometimes distorted. The letter "a" is usually written as an "e" or "ae" in an unsuccessful effort to Americanize the pronunciation – "hat", for example, will be pronounced "het" by the majority of the population, while to kowtow to American norms gimbap is often written "kimbob".

forcefully – but pronunciation guides to some of the tricky **vowels** and **diphthongs** are as follows (British English readings offer the closest equivalents):

a as in "**car**"	**e** as in "**bed**"
ya as in "**yap**"	**ae** as in "**air**"
eo as in "**hot**"	**ye** as in "**yet**"
yeo as in "**yob**"	**yae** as in "**yeah**"
o pronounced "**ore**"	**wi** as in "**window**"
yo pronounced as the British "**your**"	**we** as in "**wedding**"
u as in "**Jew**"	**wae** as in the beginning of "**whe**re"
yu pronounced "**you**"	**wa** as in "**wag**"
eu no English equivalent; widen your mouth and try an "euggh" sound of disgust	**oe** as in the beginning of "**way**"
i as in "**pea**"	**ui** no English equivalent; add an "ee" sound to *eu* above
	wo as in "**wad**"

USEFUL WORDS AND PHRASES

BASICS

Yes	*ye/ne*	예/네
No	*aniyo*	아니요
Please (asking for something)	*…juseyo*	…주세요
Excuse me	*shillye hamnida*	실례합니다
I'm sorry	*mian hamnida*	미안합니다
Thank you	*gamsa hamnida*	감사합니다
You're welcome	*gwaenchan-ayo*	괜찮아요
What?	*muot?*	무엇?

When?	*eonje?*	언제?
Where?	*eodi?*	어디?
Who?	*nugu?*	누구?
How?	*eotteokke?*	어떻께?
How much?	*eolma-eyo?*	얼마에요?
How many?	*myeokke-eyo?*	몇 개에요?
I want…	*…hago-shipeoyo*	…하고 싶어요
Please help me	*dowa-juseyo*	도와주세요

COMMUNICATING

I can't speak Korean	*jeo-neun hangugeo-reul mot haeyo*	저는 한국어를 못 해요
I can't read Korean	*jeo-neun hangugeo-reul mok ilgeoyo*	저는 한국어를 못 읽어요
Do you speak English?	*yeongeo halsu-isseoyo?*	영어 할 수 있어요?
Is there someone who can speak English?	*yeongeo-reul haljul a-neun bun isseoyo?*	영어를 할줄 아는 분 있어요?
Can you please speak slowly?	*jom cheoncheonhi mal haejuseyo?*	좀 천천히 말 해주세요?
Please say that again	*dashi han-beon mal haejuseyo*	다시 한번말 해주세요
I understand/I see	*alasseoyo*	알았 어요
I (really) don't understand	*(jal) mollayo*	(잘) 몰라요
What does this mean?	*i-geot museun ddeushi-eyo?*	이것 무슨 뜻이에요?
How do you say (x) in Korean?	*(x) eul/reul hanguk-eoro eotteokke mal haeyo?*	(x) 을/를 한국어로 어떻께 말해요
Please write in English	*yeongeo-ro jeogeo jushillaeyo*	영어로 적어 주실래요
Please wait (a moment)	*(jamggan) gidariseyo*	(잠깐) 기다리세요
Just a minute	*jamggan manyo*	잠깐 만요

MEETINGS AND GREETINGS

Hello; Good morning/ afternoon/evening	*annyeong haseyo*	안녕 하세요
Hello (polite)	*annyeong hashimnikka*	안녕 하십니까
How are you?	*jal jinaesseoyo?*	잘 지냈어요?
I'm fine	*jal jinaesseoyo/jo-ayo*	잘 지냈어요/좋아요
Nice to meet you	*bangapseumnida*	반갑습니다
Goodbye (when staying)	*annyeong-hi gaseyo*	안녕히 가세요
Goodbye (when leaving)	*annyeong-hi gyeseyo*	안녕히 계세요
What's your name?	*ireum-i eotteokke doeshimnikka?*	이름이 어떻께 되십니까?
My name is…	*ireum-i … imnida*	이름이… 입니다
Where are you from?	*eodi-eso wasseoyo?*	어디에 왔어요?
I'm from…	*…eso wasseoyo*	에서 왔어요
Korea	*han-guk*	한국
Britain	*yeong-guk*	영국
Ireland	*aillaendeu*	아일랜드
America	*mi-guk*	미국
Australia	*oseuteureillia/hoju*	오스트레일리아 / 호주
Canada	*kae-nada*	캐나다
New Zealand	*nyu jillaendeu*	뉴질랜드
South Africa	*nam apeurika*	남 아프리카
How old are you?	*myeot-sal ieyo?*	몇 살이에요?
I am (age)	*(age)-sal ieyo*	(age) 살이에요
Do you like…?	*…o-a haeyo?*	…좋아 해요?
I like…	*jo-a haeyo*	좋아 해요
I don't like…	*an jo-a haeyo*	안 좋아해요
Do you have (free) time?	*shigan-i isseoyo?*	시간이 있어요?

NUMBERS

Rather confusingly, the Korean language has two separate number systems operating in parallel – a **native Korean** system, and a **Sino-Korean** system of Chinese origin – and you'll have to learn according to the situation which one to use. To tell the time, you'll need both – amazingly, minutes and hours run on different systems. The native Korean system only goes up to 99, and has been placed on the right-hand side of the readings. Dates and months use the Sino-Korean system alone, with **il** (sun) used as a suffix for days, and **wol** (moon) for months: June 7 is thus **yuk-wol chil-il**.

Zero	yeong/gong	영/공
One	il/hana	일/하나
Two	i (pronounced "ee")/dul	이/둘
Three	sam/set	삼/셋
Four	sa/net	사/넷
Five	o/daseot	오/다섯
Six	yuk/yeoseot	육/여섯
Seven	chil/ilgop	칠/일곱
Eight	pal/yeodeol	팔/여덟
Nine	gu/ahop	구/아홉
Ten	ship/yeol	십 / 열
Eleven	shib-il / yeol-hana	십일/열하나
Twelve	shib-i/yeol-dul	십이/열둘
Twenty	i-shib/seumul	이십/스물
Thirty	sam-ship/seoreun	삼십/서른
One hundred	baek	백
Two hundred	i-baek	이백
Thousand	cheon	천
Ten thousand	man	만
One hundred thousand	shim-man	십만
One million	baeng-man	백만
One hundred million	eok	억

TIME AND DATES

Now	jigeum	지금
Today	o-neul	오늘
Morning	achim	아침
Afternoon	ohu	오후
Evening	jeonyok	저녁
Night	bam	밤
Tomorrow	nae-il	내일
Yesterday	eoje	어제
Week	ju	주
Month	wol/dal	월/달
Year	nyeon	년
Monday	wolyo-il	월요일
Tuesday	hwayo-il	화요일
Wednesday	suyo-il	수요일
Thursday	mogyo-il	목요일
Friday	geumyo-il	금요일
Saturday	toyo-il	토요일
Sunday	ilyo-il	일요일
What time is it?	myo-shi-eyo?	몇시에요?
It's 10 o'clock	yeol-shi-eyo	열시에요
10.20	yeol-shi i-ship-bun	열시 이십분
10.30	yeol-shi sam-ship-bun	열시 삼십분
10.50	yeol-shi o-ship-bun	열시 오십분

TRANSPORT AND TRAVEL

Aeroplane	*bihaenggi*	비행기
Airport	*gonghang*	공항
Bus	*beoseu*	버스
Express bus (terminal)	*gosok beoseu (teominal)*	익스프레스 (터미널)
Intercity bus (terminal)	*shi-oe beoseu (teominal)*	시외 버스 (터미널)
City bus	*shinae beoseu*	시내 버스
Airport bus	*gonghang beoseu*	공항 버스
City bus stop	*jeong-nyu-jang*	정류장
Train	*gicha*	기차
Train station	*yeok*	역
Subway	*jihacheol*	지하철
Ferry	*yeogaek-seon*	여객선
Ferry terminal	*yeogaek teominal*	여객 터미널
Left-luggage office	*jimbogwanso*	짐보관
Ticket office	*maepyoso*	매표서
Ticket	*pyo*	표
Platform	*seunggangjang*	승강장
Bicycle	*jajeon-geo*	자전거
Taxi	*taek-shi*	택시

DIRECTIONS AND GENERAL PLACES

Where is (x)?	*-i/ga eodi-eyo?*	-이/가 어디에요?
Straight ahead	*jikjin*	직진
Left	*oen-jjok (pronounced "wen-chok")*	왼쪽
Right	*oreun-jjok*	오른쪽
Behind	*dwi-e*	뒤에
In front of	*ap-e*	앞에
North	*buk*	북
South	*nam*	남
East	*dong*	동
West	*seo*	서
Map	*maep/jido*	맵/지도
Entrance	*ip-gu*	입구
Exit	*chul-gu*	출구
Art gallery	*misulgwan*	미술관
Bank	*eunhaeng*	은행
Beach	*haebyeon*	해변
Department store	*baekhwajeom*	백화점
Embassy	*daesagwan*	대사관
Hot spring spa	*oncheon*	온천
Museum	*bangmulgwan*	박물관
Park	*gongwon*	공원
Sea	*haean/bada*	해안/바다
Temple	*Jeol/sachal*	절/사찰
Toilet	*hwajang-shil*	화장실
Tourist office	*gwan-gwang annaeso*	관광 안내소

ACCOMMODATION

Hotel	*hotel*	호텔
Motel	*motel*	모텔
Guesthouse	*yeogwan*	여관
Budget guesthouse	*yeoinsuk*	여인숙
Rented room	*minbak*	민박

Youth hostel	*yuseu hoseutel*	유스 호스텔
Korean-style room	*ondol-bang*	온돌방
Western-style room	*chimdae-bang*	침대방
Single room	*shinggeul chimdae*	싱글 침대
Double room	*deobeul chimdae*	더블 침대
Twin room	*chimdae dugae*	침대 두개
En-suite room	*yokshil-ddallin bang*	욕실 딸린방
Shower	*syaweo*	샤워
Bath	*yokjo*	욕조
Key	*ki*	키
Passport	*yeogwon*	여권
Do you have any vacancies?	*bang isseoyo?*	방 있어요?
I have a reservation	*yeyak haesseoyo*	예약 했어요
I don't have a reservation	*yeyak anhaesseoyo*	예약 안했어요
How much is the room?	*bang-i eolma-eyo?*	방이 얼마에요?
Does that include breakfast?	*achim-shiksa poham-dwae isseoyo?*	아침식사 포함돼 있어요?
One/two/three nights	*haruppam/ i-bak/sam-bak*	하룻밤/이박/삼박
One week	*il-ju-il*	일주일
May I see the room?	*bang jom bolsu- isseoyo?*	방 좀 볼수 있어요?

SHOPPING, MONEY AND BANKS

Bank	*eunhaeng*	은행
Foreign exchange	*woe-hwan*	외환
Won	*won*	원
Pounds	*pa-un-deu*	파운드
Dollars	*dalleo*	달러
Cash	*don*	돈
Travellers' cheque	*yeohaengja supyo*	여행자 수표
How much is it?	*eolma-eyo?*	얼마에요?
It's too expensive	*neomu bissayo*	너무 비싸요
Please make it a little cheaper	*jom kkakka-juseyo*	좀 깎아주세요
Do you accept credit cards?	*keurediteu kadeu gyesan dwaeyo?*	크레디트 카드 계산 돼요?

POST AND TELEPHONES

Post office	*uche-guk*	우체국
Envelope	*bongtu*	봉투
Letter	*pyeonji*	편지
Postcard	*yeopseo*	엽서
Stamp	*u-pyo*	우표
Airmail	*hanggong u-pyeon*	항공 우편
Surface mail	*seonbak u-pyeon*	선박 우편
Telephone	*jeon-hwa*	전화
Fax	*paekseu*	팩스
Telephone card	*jeonhwa kadeu*	전화카드
Internet café	*PC-bang* PC	방
I would like to call…	*…hante jeonhwa hago- shipeoyo*	좀바꿔 주세요
May I speak to…	*…jom baggwo juseyo*	저는 아파요
Hello?	*yeoboseyo?*	여보세요?

HEALTH

Hospital	*byeongwon*	병원
Pharmacy	*yak-guk*	약국
Medicine	*yak*	약

Doctor	uisa	의사
Dentist	chigwa-uisa	치과의사
Diarrhoea	seolsa	설사
Nausea	meseukkeo-um	메스꺼움
Fever	yeol	열
Food poisoning	shikjungdok	식중독
Antibiotics	hangsaengje	항생제
Antiseptic	sodok-yak	독약
Condom	kondom	콘돔
Penicillin	penishillin	페니실린
Tampons	tampon	탐폰
I'm ill	jeo-neun apayo	저는 아파요
I have a cold	gamgi geoll-yeosseoyo	감기 걸렸어요
I'm allergic to...	...allereugi-ga isseoyo	...알레르기가 있어요
It hurts here	yeogi-ga apayo	여기가 아파요
Please call a doctor	uisa-reul bulleo juseyo	의사를 불러 주세요

FOOD AND DRINK

PLACES

Restaurant	sikdang	식당
Korean barbecue restaurant	galbi-jip	갈비집
Seafood restaurant	hoet-jip	횟집
Western-style restaurant	reseutorang	레스토랑
Italian restaurant	itallian reseutorang	이탈리안 레스토랑
Chinese restaurant	jungguk-jip	중국집
Japanese restaurant	ilshik-jip	일식집
Burger bar	paeseuteu-pudeu-jeom	패스트푸드점
Convenience store	pyeonui-jeom	편의점
Market	shijang	시장
Café	kape	카페
Bar	ba/suljip	바/술집
Club	naiteu-keulleob	나이트클럽
Where's (a) ... ?	...eodi isseoyo?	...어디 있어요?

ORDERING

Waiter/Waitress (lit. "Here!")	yeogiyo!	여기요!
How much is that?	eolma-eyo?	얼마에요?
I would like...	...hago shipeoyo	...하고 싶어요
May I have the bill?	gyesanseo juseyo?	계산서 주세요
I'm a vegetarian	jeo-neun chaeshikju uija-eyo	저는 채식주의자에요
Can I have this without meat?	gogi bbaego haejushilsu isseoyo?	고기 빼고 해주실수 있어요?
I can't eat spicy food	maeun-geot mot meogeoyo	매운 것 못 먹어요
Delicious!	mashisseoyo!	맛있어요!
Chopsticks	jeot-garak	젓가락
Fork	po-keu	포크
Knife	nai-peu/kal	나이프/칼
Spoon	sut-garak	숟가락
Menu	menyu	메뉴

STAPLE INGREDIENTS

Beef	so-gogi	쇠고기
Chicken	dak-gogi	닭고기
Duck meat	ori-gogi	오리고기

Fish	*saengseon/hoe (raw fish)*	생선/회
Ham	*haem*	햄
Meat	*gogi*	고기
Noodles	*myeon*	면
Pork	*dwaeji-gogi*	돼지고기
Red-pepper paste	*gochu-jang*	고추장
Rice	*bap*	밥
Rice-cake	*ddeok*	떡
Seaweed laver	*gim*	김
Shrimp	*sae-u*	새우
Squid	*ojing-eo*	오징어
Tuna	*chamchi*	참치
Vegetables	*yachae*	야채

WESTERN FOOD

Bread	*bbang*	빵
Cereal	*shiri-eol*	시리얼
Cheese	*chi-jeu*	치즈
Chocolate	*chokollit*	초콜릿
Eggs	*gyeran*	계란
Fruit	*gwa-il*	과일
Pizza	*pija*	피자
Spaghetti	*seupageti*	스파게티
Steak	*seuteikeu*	스테이크

DRINKS

Beer	*maekju*	맥주
Bottled beer	*byeong maekju*	병 맥주
Cocktail	*kakteil*	칵테일
Coffee	*keopi*	커피
Draught beer	*saeng maekju*	생 맥주
Fruit juice	*gwa-il jyuseu*	과일 쥬스
Milk	*uyu*	우유
Mineral water	*saengsu*	생수
Orange juice	*orenji jyuseu*	오렌지 쥬스
Water	*mul*	물
Wine	*wain*	와인
Whisky	*wiseuki*	위스키

Glossary

ajeossi an older or married man.

ajumma an older or married woman.

anju bar snacks.

-bang room.

-bawi boulder or large rock.

-bong mountain peak. The highest peak in a park is often referred to as *ilchulbong* ("Number One Peak").

buk- north.

buncheong a Korean style of pottery popular in Joseon times and often bluish-green.

celadon a Korean style of pottery used since the Three Kingdoms period – often pale green in colour, with a cracked glaze.

Chuseok Korean Thanksgiving.

dae- big, large, great.

Dangun mythical founder of Korea.

DMZ the Demilitarized Zone that separates North and South Korea.

-do island.

-dong city neighbourhood; part of a *-gu*.

dong- east.

dongdongju a milky rice wine much favoured by Korean students; very similar to *makgeolli*.

DPRK Democratic People's Republic of Korea.

-ga section of a major street.

-gil street.

gisaeng Female entertainers popular in dynastic times (see box, p.74).

-gu district of a city, subdivided into *-dong* neighbourhoods.

-gung palace.

gwageo civil service examinations in the Joseon era.

Gyopo Koreans, or people of Korean descent, living overseas.

hagwon private academy for after-school study. Many expats work at an English academy (*yeongeo hagwon*).

hallyu the "Korean New Wave" of pop culture, most specifically films.

hanbok traditional Korean clothing.

hangeul the Korean alphabet.

hanja Chinese characters, which are still sometimes used in Korea.

hanji traditional handmade paper.

hanok a style of traditional, tile-roofed wooden housing.

hof a Korean-style bar.

insam ginseng.

jjimjilbang Korean spa-cum-sauna facilities, often used by families and youth groups (see box, p.107).

KNTO Korea National Tourism Organization.

makgeolli a milky rice wine much favoured by Korean students; very similar to *dongdongju*.

mudang practitioner of shamanism; usually female.

mugunghwa Korea's third-highest level of train, one below a *saemaeul*. Named after Korea's national flower, a variety of hibiscus.

-mun city or fortress gate.

-myo Confucian shrine.

nam- south.

-ni village; sometimes pronounced *-ri*.

-no large street; sometimes pronounced *-ro*.

nocheonnyeo an "over-the-hill" female – Korean women have long been expected to marry by the age of thirty, though this is slowly changing.

noraebang a "singing room", often the venue of choice for the end of a night out.

ondol traditional underfloor system of heating, using wood fires underneath traditional buildings.

pansori Korean opera derived from shamanistic songs, sung by female vocalists.

pyeong Korean unit of measurement equivalent to approximately 3.3 square metres; still commonly used to measure the floorspace of housing or offices.

-ri village; sometimes pronounced *-ni*.

-ro large street; sometimes pronounced *-no*.

ROK Republic of Korea.

-sa temple.

-san mountain; often used to describe an entire range.

sanseong mountain fortress.

seo- west.

Seon Korean Buddhist sect proximate to Zen in Japan.

seonsaengnim title for a teacher, which goes before the family name, or after the given name. Hence, a teacher will be referred to as "Martin *seonsaengnim*". It's also used as a version of "Mister".

seowon Confucian academy in Joseon times.

-si city, subdivided into *-gu* districts.

sijang market.

soju clear alcoholic drink (around 25 percent alcohol by volume) which is often compared to vodka.

ssireum a Korean wrestling style to Mongolian or Greco-Roman styles.

STO Seoul Tourism Organization.

taekwondo Korean martial art.

tongil unification, a highly important concept on the divided Korean peninsula.

woeguk-in foreigner; pronounced "way-goog-in". *Woeguk-saram* is also used.

yangban the scholarly "upper class" in Joseon times.

yeogwan Korean form of accommodation, similar to a motel but privately run and almost always older.

yeoinsuk Korean form of accommodation, similar to a *yeogwan* but with communal toilets and showers.

Small print and index

ABOUT THE AUTHOR

Martin Zatko has been on the road more or less continuously since 2002, and has spent some of his more productive moments writing the Rough Guides to Korea, China, Japan, Vietnam, Myanmar, Turkey and Europe. More than a hundred countries into his quest to see all of everywhere, Seoul still ropes him in with pleasing regularity – you'll often find him surveying the city from the top of the Jinyang Building, bottle of *makgeolli* in hand, or scoffing seafood with his buddies in a Jongno *pojangmacha*.

ACKNOWLEDGEMENTS

Martin Zatko would like to thank the Seoul Tourism Organization for their assistance with this guide, as well those who made the project such a pleasure – thanks to Jason Strother for storage space and restaurant recommendations; David Carruth for some grand nights out and use of his floor (and to his hedgehog Goldilocks for not dying on my watch); Matt Crawford for the kind loan of his apartment; Mike Spavor for the entertaining cameo; Jane and the staff at Hide & Seek for putting up with me for a month; Yeongae Min for the ride to Yangsu-ri; Yuhyun Lee for the *churros*; Laura Hong for the wow factor of her transition from stewardess to pilot; Mina Kim for showing me around Suwon; Sally Dinh for putting up with below-par Vietnamese food; and father Zatko and sister Nicole for putting up with me during the writing process.

READERS UPDATES

Thanks to all the readers who have taken the time to write in with comments and suggestions (and apologies if we've inadvertently omitted or misspelt anyone's name):

David Brengelmann; Stephen P. Cahill; Kiri Center; Rolf Mattes; Prakash Menon; Brenda Patterson; Kara Richardson; Thorsten Schmidt; and Flavia Woodwark.

HELP US UPDATE

We've gone to a lot of effort to ensure that the second edition of **The Rough Guide to Seoul** is accurate and up-to-date. However, things change – places get "discovered", opening hours are notoriously fickle, restaurants and rooms raise prices or lower standards. If you feel we've got it wrong or left something out, we'd like to know, and if you can remember the address, the price, the hours, the phone number, so much the better.

Please send your comments with the subject line "**Rough Guide Seoul Update**" to ❶mail@uk.roughguides.com. We'll credit all contributions and send a copy of the next edition (or any other Rough Guide if you prefer) for the very best emails.

Find more travel information, connect with fellow travellers and plan your trip on ❶**roughguides.com**.

Rough Guide credits

Editor: Amanda Tomlin
Layout: Nikhil Agarwal
Cartography: Swati Handoo
Picture editor: Aude Vauconsant
Proofreader: Jan McCann
Assistant editor: Payal Sharotri
Production: Jimmy Lao

Cover design: Nicole Newman, Aude Vauconsant, Nikhil Agarwal
Editorial assistant: Freya Godfrey
Senior pre-press designer: Dan May
Programme manager: Gareth Lowe
Publisher: Keith Drew
Publishing director: Georgina Dee

Publishing information

This second edition published November 2015 by
Rough Guides Ltd,
80 Strand, London WC2R 0RL
11, Community Centre, Panchsheel Park,
New Delhi 110017, India
Distributed by Penguin Random House
Penguin Books Ltd, 80 Strand, London WC2R 0RL
Penguin Group (USA), 345 Hudson Street, NY 10014, USA
Penguin Group (Australia), 250 Camberwell Road,
Camberwell, Victoria 3124, Australia
Penguin Group (NZ), 67 Apollo Drive, Mairangi Bay,
Auckland 1310, New Zealand
Penguin Group (South Africa), Block D, Rosebank Office
Park, 181 Jan Smuts Avenue, Parktown North, Gauteng,
South Africa 2193
Rough Guides is represented in Canada by DK Canada, 320
Front Street West, Suite 1400,Toronto, Ontario M5V 3B6
Printed in Singapore
© Rough Guides 2015
Maps © Rough Guides

208pp includes index
A catalogue record for this book is available from the
British Library
ISBN: 978-0-24120-131-2
The publishers and authors have done their best to
ensure the accuracy and currency of all the information
in **The Rough Guide to Seoul**, however, they can accept
no responsibility for any loss, injury, or inconvenience
sustained by any traveller as a result of information or
advice contained in the guide.
1 3 5 7 9 8 6 4 2

Photo credits

All photos © Rough Guides except the following:
(Key: t-top; c-centre; b-bottom; l-left; r-right)

p.1 Corbis/Topic Photo Agency
p.2 AWL Images/Gavin Hellier
p.4 AWL Images/Gavin Hellier
p.8 Corbis/YONHAP/epa
p.9 Alamy Images/SFL Travel
p.11 Dreamstime.com/Sean Pavone (t); SuperStock/Tips Images (c)
p.13 Alamy Images/dbimages (t); Robert Harding Picture Library/Tibor Bognar (b)
p.14 Dorling Kindersley/James Tye (r)
p.15 Robert Harding Picture Library/Andre Seale (t)
p.16 Corbis/Topic Photo Agency (t); Corbis/LEE JAE-WON/Reuters (c); Robert Harding Picture Library/Christian Kober (b)
p.17 Corbis/Atlantide Phototravel (t); Getty Images/Seongjoon Cho (cl)
p.19 123RF.com/crystaltmc (c)
p.20 Corbis/Massimo Borchi
p.36 Robert Harding Picture Library/Eurasia
p.41 Alamy Images/Hemis (b)
p.47 Getty Images/Glenn Sundeen/TigerPal
p.51 Robert Harding Picture Library/Pietro Scozzari (bl); Getty Images/Alex Barlow (br)
p.55 Corbis/Topic Photo Agency
p.59 Robert Harding Picture Library/Tibor Bognar (t); Alamy Images/National Geographic Image Collection (b)
p.63 Corbis/Massimo Borchi/Atlantide Phototravel

p.67 Corbis/Atlantide Phototravel (t); Robert Harding Picture Library/Christophe Boisvieux (b)
p.75 Corbis/Emilie CHAIX/Photononstop (t); Corbis/Topic Photo Agency (b)
p.80 Corbis/R. Ian Lloyd/Masterfile
p.85 Corbis/Topic Photo Agency (t); Corbis/Atlantide Phototravel (b)
p.89 Robert Harding Picture Library/Christian Kober
p.93 Corbis/Atlantide Phototravel
p.99 Corbis/Topic Photo Agency
p.115 Corbis/Topic Photo Agency (t); Alamy Images/SFL Travel (b)
p.122 Corbis/Topic Photo Agency
p.128 SuperStock/Photononstop
p.138 Alamy Images/ASK Images
p.142 AWL Images/Travel Pix Collection
p.147 Dreamstime.com/Thejipen (b)
p.153 Robert Harding Picture Library/Michael Runkel
p.160 Corbis/Topic Photo Agency

Front cover and spine LED illuminated wall in Seoul © Getty Images/EschCollection
Back cover Gyeongbokgung Palace © AWL Images/Jane Sweeney (t); *Kimchi* at *Korea House*, Jung-gu © Rough Guides/Martin Richardson (bl); Ceremonial guard at Gyeongbokgung Palace © Rough Guides/Martin Richardson (br).

Index

Maps are marked in grey

Map index

Listings key

- ■ Accommodation
- ● Restaurant/café
- ■ Bar/club
- ● Shop

City plan

The **city plan** on the pages that follow is divided as shown:

0   250
metres

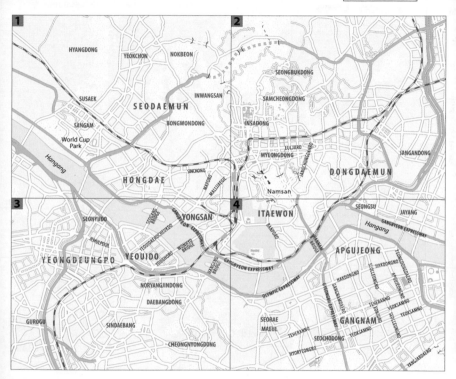

Map symbols

♦	Point of interest	⊠	Gate	▨	Motorway	▨	Building
ⓘ	Information office	⊙	Memorial/statue		Main road	⬭	Stadium
Ⓜ	Subway station	⌂	Shrine		Minor road	▭	Park
✈	Airport	♠	Buddhist temple	⌇⌇⌇	Tunnel	🞢	Cemetery
⊠	Post office	🏛	Monument	- - - -	Path	▪▪▪	International boundary
⊞	Hospital	🏛	Palace		Wall	- - -	Regional boundary
♠	Museum	⚐	Border checkpoint	— -	Ferry	— — —	Chapter boundary
▲	Mountain peak	⌣	Bridge	▭▭	Railway		Subway line
⛰	Tower	Ⓔ	Embassy	●- ▪●	Cable car		

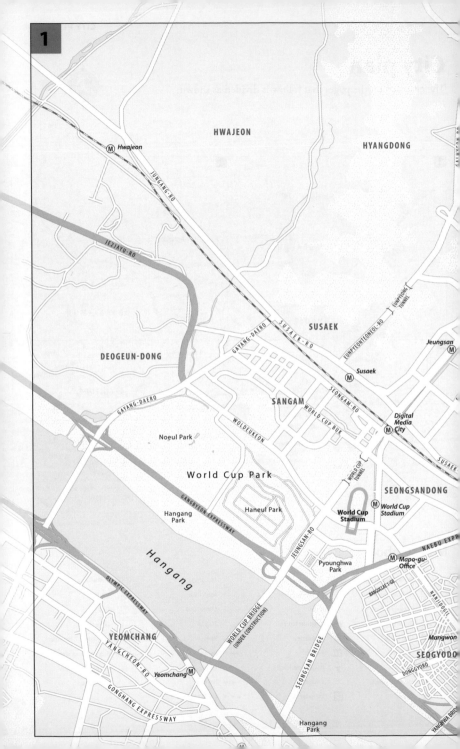

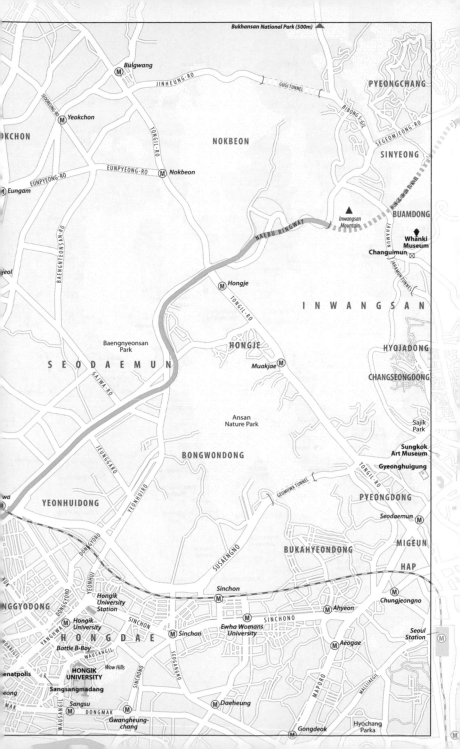

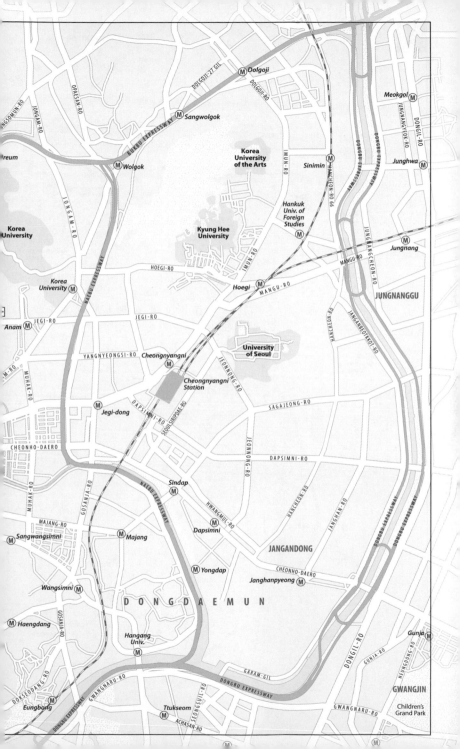

SEONYUDO

Hangang Park

Hangang

Seonyudo Ⓜ

OLYMPIC EXPRESSWAY

YANGHWA BRIDGE

Dangsan Ⓜ

SEOBU EXPRESSWAY

MOKDONGJUNGANG-RO

MOKDONGSEO-RO

MOKDONGDONG-RO

Pari Park

SEONYU-RO

DANGSAN-RO

BEODNUMARU-RO

GUKHOE-DAERO

Mokdong Stadium

Yeongdeungpo-Gu Office

YEONGDEUNGPO OVERPASS

YEONGDUNG-RO

Omok Park

MOKDONGDONG-RO

JEMULPOGIL

Mok-dong Ⓜ

OMOK-RO

Omokgyo Ⓜ

Yangpyeong Ⓜ

Yeongdeungpo Market Ⓜ

YEONGDEUNGPO-RO

DANGSAN-RO

YEONGDEUNGPO-RO

MOKDONGSEO-RO

MOKDONGDONG-RO

SINMOK-RO

SEONYU-RO

Mullae Ⓜ

YEONGDEUNGPO

Yeongdeungpo Ⓜ

MOKDONG-RO

ANYANGCHEON-RO

DORIMCHEON-RO

DANGSAN-RO

Yeongdeungpo Park

Dorimcheon Ⓜ

GYEONGIN-RO

Yangcheon-gu Office Ⓜ

SINDORIM-RO

Sindorim Ⓜ

DOSIN-RO

JOSIN-RO 29 GIL

GAMASAN-RO

DAEBANGCHEON-RO

JOSIN-RO

Guro Ⓜ

GYEONGIN-RO

GONGWON-RO

Sinpung Ⓜ

SINPUNG

SEOBU EXPRESSWAY

BEOTKKOT-RO

GAMASAN-RO

DAERIM-RO

DORIM-RO

DIGITAL-RO

Guil Ⓜ

ANYANGCHEON-RO

NAMBU EXPRESSWAY

GURO-RO

GUROJUNGANG-RO

DORIM-RO

Daerim Ⓜ

BONGCHEON-RO

YEOUIDAEBANG-RO

GURO-GU

SICHEONG-RO

GAMASAN-RO

GURODONG-RO

Namguro Ⓜ

Guro Digital Complex Ⓜ

JAWONJUNGANG-RO

ANYANGCHEON-RO

GASAN DIGITAL

BEOTKKOT-RO

Gasan Digital Complex

NAMBU EXPRESSWAY

MUNSEON

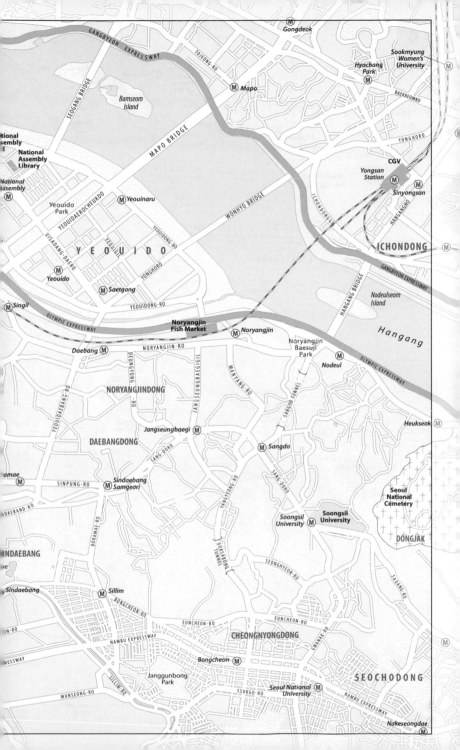

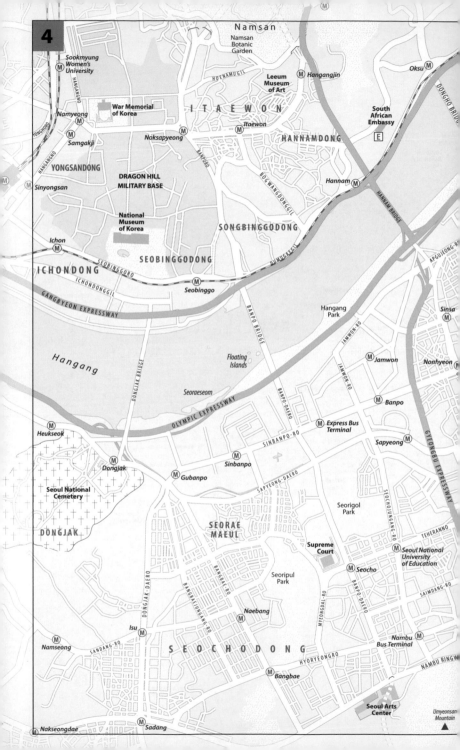

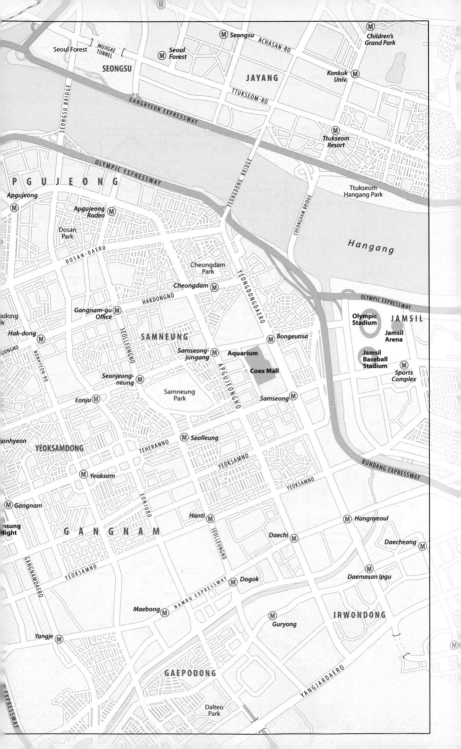

SEOUL SUBWAY

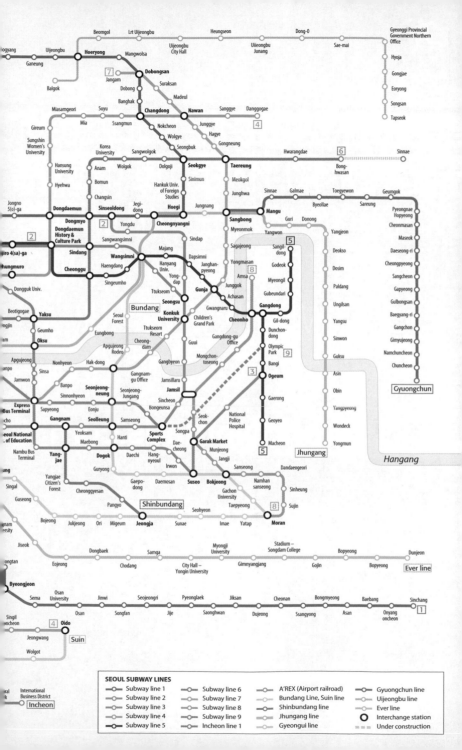